What people are

The Bullet in

The Bullet in the Pawpaw is a compelling page-turner that traces Kim Hope's ground-breaking years as a theatre professional in South Africa. But this is no star-struck memoir. It begins in the years of apartheid and follows the author's growing belief in the power of drama to change lives, her struggle against the odds to found the brilliantly innovative Themba Project, and her realisation, during the HIV/AIDS epidemic, that her skills as a director could help break the silence surrounding that terrible disease. Beautifully and atmospherically written, her book shines with optimism, courage and an irrepressible sense of adventure. As it drew to a close I found myself so moved that I went straight back to the beginning and read it again.

Geoffrey Durham, Quaker, and author of *The Spirit of the Quakers* and *Being a Quaker: A Guide for Newcomers*

This frank and compassionate account of the apartheid years and the AIDS epidemic in Southern Africa brings back many memories for me. It is a most valuable record of a Project that without question has been of immense value to so many people. Kim Hope writes directly and frankly and in so doing demonstrates how individuals with dedication and purpose utilised their own skills to help create a better quality of life for all regardless of creed or colour. This is not only a compelling story it is also a valuable historical record.

Terry Waite CBE, Anglican and a Quaker, and author of several books including *Out of the Silence* a book of poems and reflections, and *Solitude* an exploration of solitary places and solitary people.

The Bullet in the Pawpaw is a story of hope (ithemba) and triumph at a time in South Africa when denial and ignorance around HIV and AIDS was killing people and threatening to rip the nation apart. The Themba HIV and AIDS Project, built on the Alternatives to Violence Project and Forum theatre, is a story of courage, resilience, empowerment and love. It is the story of individual and collective action at a time of crisis. Kim Hope took up the challenge and transformed her love for theatre into something that gave young South Africans hope and the power to overcome ignorance and fear. As she puts it: "It began to look as if we had created something which was not only unique, but also valuable." I highly recommend this book.

Nozizwe Madlala-Routledge – Quaker, and Deputy Health Minister of South Africa (2004–2007).

In this enchanting and important book Kim Hope takes us with her through her years in South Africa involving young people in theatre projects helping to overcome the stain and pain left by apartheid. And confronting and dealing with violence, abuse and HIV&AIDS.

Angela Neustatta, Journalist and author of *The Year I Turn: A Quirky A–Z of Ageing*

Congratulations to Kim on her vivid and moving account of how she went about the onerous task of setting up and running the innovative Themba ("Hope") Project. At a time when people were beginning to be open to testing for HIV but were overwhelmed by the implications, she and her colleagues helped many to comprehend the enormity of the Aids pandemic. I hope this book will affirm the work she and Themba did, recognise those who were given the courage to be tested, and constitute a tribute to those who did not survive the scourge.

The Most Revd Thabo Makgoba, Archbishop of Cape Town, and author of *Faith and Courage – Praying with Mandela*

The Bullet in the Pawpaw

Theatre and AIDS
in South Africa

The Bullet in the Pawpaw

Theatre and AIDS in South Africa

Kim Hope

IFF
BOOKS

Winchester, UK
Washington, USA

JOHN HUNT PUBLISHING

First published by iff Books, 2019
iff Books is an imprint of John Hunt Publishing Ltd., No. 3 East Street, Alresford,
Hampshire SO24 9EE, UK
office@jhpbooks.com
www.johnhuntpublishing.com
www.iff-books.com

For distributor details and how to order please visit the 'Ordering' section on our website.

A CIP catalogue record for this book is available from the British Library.

Design: Stuart Davies

UK: Printed and bound by CPI Group (UK) Ltd, Croydon, CR0 4YY
US: Printed and bound by Thomson-Shore, 7300 West Joy Road, Dexter, MI 48130

We operate a distinctive and ethical publishing philosophy in
all areas of our business, from our global network of authors to
production and worldwide distribution.

Contents

Kim as Luciana in *The Comedy of Errors* in Soweto. 1964.
Photo: Patrick Eagar

This book is for my children, Sally and Andrew, and my grandchildren Elliot, Niamh and Esme.
Also for Bongani, Mary, Thabo and all the actor-educators who joined Themba.
And, of course, for Theresa.

* * *

In memory of Richard and Sheila Attenborough
and Mary Mpho Masita

* * *

* * *

Let us then try what love can do to mend a broken world.
William Penn, Quaker, 1644–1718

* * *

This is my story – it is my account of events.
It may not always accord with other people's memories.

* * *

Part One

1964–1965

There is a lovely road that runs from Ixopo into the hills. These hills are grass-covered and rolling, and they are lovely beyond all singing of it ... the grass is rich and matted, you cannot see the soil. It holds the rain and the mist, and they seep into the ground, feeding the streams in every kloof.
Alan Paton, *Cry, the Beloved Country*

Prologue

South Africa, 1964

The wooden hut is packed with an audience of old men and matrons, teenagers and children. There are women with babies humped on their backs, strapped on with colourful towels secured with huge safety pins. More than three hundred people are gathered here. We even have a semi-circle of ragged little ones, three rows deep, sitting bunched together behind us on the stage, and we can see more children, most of them barefoot, peeping in through the door at the back. Some members of the audience are standing squashed up against the walls while others perch on rickety chairs and benches. We are a company of young actors from Britain performing *The Comedy of Errors* in the dusty Mofolo Community Hall in Soweto. The sun streams through the broken windows and onto the backs of the spectators as they lean forward. English is their second or even third language. They furrow their brows in concentration as they try to catch the unfamiliar words.

The character of Doctor Pinch, a conjuror and exorcist, terrifies the audience. They shriek in fear as he climbs his ladder and frightens them with his magic. Scattering glitter, he intones, *Mistress, both man and master is possess'd; I know it by their pale and deadly looks. They must be bound and laid in some dark room.* There are howls of laughter at the lines *In what part of her body stands Ireland? Marry, sir, in her buttocks.* The audience is enthralled; gripped by the misunderstandings in the story, fascinated by the different characters and shocked by the sexual innuendos. They boo the baddies, and cheer when the dénouement arrives.

After the performance the headmaster of the local school stands up. He is a short, square man with a wide smile. He mops the sweat from his forehead then tucks the hankie back into the breast pocket of his dowdy suit.

"You have entertained us, so now we will sing for you," he announces as he strides from his bench to the makeshift stage. The children from the local primary school shuffle to their feet – they have learnt and practised a song especially for us. We, the actors, dressed incongruously in Regency costume, sit along the edge of the low platform, while in perfect African harmony the children sing *If You Ever Go Across the Sea to Ireland*.

The fourth verse runs:

Yet the strangers came and tried to teach us their way.
They scorned us just for bein' what we are.
But they might as well go chasing after moonbeams
Or light a penny candle from a star.

I gaze at these smiling children standing bright-eyed, their faces turned up, singing this song of beauty, longing and oppression, and I wonder about their lives. What do they learn in school? What sort of future is in front of them? It's obvious from their bare feet and worn school uniforms that they are poor. What chances do they have in life under an apartheid regime that thwarts every opportunity for them to reach their potential?

Now everyone in the audience rises up and, flouting the law, they stand with right fists raised in defiance as they sing *Nkosi Sikelel' iAfrika*.

We stand too, wipe our cheeks, and raise our right fists in solidarity. We don't know the words, but as the black audience and the white actors face each other across that dirty wooden shack, in the heat and dust of the afternoon, there is a moment of profound connection as the hymn bursts forth:

Nkosi Sikelel' iAfrika (Lord Bless Africa)
Maluphakanyisw' uphondo lwayo (May her glory be lifted high)

3

Yizwa imithandazo yethu (Hear our petitions)
Nkosi Sikelela (Lord bless us)
Thina lusapho lwayo (Us your children)
Woza Moya, (Come Spirit)
Woza Moya, woza Moya,
Woza Moya,
Woza Moya, woza Moya,
Woza Moya oyingcwele (Come Holy Spirit)
Nkosi Sikelela (Lord bless us)
Thina lusapho lwayo. (Us your children)

One day, *Nkosi Sikelel' iAfrika* will be incorporated into the national anthem of South Africa. Now, in 1964, it is prohibited by the Government. Singing it is an illegal act, and if we are discovered we could all be arrested.

Chapter 1

London/South Africa, 1964

Margaret Dalton, an attractive, dark-haired woman, approached me and whispered, "How do you fancy auditioning for a theatre group going to South Africa?"

"What?" I was leaning against the tiled wall at the back of a school hall in South Kensington. I was part of a drama evening class, where Margaret, too, was a member, and I was watching a rather dreary rehearsal.

"A theatre company. They're going to take a couple of Shakespeare plays to South Africa. If you want to audition, I'll give you the details."

"Oh. Okay. Thanks."

Margaret wasn't the most reliable bearer of information, and I had no idea how she came to know about the auditions. Nevertheless, I was intrigued. At the time, I was working as a children's journalist, enjoying London in the "Swinging Sixties". I had a reasonable salary, a small flat and lots of friends. I was twenty-one years old, naïve and immature. The Beatles, who had exploded onto the scene, the Twist, music, night clubs, coffee shops in Soho, Biba in Kensington Church Street and Mary Quant in the King's Road, had drawn me into a carefree, fun-filled existence. I didn't bother to take a daily paper. I had no interest in politics, let alone in a faraway country like South Africa, about which I knew almost nothing.

Four years earlier, in March 1960, I'd been standing by the balustrade overlooking Trafalgar Square watching hundreds of people at a rally. They were protesting about a massacre that had occurred in a place called Sharpeville. I learnt that the police in the township had fired on the crowd who had been standing outside the police station demonstrating against something called the "pass laws". Sixty-nine people had been killed – most of them shot in the back as they'd tried to run away.

I remember turning to my companion as I watched the protest and asking him, "What has this to do with us here in England?"

The following morning as I walked from Charing Cross Station I saw red paint had been poured down the steps of South Africa House. I supposed it was to symbolise the blood of the people who had been killed. I was shocked at the vandalism, and "tut-tutted" to myself. But at the same time, I sensed the paint held great significance and was ashamed by my reaction.

I was confused. Never having had the sort of schooling which encouraged independent thought, or an interest in world affairs, I was unsure how I felt about people protesting in such a public manner. I'd had a sheltered upbringing, and was bored and naughty at school. My sister and I had been sent to a private girls' school in Eltham, south-east London, the full title of which was "Babington House – an Establishment for Young Ladies". It sounded, and was, very like an old-fashioned "Dame" school. There were four Houses, each one named, bizarrely, after a military commander from World War One: Kitchener, Jellicoe, French and Haig. I was in Kitchener House, and our verse from the school song ran:

Kitchener stands for courage and strength,
Not yielding to sloth nor wrong.
Duty the watchword, steadfast the will,
Kitchener House be strong!

Incredibly inappropriate for little girls.

Eventually, I was expelled for a minor misdemeanour: touching a teacher's tin of Sharp's toffees. Touching other people's belongings – especially those of a teacher – was expressly forbidden, so I was told to "put on your hat and coat, girl, and go home."

I couldn't imagine "behaving badly" in public. But this protest in Trafalgar Square showed me that people were prepared to risk censure or even arrest in order to voice their anger about injustice. I was intrigued, but put the whole affair out of my mind. Nonetheless, a seed had been sown.

What harm could auditioning for the Shakespeare theatre company do? If I succeeded, I would have the chance to see something of the world. I decided to phone the number Margaret had given me, and was told to go to an address in Fulham.

Alexandra Dane, a striking South African actress and one of the two directors responsible for the tour, answered my ring at her door. She was tall, big-busted and voluptuous, with blonde hair flowing down her back. She ushered me into a high-ceilinged room with dark red curtains draped at the long windows. We ran through a couple of scenes from Shakespeare, and then Sandy (as she liked to be known) gave me direction, telling me how she wanted me to stand, gesture and speak the lines.

"Good," she said after about ten minutes' work, "you take direction well – and you look right. You're not tall, and your hair is good too – I need someone fair to contrast with Jean Dempsey – she's one of the other actresses. You'll have to wear it up, though, for both plays."

"D ... do you mean I've passed the audition? You want me to come on the tour?"

"Definitely. You're what I'm looking for. Any questions?"

I was dazed and my brain wasn't functioning properly. Was it really this simple? I tried to think of things I should ask, but nothing surfaced.

"Stephen'll send you a pack of information about everything: departure dates, money, jabs, that sort of thing. Okay? He's the other director."

I nodded dumbly.

"Oh, and one more thing: do you sew? I need you to make your own costume. An Empire-line dress. I'll post you the material. Can you do that?"

I could.

"Good. See you in a couple of months. In Cambridge. That's where we're going to begin our rehearsals."

As I left Sandy's flat, I thought my head might explode. I had passed the audition! I was going to South Africa! I wondered what had made Margaret come and speak to me as I'd leant against the wall at the school. Why hadn't she talked to Anne or Vicki, or any of the other young women who'd been at the drama class? Perhaps she had, but they weren't interested. Perhaps I had just happened to be standing there at exactly the right moment.

Two plays, *The Comedy of Errors* and *Love's Labour's Lost*, had been chosen for the tour to celebrate the four hundredth anniversary of Shakespeare's birth. A few days after the audition, Stephen Gray sent me copies of the scripts and the paperwork from the English Academy of South Africa – an organisation dedicated to enhancing all things English in the Afrikaner-led Republic. Stephen, a student at Cambridge University, and Sandy Dane, a professional actress and director, had been invited to put together a company of actors for the tour. The Academy had written:

First and foremost the object of the tour is to present the plays to people who wouldn't normally get to a theatre – Black and Coloured schools, particularly. To quote from the English Academy secretary's letter: "We are perfectly well aware of how bitter the feeling is overseas about our racial policies (nobody abhors them more than the English Academy). But the University Great Hall here in Jo'burg is one of the few theatres in the country where we can have mixed audiences, and Non-whites will be free to come to any of the performances you have here ... the few performances we will ask you to do for Whites only will be to fleece them of their money in order to bring you out here at all."

I didn't understand any of this, so decided to simply get on with learning my lines. I was lucky that Shakespeare's language held no terrors for me. My mother had been an actress at the Old Vic Theatre before the war, and had performed in a number of Shakespeare plays. I had imbibed a love of the Bard from her. I used to run up and down the garden yelling (and misquoting) lines from *Romeo and Juliet*:

A rose by any other name would smell as sweet. So Romeo would, were he not Romeo called, retain that dear perfection which he owes without that title ....

Back then, I had thought it was Romeo's own sweet smell Shakespeare was referring to.

I remember coming home from Brownies one day and hearing a strange, strangled noise emanating from the sitting room. I peered around the door and saw my mother, hands clasping her neck, flinging herself backwards onto the sofa with a cry of *Oh my dear Hamlet, the drink, the drink! I am poisoned* ... She had joined the local Eltham Players and was rehearsing for Queen Gertrude.

My father, meanwhile, would have been happier if he could have stayed in the Royal Navy after the war. He'd been a Lieutenant Commander on the HMS Ulster Queen, travelling in hideous, freezing conditions back and forth to Russia with the Arctic convoys. Toiling behind a desk at Imperial Chemical Industries for the rest of his working life was – to say the least – extremely tough.

My parents had been next-door neighbours when they were children, and once they had grown up (she extremely beautiful, and he handsome in his naval uniform) they had fallen in love and married. My father had not wanted to be a "stage-door Johnny" so my mother gave up the professional stage to have her three children: my sister Hazel, who became a nurse, then me, and then my younger brother Mike, who grew up to be an artist and art teacher. I had always wanted to be an actress like my mother, but hadn't the confidence to audition again and again for drama school. One rejection from the Royal Academy of Dramatic Art had been enough for me so I had trained instead as a journalist.

* * *

A few weeks after my audition in Fulham I travelled to St John's College in Cambridge for six days of rehearsals. The other actors were a mix of professionals and Cambridge undergraduates, who talked knowledgeably about South Africa and the tour we were about to embark on. There would later be a vehement row in the Cambridge press about it, with a large, vociferous section of the student population demanding that it be cancelled because of the apartheid regime. The University eventually stepped in and decided that, as long as the word "University" was not used in any publicity material, the tour could go ahead. I knew nothing of this at the time, and even though I was a bit older than most of the students, I felt lost: I had no experience of higher education, and didn't know how to converse with these people who seemed to me to be exceedingly intelligent. My life had not prepared me for intellectual conversation or even for having my own opinion on anything that mattered.

I did, however, understand Shakespeare, and I knew how to speak the verse. I had also had more "life experience" than the undergraduates, and so, as the week progressed, I began to feel a little more comfortable, and started to enjoy the rehearsals.

On 21 June 1964, our group set off from Stansted Airport in a juddering, propeller-driven aeroplane. It was a scary, two-day flight with frequent stops for re-fuelling and a traumatic roller-coaster of a ride through a massive electric storm. Richard Huggett, one of my fellow actors, said his rosary as the plane lurched, dipped and rattled. Colin Harris was repeatedly sick into a paper bag.

At Jan Smuts airport we staggered exhausted down the steps of the plane and across the tarmac, shielding our eyes from the bright sunlight. Sandy Dane's mother was there to greet us, surrounded by a crowd of people who had volunteered to be our hosts.

"Hello, dear, it's very good to meet you. Welcome to South Africa." Mrs Hodgson, a tall, imposing woman, heavily made-up and wearing a navy blue suit, looked down at me. She welcomed me kindly, if somewhat formally. Then she turned and her manner changed completely as she stridently instructed a porter, "Won't you put the bags in the boot?"

Suitcases stowed, Sandy and I were driven off to her family home in the smart northern suburb of Morningside in Johannesburg. With a crunch of tyres we swung through the gates onto the gravel drive, drawing up in front of an imposing house. A male servant came out to take our suitcases. I felt embarrassed as I could easily have carried mine myself, but that clearly wasn't expected. The house was cool and light, and smelled of Johnson's Wax furniture polish and baking. A black woman with a sweet face and wearing a pretty floral overall came forward to greet Sandy. They didn't hug or shake hands even though I could see by their smiles they were glad to see each other again.

"Welcome home, Miss Sandy," said the servant, and she bobbed a brief curtsey.

In the sitting room we sat on large, squishy sofas and were served tea in china cups, along with freshly-baked cakes. The walls were covered with flowery wallpaper; French windows opened onto a beautiful garden of trees and shrubs. It was winter in Johannesburg, but the sun was shining brightly and it was warm. Shown to my room, I lay on the bed, looking out through the window at the clear blue sky. I soon nodded off to sleep.

Mrs Hodgson was a kind hostess and tried to make me feel at home, but I was on edge much of the time. Her moods seemed to fluctuate unpredictably: one minute she was sweet and charming, the next, severe and authoritative. The frequent changes in my hostess' behaviour confused me and I wondered if she really wanted me in her house. Then on the morning of the third day, sitting at the laden breakfast table, the sharp sunshine streaming in through the windows, I suddenly saw what had been in front of me ever since I'd arrived. The difference in Mrs Hodgson's attitude and tone of voice depended on the skin colour of the person she was speaking to. I was flabbergasted.

Now that I'd recognised what was happening I saw this dual behaviour in other white South Africans. I began to watch and listen closely. I heard whites speaking to blacks in voices which were a mixture of patronising and aggressive, and I saw how black Africans gave way to white people on the pavements in the town. In the suburbs, during their brief time away from work, black servants would sit together on the neatly-cut grass outside the houses where they were employed. The maids, dressed in uniforms of pink or blue with white aprons and caps, would chat quietly while white South Africans drove past in their shiny cars, never acknowledging the presence of the black people only inches away.

* * *

We went to South Africa a disparate bunch of actors – twelve men and five women, and a stage manager – but after two weeks of rehearsal in a large wooden hut on the campus of Witwatersrand University, a close-knit theatre company had emerged. We built our sets, gathered and organised props, and helped each other with costumes. Then we set off on the tour, me clasping my mother's stage make-up box proudly on my lap.

Nothing had prepared me for the vastness of South Africa, the friendliness of the people, nor the brilliant blue of the sky. As our coach, with the words "Cambridge Shakespeare Tour of South Africa" emblazoned on each side, trundled through the country, I gazed out of the window at the sensuous hills, inhaling the warm air and pungent earth-smell. I watched small boys with sticks herd black-and-white cows towards the cattle kraals; saw yellow weaver birds fly between dried-up shrubs, piercing the air with their "zik-zik-zik" cry. Xhosa women dressed in wrap-around skirts and thick jumpers carried burdens on their heads to their rondavels, hips swaying as they walked, etched by the winter sun against the green-grey scrub.

Our first stop was Pietermaritzburg, Natal, where we performed to audiences of dignitaries and members of the public. We received an enthusiastic reception, and were accommodated by local people in their homes. These rather staid South Africans welcomed our youthful, lively and somewhat irreverent approach to the plays. They told us they enjoyed hearing Shakespeare spoken "properly", with English accents. We travelled on, playing in Grahamstown, Cape Town, Bloemfontein and Pretoria.

Throughout the tour we performed only in university theatres where it was legally possible to play to mixed audiences. Almost all the faces we saw, however, were white. Most black people lived outside the towns, and it was difficult, if not impossible, for them to travel into the cities at night. I imagined it would be intimidating for a black person to enter the hallowed university halls, filled to capacity with white people. This made me upset and angry. I wanted everyone, regardless of the colour of their skin, to have the opportunity to see the plays.

After two months on the road, we returned to Johannesburg and set up an alternative tour for people who lived in the townships. But we needed authorisation first: whites were forbidden from entering black areas without special permission. We applied for permits, a few strings were pulled, and we were successful. We set out in the afternoons in our bus, visiting some of the towns and townships around Johannesburg and Pretoria: Evaton, Luipaarsdsvlei, Benoni, Springs and Soweto. Although these were the areas where black and coloured South Africans lived, I felt more at home here than in the white areas of Johannesburg or the houses we had stayed in during the tour. We were given lively and enthusiastic welcomes in the townships. After one particularly animated afternoon, we returned to the State Theatre in Pretoria to perform to the "great and good" of South Africa. The audience consisted of dinner-jacketed white men, many of them in the government, and white women dripping with pearls and diamonds. It was hard not to spit Shakespeare at them as they sat upright in the stalls watching the play.

By contrast, our audiences in the townships were excited and enthusiastic, cheering and clapping.

"Please come back. Come back and show us your other play."

"Thank you for coming."

"Thank you, madam, thank you."

At the end of these shows helping hands lifted our scenery into the coach, although most of our props ended up given away or purloined. Children dashed around in excitement, proudly displaying their newly-acquired helmets and having play fights with our wooden swords.

Travelling through South Africa, I had already fallen in love with the landscape. Here, in the dirty community halls of the townships, I fell in love with the country again – this time, with its people.

Chapter 2

Johannesburg, 1964–1965

A strange metamorphosis had happened during the tour: South Africa had begun to feel more like home than England. I was enjoying being a free spirit, away from the constraints of my suburban upbringing. I had never questioned the views held by my parents, my teachers or my friends, and I had certainly never dwelt on the big questions about Life. But this country had set me interrogating all my previous assumptions – assumptions I didn't even realise I'd had.

There were stirrings, awakenings in me. I needed to find out more about South Africa, bursting as it was with contrasts and surprises. There were secrets locked in the rust-brown earth, in the dusty townships and in the sprawling, white-owned homes in the smart northern suburbs of Johannesburg.

In London I had a South African friend, Ian Strauss, a drama student at the Royal Academy of Dramatic Art. I contacted his parents in Jo'burg.

"You must come and stay with us," they insisted, "while you get yourself sorted out."

Number Sixteen, 8th Street, Houghton, was spacious and imposing (at least to my eyes), with a huge garden of sweeping lawns. Tall pillars stood each side of a wide front door with a triangular portico above. I felt intimidated by the grandeur, but Mr and Mrs Strauss were kind to me and did their best to make me feel at home.

Jacobus Gideon Nel Strauss (known as JGN) was a retired politician and had been the leader of the United Party from 1950 to 1953, when the Nationalist Government was developing its apartheid policies. As leader of the opposition, JGN had tried, but failed, to halt the progress of the draconian laws which relegated black, Indian and coloured people to the lower echelons of society.

Joy Strauss was part of the women's "Black Sash" organisation. Its members, most of whom were white and middle class, stood silently at street corners in the centre of Johannesburg wearing wide black ribbons draped over their shoulders, protesting against the injustices inflicted on the black and coloured population. I often saw these women standing on the pavement in their neat hats, short white gloves and 1950s-style cotton frocks, enduring catcalls and insults from the occupants of cars driving past. Many Black Sash women were married, and their husbands were sometimes threatened with dismissal from their jobs if they didn't keep their wives under control.

JGN and Joy shared their insights into South Africa with me, and life in their house was easy, comfortable and secure. But as I began to find my way around Johannesburg, I wanted more independence. I didn't need to apply for a work or residence permit: I was young, British and white, which meant if I wanted to stay, I could. It wouldn't have been so easy if my skin had been of a darker hue or if I hadn't been from the Commonwealth.

I found a room to rent in a house in Parktown, a place very different from the comfort and elegance of the Strauss family home. It was grubby, bohemian and untidy, and shared by subversive young people. The men were bearded and played guitars; the young women flounced about in long skirts and floppy blouses. They spent every evening around the big pine table in the communal kitchen loudly discussing politics over supper, and debating whether sabotage was a legitimate form of protest.

"These pass laws are an infringement of personal liberty," said Johan. "Can't we do something about them?"

"*We* don't have to carry passes," argued Piet.

"Joseph does," countered Marieka. "We could protest on his behalf. It would be too dangerous for him."

"Maybe for us, too," Piet said.

Joseph was the servant who cooked and cleaned, but he was treated with respect and ate his meals with the rest of us.

Sometimes, we held parties with both black and white guests, which was illegal unless the front door was left open and our black friends were given no alcohol. A young woman who lived in the converted stable block at the back of the house had a black lover who sometimes stayed with her at night. The Immorality Act of 1957 prohibited sexual or "immoral or indecent" acts between white people and anyone not white. The penalty was up to seven years imprisonment for both partners, so they were taking a big risk. They were putting the rest of us in danger too, because if they were discovered, we'd all be rounded up for questioning.

I was thrown into a heady mix of subversion, protest and anti-government activity. It was exciting and scary.

One hot summer afternoon some of us went to the family home of a young man who camped out occasionally at our house. There was a swimming pool set in beautifully manicured gardens, and I lay on a li-lo letting the sun soak into my body. I was wearing an orange bikini and sipping gin and tonic. I listened to the subdued conversation of the young people lolling around the pool in their swimsuits.

"We should blow up the pylons out on the East Rand," said Johan.

"That's too risky," Marieka replied.

"Not if we plan carefully."

"I don't like the idea of using explosives."

"What do you suggest we do? It's okay as long as no one gets hurt."

"But how can we guarantee that?"

"Ag, man, you're too soft," answered Johan, and turned to talk to the others.

"Sabotage is the only way forward," he said, and they nodded in agreement.

They were members of one of the many resistance movements in South Africa, and prepared to use force in the fight against apartheid. The irony was not lost on any of us: here we were, benefitting from our pale pigmentation, surrounded by luxury and servants, while attempting to subvert the very government which was responsible for our privilege.

As I sipped my drink and listened to the talk, I asked myself what I thought about the use of violence. Was I equipped to join the struggle? Was it my fight? I was not, after all, a South African. What if I was arrested – did I know anything that would be useful to the authorities? How would I cope under questioning? I had no confidence that I would survive torture or solitary confinement.

* * *

I decided to audition for the South African Broadcasting Corporation (SABC). Here was an opportunity to fulfil my ambition to be a professional actress. I could do a range of English accents, and because I could pass for a boy as my voice was low and my name genderless, I was given a range of roles. No television was allowed in the country because the Calvinist government believed it was a corrupting influence, so radio was the only broadcast medium of entertainment. I played John in *Peter Pan,* and a little round red cheese for *Listen with Mother*. One afternoon I was a prostitute, a boy scout and a housewife – all in the same play. I worked in the theatre, too, and played Lydia Languish in *The Rivals*, by Sheridan.

Now I had a little money coming in, I decided to move into the centre of town. I found a one-room flat on the twelfth floor of a tall apartment block in Hillbrow, on the corner of Twist and Pietersen Street. Although the building was relatively new, cockroaches had taken up residence. In the evenings I lay in bed propped up against the wall reading, a book in one hand, a shoe in the other. I became adept at whacking the roaches behind me without turning my head. In the morning there would be splashes of blood and squidgy carcasses splattered across the wall like surreal modern art.

I was beginning to take a serious interest in current affairs and although the domestic press was circumspect about reporting the rest of the world's attitude to South Africa, I was nevertheless learning. I discovered that I'd arrived in South Africa with the Cambridge Shakespeare tour only two weeks after Nelson Mandela and his colleagues had begun their life sentences on Robben Island.

Homesickness suddenly and unexpectedly descended like a grey cloud. There was a hole in the pit of my stomach, sometimes echoingly empty, sometimes filled with lead. I dreamt of England and my family. I was still uncertain whether I had any role in the struggle against apartheid, or what I felt about the use of violence. I also sensed that the net was closing in as I got to know more people in the resistance movements.

One evening a hurried meeting was called because one of our friends had disappeared – I heard later that he'd managed to get over the border into Lesotho and had travelled to England. We never discovered who informed on him, forcing him to flee. Another young man we knew was arrested and jailed. I become aware, by the slight "click" as I lifted the receiver, that my phone was being tapped. I feared I might be picked up at any moment by the security police. The situation was becoming nerve-wracking.

On 1 April 1965, the schoolteacher John Harris, a member of the Armed Resistance Movement and Chairman of the Non-racial Olympics Committee, was hanged for exploding a bomb in Johannesburg Park Station in July the year before. Although I was an insignificant member of our group and had never been asked to engage in acts of sabotage, or even to distribute propaganda leaflets, I realised that I knew too much about too many people.

I was a weak link who was sure to crack under interrogation, and even if it didn't come to that, was probably no use to the movement. I abhorred apartheid, but I was questioning again whether this was my fight.

Reluctantly, it was time to pack my bags and fly home.

Part Two

1993–1997

No one is born hating another person because of the colour of his skin, or his background, or his religion. People must learn to hate, and if they can learn to hate, they can be taught to love, for love comes more naturally to the human heart than its opposite.
Nelson Mandela, *Long Walk to Freedom*, 1994

Chapter 3

London, 1993–1994

"I completely disagree with everything you've just said, and I hope very much that I never, ever see you again."

These were the first words Theresa Lynne spoke to me, very firmly, gripping my hands and staring up into my eyes. It took me a moment to realise that she meant precisely the opposite. We were taking part in an exercise during a drama therapy training course in London in 1993, where participants had to say the reverse of what they meant. Theresa had sought me out among the group in order to speak these back-to-front words to me – words that were, it turned out, prophetic. She was a skinny, flat-chested New Zealander, with an attractive, laughter-lined face, a broken nose and high, almost Slavic, cheekbones. Her fine grey hair was pulled into a French pleat and her green eyes shone mischievously as she spoke. After a second or two I managed to interpret what she actually meant: she very much wanted to keep in touch, and she agreed with everything I'd said.

The drama therapy course was being held in an old Victorian school building in Holborn. I had had a "portfolio career" in journalism, public relations, fundraising, staff management and teaching – as well as in the theatre. I was now head of a drama department in a large comprehensive school in Sussex, and had joined the course to try to discover the dividing line between drama therapy and drama teaching. What I learnt was that there was no "line" as such, and that similar games and exercises were employed in both activities. It was the *contract* with the participants that made the difference: they were either students or people in therapy.

My experiences in South Africa in 1965 had made me recognise how profound my ignorance was and when I'd returned to

England after that first visit, I had vowed to make up for the deficit in my education.

Once I'd re-established myself back in London with a job and a flat, I'd enrolled for evening classes. Studying alongside jaded, chewing-gum-flicking sixteen-year-olds in a dark Victorian school in Hammersmith, I had succeeded in gaining one further O level to add to the two I already had. I applied to London University to be trained as a teacher, even though I didn't have the necessary minimum qualifications, and was surprised and pleased when I was called for an interview.

My trepidation, as I walked along Bedford Way to the Institute of Education, was intense. Afterwards, I was sure I'd blown it.

"So, what makes you want to be a teacher?" I was asked.

I took a deep breath, paused for a moment, and decided the only thing to do was to tell the truth.

"I – it's not that I specially want to be a teacher," I said, "but I *must* get an education. While I was in South Africa I realised what I had missed when I was at school, and now I am determined, somehow, to be educated. I want – I *need* – to learn."

It sounded so pathetic – yet a few weeks later, an offer came for a place at Furzedown Teacher's Training College. I was completely overwhelmed. I stood in the kitchen of my flat reading the letter, and my eyes blurred and my hands trembled. I felt intensely grateful.

I loved being a student. It felt romantic to be cycling to college along Tooting High Street with my briefcase strapped to the carrier behind me and the wind in my hair. Towards the end of the three-year course, we were informed that if we achieved a distinction in the Teacher's Certificate, we would be allowed to register with the University of London and study for a degree. Thus, after four years, I became a Bachelor of Education – the first person in my family to graduate from a university. I was incredibly proud when I donned my academic gown and received my diploma from the Queen Mother at the Royal Albert

Hall in London. My mother and father and my new husband were all there to cheer me on.

Since then, I'd had two children and been divorced. I had found my spiritual home in the Religious Society of Friends (the Quakers) where my ambivalence and doubt about Christianity was accepted – as was my questioning the existence of God. I had become a Quaker through my involvement with the peace movement in the 1980s. I was also now a trainer with the Alternatives to Violence Project (AVP), a volunteer-led Project created in New York in 1975. Inmates at Green Haven Prison had approached the local Quakers and asked them to devise programmes to help reduce some of the violence within the penitentiary, and to work with the youth to resolve conflicts. The Project had spread to a number of countries in the world, with workshops being held in many different settings.

Theresa worked in prisons using drama techniques with inmates to explore issues like sexual health, HIV and drugs. She was, like me, an AVP trainer. We had much in common, notwithstanding our very different earlier lives: she was an only child raised on the wild West Coast of the South Island, New Zealand. Her father had been killed in the Strongman mining disaster of 1967.

Meeting Theresa was to have far-reaching consequences for us both, though neither of us had any idea at the time how far-reaching these would be. After the drama therapy course, she and I met occasionally. Sometimes she came to stay at my house in Sussex and we'd walk along the river near my home, putting the world to rights. Or we'd get together in London and go to the theatre. Despite the differences in our backgrounds, there were similarities in our spiritual quests, and we had other things in common, too: our work, our left-leaning political views. We became firm friends.

One afternoon I met Theresa in London for a sandwich. That morning, 29 October 1994, I had been at a celebratory event in

Congress House, the headquarters of the Trades Union Congress. There, the Anti-Apartheid Movement (AAM), a British-based organisation which had campaigned for years for an end to apartheid and the release of political prisoners in South Africa, had just made a decision to dissolve itself following the first democratic South African elections in April 1994. The same day, a new organisation was born: Action for Southern Africa (ACTSA), which was to launch campaigns in Swaziland and Zimbabwe as well as in South Africa.

As Theresa and I walked along Great Russell Street, I said in an overly casual tone of voice, "I'm thinking of going back to South Africa to see if there's anything useful I might be able to do. Do you want to come?"

Without hesitation Theresa replied, "Yes." This time she meant what she said.

We talked for a long time over lunch.

I had marched on the streets of London with the Anti-Apartheid Movement, protested outside the South African Embassy, at Shell garages and Barclays banks, but I had always believed I should have done more. For thirty years I had longed to go back to South Africa, and maybe now was the time. Even from a distance of six thousand miles, Theresa and I were aware that there was a great deal of tension in the country during the transition from the old apartheid government to the new democracy. We agreed ours would be a short visit to meet people and to explore our ideas of running conflict-resolution workshops in communities, using a combination of our drama skills and non-violence training.

And it turned out that our ideas had support.

A month later, on a cold, grey November day, I was talking with Rev. Thabo Makgoba, the priest-in-charge at the Church of Christ the King in Sophiatown, Johannesburg. We'd agreed to meet in the crypt of St Martin-in-the-Fields Church in London, next door to South Africa House. Our meeting had been arranged by Tricia Sibbons, a friend who was an exceptional networker and fundraiser. I had told her of my desire to go back to South Africa to run workshops, and she had invited me to meet Thabo who was in London for meetings to do with his role in the Anglican Church. Tricia had raised many thousands of pounds to help educate disadvantaged young people in South Africa and it was through this work she had met Thabo. We sat with our coffees and talked.

"I like your ideas," Thabo had said after I'd outlined briefly what I had in mind, "and I don't know of any drama practitioners involved in conflict resolution. Why don't you go on your trip and find out?"

Thabo had brought his wife, Lungi, who was pregnant with their first baby – a boy who would grow up in the new South Africa with all its possibilities and potential. While Thabo and I talked, I began to believe that my ideas to lead interactive drama workshops for conflict resolution and reconciliation might actually be helpful. And there was another consideration that weighed in my deliberations as I wondered whether to return.

Eight months earlier, I had been sitting with a dozen or so people from different local groups (Church of England, Unitarians, Roman Catholics, Quakers and anti-apartheid activists) in the lady-chapel of St Mary's parish church in Billingshurst, Sussex. It was the evening before the day of the first democratic elections ever to be held in South Africa: 27 April 1994. We were holding a vigil, and praying that the next day's events would be peaceful.

I sat silently, thinking back to the South Africa I had known when I'd been a confused girl in my twenties. I was completely absorbed in my own thoughts and reminiscences. Then out of the silence I heard a tender voice in my right ear. "You can go back now."

The voice was male and quite distinct. There was no one on my right. I continued sitting quietly but the words were insistent.

"You can go back now, you can go back ..."

I suppose if I was a Christian I might have thought this was Jesus. I soundlessly told the voice to go away. *Leave me alone. I'm vigiling.*

I am not one for hearing voices; in fact, this was the first and only time it happened to me. The memory of it stayed with me and preyed on my mind. Over the next days and weeks, I wondered about the voice, but told myself it was just a silly notion. It was merely wish-fulfilment, my own unconscious desires creeping into my thoughts. But the idea of going back to South Africa had entered my consciousness, and wouldn't go away. It had felt impossible for me to visit South Africa as a tourist while the apartheid government was in power. But now, I felt I could finally return to the "beloved country".

Chapter 4

Johannesburg, April 1995

I was in touch with people in the UK who had contacts in South Africa and through them, I arranged for Theresa and me to stay at St Benedict's convent in the suburb of Rosettenville, south of Johannesburg. St B's, a collection of red brick buildings with concrete floors and corrugated iron roofs, was a retreat centre run by the Sisters of the Order of the Holy Paraclete. The word Pax was emblazoned on one of the chimneys above the roof, contrasting incongruously with the high metal fences topped with razor wire.

Throughout the apartheid years, St B's had played a significant role in the fight against oppression. The security police had sat all day in their cars in the street outside, keeping an eye on the comings and goings in the convent. The Sisters would go out and offer the patrolmen cups of tea and cake and engage them in conversation. Sister Jane told me, with a mischievous smile, that this unnerved the police. They attempted to remain surly and watchful, but the gentle manner of the nuns and the welcome refreshments meant that the officers were forced, somewhat against their will, to be civil.

Across the road was St Peter's, the ecumenical centre of the Community of the Resurrection. This was a monastic community of men who had committed themselves to a religious life of service, and it was here that Trevor Huddleston had written *Naught for Your Comfort* in 1955. The Fathers from St Peter's discovered that the police had heard about the manuscript and were planning to raid the Centre and confiscate the book, so the Sisters smuggled it into St Benedict's and hid it. When the police arrived to search St Peter's it was nowhere to be found. Next day, a Sister crossed the street with the book secreted under her habit, right under the noses of the police who were, as usual, sitting in their car. That night St Benedict's was raided. The manuscript was never discovered, and was later secretly taken out of South Africa and published in the UK, alerting the world to the horrors of apartheid.

It was Sister Maureen, dressed in the pale grey habit of her order with a large silver cross on a black cord around her neck, who greeted Theresa and me. As she was leading us upstairs to show us our rooms, she turned to me and asked, "Is this your first time in South Africa?"

I sank onto a concrete step and burst into tears. I was exhausted after the flight, and overwhelmed by a powerful mix of emotions. I explained that I'd been in the country thirty years before. Sister Maureen sat down beside me, and put her arm around my shoulder.

"Many people react like this when they first return. Have a good night's sleep and you'll feel better in the morning."

After breakfast the following day, Sister Maureen suggested a trip.

"Sister Jane and Patricia are going to the supermarket to collect the past-the-sell-by-date produce. We collect it so we can give it to the homeless people who live around here. If you'd like a ride you could go with them. But you'll have to make your own way back because the car will be full of food."

Theresa and I had no idea how we would get home, but with the assurance that there were buses, we readily accepted the offer. Rosettenville was a suburb inhabited mainly by Portuguese residents who lived in small, run-down, single-storey houses. We were keen to venture further.

I stared out of the car window as the Sisters drove us to the Eastgate shopping mall. The streets we drove through and the buildings we passed seemed familiar, but at the same time, unrecognisable. I felt disorientated, as if in a dream where everything is simultaneously known and not known, and reality shifts obliquely.

The tangy smell of the Johannesburg air – eucalyptus and acacia trees mixed with diesel fumes and the dust from the gold mine dumps – transported me back to my time here as a young woman. The sky was familiar, too: an intense blue unknown in the gentle English landscape. The shopping centre, however, with its modern outlets and shiny pedestrian walkways was disconcertingly new and unexpected. The Sisters made their way to Woolworth's food section, where they were allowed to clear all the out-of-date produce in return for cleaning the shelves. Meanwhile, Theresa and I went exploring.

Outside we found a bus rank but there was no timetable or information to be seen. After waiting fruitlessly for a while, we asked the people who were hanging about, laden with shopping:

"Excuse me, could you help us? We need to get a bus back to Rosettenville."

"Where?"

"Rosettenville."

"Eish, man, never heard of it."

We eventually discovered that there was no direct route and we'd have to take a bus to the terminus in the middle of town for a connection. This sounded straightforward, so we boarded a bus going in the direction of the centre of Johannesburg and paid our fare. I sat back, looking out of the windows. After about half an hour, I saw that we were heading for Hillbrow. As the bus began to make its descent to Twist Street I approached the driver.

"Please could you stop near the corner of Twist and Pietersen?" I asked him.

He shook his head, looking at me as if I was crazy. "Ag, man, you don't want to get off there," he said.

"No, I do. I used to live there," I insisted.

With great reluctance he stopped the bus and we jumped off.

Immediately I realised my mistake. This was not the Hillbrow

I had known. The Sisters had assured us it was now an "arty" area and had seemed to think we would be safe enough, but I wasn't so sure. I tried to get my bearings. There was the block of flats where I had once lived, but gone were the flowers, the tidy balconies, the clean, well-ordered streets. The whole area was now run-down and dirty, teeming with people, mostly looking poor, unkempt and hungry. Passers-by gave us unfriendly glances as we stood on the pavement looking around, clearly at a loss. I didn't know if it was my imagination, but it felt to me that the looks we were getting were full of animosity. We were the only white people on the street.

We waited at the bus stop, attempting nonchalance, vainly hoping there would be a bus to take us to the city centre. Most of the people on the street were men – the few women around appeared to be coming back from market, their plastic bags filled with vegetables. By now it was late morning and they would be going home to cook.

"Let's walk round the block and try to look as if we know where we're going." Theresa suggested.

Johannesburg is built on a grid system which was laid out when it was established as a gold rush town in the 1880s. Theresa and I set off, shoulder-to-shoulder, marching down Twist Street. Then left into Pietersen Street, until we arrived at Quartz. Here we turned left again, going uphill now, as far as Esselin. The roads we walked along were strewn with litter. Tall apartment blocks had a variety of shops on the ground floor: mini-markets, cafes, dress shops, stores selling electrical goods, liquor, meat, and stalls loaded with used spare motor parts and second-hand clothes, goods spilling out onto the pavement so pedestrians had to manoeuvre their way around them. Everywhere there were billboards advertising hair cream, deodorant, shampoo and financial services. The lamp-posts were covered in fading placards displaying the news headline, *Winnie Sacked!*

We did our best to look as if we knew where we were going

as we turned left into Twist Street again and returned to the bus stop.

"Now what?" asked Theresa.

"Let's grab the first bus that comes along and get out of here," I said.

We stood and waited. I saw a notice across the street pointing down a dark, narrow alleyway.

"Look, that sign says 'police station'. Maybe we could run down there if things get dodgy."

"I don't fancy getting stuck in that passageway," said Theresa.

We were speaking to each other through the corners of our mouths, not because we were pretending to be gangsters, but because we were now standing back-to-back so that between us we had a 360-degree field of vision. It felt as if the people walking past were giving us increasingly hostile stares. Or was it my imagination? A young man passed much too close for comfort, looking at us intently. He went down the hill a few yards and I watched as he turned and began to come back. This time he had his right hand tucked into his jacket and I guessed he was fingering a weapon.

"You see that young man?" I said. "I think he has a knife."

Was I now completely delusional, or was he really about to attack us? We watched apprehensively as he walked past again and up the hill. Then he turned back towards us ...

A bus came. We jumped in and fell on the seats with relief.

It was now early afternoon, and the streets in the Central Business District of Johannesburg were, in contrast to the bustle of Hillbrow, almost empty. It was eerily quiet. Blocks of offices towered above us as we stepped down from the bus. At the terminus, we asked the few people who were wandering about how to get to Rosettenville, but no one seemed to know.

Suddenly Theresa began to feel unwell. She was dizzy and nauseous, and sat down on a metal bench with her head between her knees. I stood by, feeling helpless. The wind picked up the dust, gritting my eyes. Old newspapers flew about, empty Coke cans rolled over the tarmac. Within about five minutes Theresa was feeling very ill indeed – her face had turned grey, she was sweating profusely and shaking. A scruffily dressed white man smelling of drink sat down near us and began ranting incoherently.

"Eish, man, all these people ... all these people. The blecks only come to Jo'burg for the gold, man." We tried to ignore him.

Another man, tall and rather faded with a military bearing, noticed Theresa, and came over and asked if he could help. I felt apprehensive because he was wearing what looked like a South African army jacket. Had he been one of the soldiers who had shot and killed people in the townships in the days when there was rioting? I asked if he knew how I could get Theresa to a doctor, and he pointed to the ticket office.

"Go and ask over there," he said, with a strong Afrikaans accent. "They might assist."

Without much hope of finding anyone, and feeling nervous about leaving Theresa, I ran off, jumping over the kerbs of the terminus bus bays. I left her lying on the bench with my coat draped over her, leaning her head on her arms. The "military" man fanned her vaguely with a newspaper.

The building was a low wooden structure with flaking blue and white paint. Three white men lounged in a smoke-filled room which stank of stale cigarettes. One had his feet on the table, another was reading a newspaper. The third looked up from his mug of tea as I appeared.

"Ja?"

"I need some help. My friend's been taken ill. I must get her to a doctor."

"There's a tickey-box round the corner," he said unhelpfully.

"Can't you call an ambulance for me?"

"There's a tickey-box round the corner," he repeated. He dismissed me with a shrug, put down his mug and picked up a newspaper. I hadn't heard the expression *tickey-box* for thirty years.

I ran across the road, really worried now. Would Theresa be able to withstand the ranting man? Would the military man steal my jacket – which I now remembered had my passport in the pocket – while she didn't have the strength to resist? *Where was the tickey-box?* I stood at the kerb on the corner desperately looking around, but I could see no sign of a phone box. *Maybe it's down that road,* I thought. I was undecided: should I move further away from Theresa, leaving her unprotected, or go back in the hope of finding someone who would phone an ambulance for me?

Just then I saw a police car approaching. I flagged it down before I had a chance to wonder if this was safe. I'd been warned that in South Africa one could never be sure whether a police vehicle was occupied by bona fide officers, or by criminals who had stolen it.

I explained our predicament. The driver said, "Jump in. We'll get you back to the bus station."

Theresa was worse when we found her. One of the police used his walkie-talkie and called for an ambulance.

"Where do you want it to take her?" he asked.

I had no idea.

"OK," he said to the people on the line, "Get her to the Jo'burg Gen, would you? Ja, man."

The police car sped off. The raving man had now moved to the other end of the bench and was quietly muttering to himself. The military man had disappeared, and the few other people waiting for buses took no notice of us. I sat down and lifted Theresa's head onto my lap, tucking my jacket around her – my passport, thankfully, was safely in the pocket. She looked terrible – her face was pallid and her hands were trembling.

After fifteen long minutes I heard a siren and an ambulance screeched into the bus station. We hurtled to the Johannesburg

General Hospital, bumping over pot-holes, dodging pedestrians and swerving around corners while a student paramedic attempted, unsuccessfully, to take Theresa's blood pressure.

The deserted reception area at the Jo'burg Gen had the universal hospital smell of disinfectant mixed with the faint odour of urine and shit. I followed signs for Casualty and, with Theresa hanging on to my arm for support, walked the wide, empty corridors. After a quarter of an hour we found the right department down a narrow passageway, where two rows of plastic chairs faced each other. They were all occupied by exhausted-looking women from the townships, sitting slumped as if they had become embedded. Some had nodded off, others sat with their chins propped in their hands, elbows leaning on the arms of their chairs. Unusually for a group of township women, none of them was talking. Small children played silently at their feet. At the end of the passage was the door to casualty with the instruction *KNOCK BEFORE ENTERING* painted in large blue letters.

I didn't know what to do. Here we were, two foreign, white women, about to walk straight through the lines of black women as if by the nature of our skin colour we had a right to pass. How could we just barge our way in? I stood hesitating, holding Theresa up, and wondered if I dare move forward. Some of the women looked up, and one of them gestured that we should go past. I suspected we were jumping the queue, but Theresa was now in a state of near collapse. Feeling distinctly uncomfortable, I supported her as we walked through. I knocked on the door, and we went in.

The first thing I saw was a line of six gurneys at the far end of the room, each bearing a wounded black man. The bloody gashes in their clothes suggested they had been shot or stabbed. Although they must have been in pain, they lay quietly, occasionally letting out a gentle sigh or groan. Glistening, bright-red blood, illuminated by the glaring overhead strip lights, dripped into pools on the floor.

It was a large room with a high ceiling and in the centre, at a huge mahogany table covered with papers, sat a man of about forty-five. With his sallow skin and a dark, well-trimmed beard, he looked as if he could be Lebanese. He was supporting his head with one hand and writing notes with the other. His shoulders sagged and he looked the picture of dejection. A stethoscope hung from his neck.

Cubicles lined three sides of the room and, on the fourth wall, there was an area with a desk where a few nurses sat and chatted in low voices. No one seemed to be paying any attention to the men on the trolleys. Everything was still, as if we'd walked into the freeze-frame of a silent film. Here, the smell of disinfectant mingled with the aroma of blood and fear.

Theresa and I stood at the table until the man looked up. He seemed surprised to see us, but led us silently to a cubicle. Then he plodded back to his desk. Theresa lay down on the hard bed, and we waited. The nurses stayed where they were, and the doctor sat surveying his paperwork. It was very quiet. After waiting for about half an hour, I went over to the nurses' desk.

"Do you think someone could come and have a look at my friend?" I asked.

"Have you signed in, and paid, and got your pink slip?"

"No, I ..."

"Go to the registration office and sign in. We can't look at her till we've got the slip."

I set off again down the empty, echoing corridors and passed a black and white sign peeling off the wall with a cartoon drawing of a skeleton. Underneath were the words, *Please be patient. We have a skeleton staff today*. When I arrived at the office there was another notice behind a metal grille with a picture of a gun. This instructed, *Hand In All Your Weapons Hear*.

"Can you help me? My friend's in casualty. I need a pink slip."

The man at the desk looked up.

"That'll be a hundred and thirty rand."

I handed over the cash and, armed with the piece of paper and a receipt for the money, returned to the ward. As I passed the women still stuck in their chairs, one of them looked up and smiled encouragingly at me. I was grateful. It felt as if she'd given me permission to queue-jump. Later I discovered that the women and children were not patients, but relatives of the men on the gurneys waiting to take them home. I gave the pink slip to a nurse, sat down in the cubicle with Theresa, and waited.

Ten minutes or so passed. Then a wheelchair burst through a door in one corner of the room. In it was a bedraggled woman wearing a washed-out hospital smock, all awry. She had long straggly hair and a pasty complexion with a bright red gash of lipstick. She wheeled herself across the room into an empty cubicle opposite Theresa's. No one paid attention to her while she proceeded, with great concentration and very methodically, to remove glass phials from a sectioned tray on a small side table. She flung the ampoules one after another into a metal waste bin where they crashed and splintered, showering the floor with coloured liquid and shards of glass. Theresa and I watched in amazement. No one else seemed concerned.

Soon another woman appeared from the same direction, wearing a very short black mini-skirt, startlingly long boots, and a bright red top with a heavy belt around her slim hips. She wore a great deal of make-up and her crimson fingernails were like talons. Her long blonde hair came down almost to her waist. The "Lebanese" man looked up.

"Hi," he said, "she's over there …" He waved a hand in the direction of the phial-flinging woman. "Won't you take her back? She's being a bit of a nuisance."

The woman with the boots gently wheeled her bedraggled charge away.

The man at the table came over to Theresa's cubicle with the pink slip in his hand. He introduced himself as Dr Mohammed Khalif, the Accident and Emergency Registrar.

"Sorry about that," he said in a gentle Afrikaans-sounding voice. "She's a patient from the psychiatric ward. That was my colleague who came for her." Then he added wearily, "It's not the first time it's happened."

His speech trailed away as he sat heavily on the bed, his body sagging. He was gracious, but seemed very, very tired. Then he looked up and gestured towards the men on the trollies.

"And those men over there – they shouldn't be here. They should go to Baragwanath in Soweto. But they're scared the police will come to the hospital so their relatives bring them here instead. We don't ask questions. They've probably all been in fights. It's Saturday."

He paused, then went on, "To be honest I could do without them – they just add to my workload." Theresa and I watched him as he stared, apparently absent-mindedly, at the men. Then he shook himself and said, "There used to be a zoning policy here, but that's been scrapped and anybody can come: blacks, Indians, everybody."

I guessed he was telling us this because we were from overseas, and might be sympathetic.

"Now let's have a look at you," he continued, and proceeded to check Theresa for symptoms.

"I think it's a simple case of mild altitude sickness and low blood pressure," he said. "We're very high up here, about six thousand meters, so you're not used to it. Drink lots of water and suck barley-sugars. I'll give you an injection and you'll be fine in a day or so."

Dr Khalif put a line in to get fluids into Theresa quickly. Then he gave her the jab. He looked for a place to put the syringe down, but there was no table in the cubicle. Instead he sat down again on the bed, and plunged the needle into the side of the plastic-covered mattress, apparently unconscious of the danger this posed. There was no stand for the drip, so he handed the bag to me to hold. I stood as still as I could, clasping the pouch high above my head, until my arm ached.

Dr Khalif went on, "... and they've cut our budget by twenty-five per cent. We used to have four million rand, but it's been reduced to three. How are we supposed to manage on that? And now we're getting all these extra patients from out of town." He sounded exhausted as he ambled back to his desk. A nurse eventually wheeled over a stand for the saline drip and I massaged my arm back to life.

"I'll go and find a phone," I said, "so I can let the Sisters know where we are."

Once more I trekked down the silent hallways until I found a public phone – a tickey-box – that worked. I talked to the Sisters and ordered a taxi.

Later, when we were safely back at the convent, Sister Jane asked, "Why did you go to the Jo'burg Gen? Didn't you take out health insurance? You could have gone to the Rosebank Clinic."

Theresa and I looked at each other blankly.

"I never gave it a thought," I said. "In England you just automatically go to the local hospital."

"And you were lucky the police were genuine," said Sister Maureen. "You could easily have been driven into the veld and raped. Killed even. It's happened before."

That night I lay in my narrow bed in the quiet haven of St Benedict's, hemmed in by the restless city of Johannesburg, thinking over the thirty-year journey that had brought me here. A police siren strafed the Rosettenville suburb. A dog barked, and a shout and a cry pierced the thick wooden door of the convent. I thought of my son and my daughter, now in their twenties, who I had left behind in England. I wondered how they felt about my love affair with South Africa. They had encouraged me to come on this fact-finding visit, but none of us had any idea where it might lead.

Earlier I had noticed a poster on the wall in the stone-flagged corridor which read, *Ask not what you can do for Africa ... ask what Africa can do for you.* It was a timely reminder and I questioned for the hundredth time what on earth I thought I was doing here. Yet I reflected with gratitude it was my time in South Africa all those years before that had helped me discover that, despite being so poorly educated, I did after all have a brain. I had been able to hold my own in discussions with the student actors from Cambridge University, and I'd learnt from the young subversives I'd lived with in Johannesburg how to be discerning in listening to arguments about injustice and discrimination.

Now that apartheid was over, I wanted to use the skills I'd acquired over the years to help reduce some of the conflict and violence that was still widespread in the country. It didn't occur to me that this was a preposterous idea. Nor did I consider that there might be hundreds, perhaps thousands, of other conflict-resolution practitioners, all of them much more experienced than me and certainly more attuned to the specific difficulties in South Africa, already doing everything they could to deal with the problems in the country.

It was only later that I began to realise the enormity of my presumption.

Chapter 5

South Africa/England April 1995

Thabo and Lungi had been encouraging when I'd met them in the crypt of St Martin-in-the-Fields, but I was acutely conscious that Theresa and I were outsiders in their country. Would we be perceived as meddling in a situation about which we knew little? To find out, we needed to make contact with as many people as possible from different organisations and bounce our ideas off them. Once Theresa was fully recovered, we set forth.

Our first meeting was with Vanessa Cooke. She was a legend in the world of South African theatre, and a founder of the Market Theatre itself. This theatre, a beacon of light to many in the profession, had managed, since its opening in 1976, to successfully maintain its independent non-racial status throughout the apartheid years. Vanessa had spent decades bending apartheid's rules. As well as being an accomplished actress, she'd directed plays with mixed casts and given acting training to talented young black people from the townships. It was important to have her support.

We met her in her cluttered office at the Market Theatre Laboratory. Two cats nested on her desk among folders, papers and files. Posters of past productions peeled off the walls. Vanessa was a small, fierce white woman with untidy black hair and round spectacles. "Your ideas sound interesting," she said, after we'd outlined what we hoped to do. "And there's enough work for everybody to try and sort this country out. I think you could probably help."

Theresa and I had introductions to people in a range of institutions: churches, theatres, non-government organisations (NGOs) and in provincial government. Some were working on voter registration as there were soon to be elections for local councils. Others ran workshops attempting to reduce the level of violence and conflict. We hired a car and travelled to towns, townships and rural areas.

Everyone we met seemed to have one thing in common: utter exhaustion. People had been working for years – sometimes for decades – against the apartheid regime, with all the dangers that entailed. Now, after Mandela's release from prison and with the first democratic election over, they were attempting to create a new country where the hurts and injustices of the past could be forgiven. Everyone – black, white and coloured – wanted to talk to us about the changes since the election. In spite of the euphoria many people felt, some were worried; it seemed that creeping materialism was replacing the struggle for justice and equality. And the freedom which had been promised was a long time coming.

After talking over our ideas with a variety of key people in Johannesburg, Theresa and I travelled to Cape Town to see if we would be welcome there too. We said goodbye to the Sisters at St Benedict's and set off to take the train.

We arrived at the cavernous Park Station in the centre of Jo'burg in good time and walked up and down the brightly-lit tiled concourse looking for our platform. The station was thronged with hurrying early morning commuters, and there were stall-holders selling a variety of goods: fruit, neck-ties, soft drinks, handbags, umbrellas and snacks. We'd been warned that the station was a favourite haunt for pickpockets and thieves. Many unwary travellers had lost their luggage.

A notice directed us down a long set of grimy concrete steps to a dark, dingy platform. It was like sinking into the bowels of the earth, and the pungent smell of coal and steam reminded me of train journeys in my childhood. A sign on a noticeboard told us we would be sharing our carriage with "The Misses Mitchell". We prayed they wouldn't be old white racists, but the name gave nothing away.

Johannesburg to Cape Town is a distance of nine hundred and ninety-nine miles and the journey was scheduled to last twenty-six hours. The Trans-Karoo Express, drawn by two gigantic steam engines, finally pulled into the station two hours late with much huffing and puffing.

There were third- second- and "tourist"-class carriages, the third being hardly better than cattle trucks with only the bare wooden floor to sit on. We saw a family heave two floral-print chintz-covered armchairs up into a carriage to provide them with a relatively comfortable ride. Other third-class travellers wrapped themselves in blankets and curled up on the boards overnight. The second-class had rows of hard plastic seats and the passengers sat upright for the whole journey, many of them playing cards or nibbling snacks and drinking beer or Coke. The "tourist" accommodation was sumptuous by comparison, with only four people per compartment and vinyl-upholstered benches which converted into bunks at night. There was a small basin in each compartment with hot and cold water, two sets of hot showers at each end of the carriage, and clean sheets, blankets and pillows for hire from the attendant.

To our relief, the "Misses Mitchell" turned out to be two young coloured women: Faye, in her twenties, and her leggy, eleven-year-old sister, Roselle. How things had changed. Only a few years previously, white and coloured passengers could not have shared a compartment. We chatted as we prepared for the journey and waited for the other travellers to board. Faye told us that she and her sister were from Westbury, a suburb of Johannesburg.

I asked Roselle about her school. As a teacher, I was interested to hear how her education compared with the English system.

She said, "I go to rape classes after my lessons."

"Rape classes?"

"Yes. I learn about contraception, AIDS, pregnancy, drugs and what I should do if someone tries to rape me."

"I don't think children in England learn all that in school," I said.

There was a shout, a jolt and a clang, and the noise of an enormous monster sucking air into its lungs. Then more shuddering, a vast out-breath, and the giant engines heaved into life, pulling behind them twenty long carriages. We inched out of the gloom and into the sunlight.

A mile or two outside the station, Roselle stood up and pointed excitedly out of the window.

"Look," she said, "that's our block of flats." She stood gazing as her home passed slowly by.

When Roselle had settled herself again I asked, "What's it like, where you live?"

She hesitated, then said, "Sometimes when I'm alone in the flat, I hear fighting in the street. People killing each other."

"I want a gun," she went on, "I'd feel safer with a gun."

"Are you frightened?" I asked.

"At night I'm frightened."

Then she brightened up and said, "I want to go to University. I want to do business studies and then I'll be an air hostess."

Faye looked at her little sister with pride. "If she does, she'll be the very first person in the family to go to university. And that'll be because of the New South Africa." She paused and thought for a moment, then said, "There was a young man once who made a comment about Roselle, and another man took out a gun and shot his head off."

I didn't have any reason to suspect this was untrue. It was said with such simple conviction that it was impossible not to believe her. I sat on my side of the carriage surveying Roselle and wondered how this young girl could be so friendly, smiling and mature after seeing so much violence. Where did the spark, the clear-sightedness, the generosity of spirit come from?

Faye told us that she had decided not to get married, but to stay at home and make sure that Roselle was cared for. "How could I trust a husband to look after my little sister?" she said. "I am not prepared to take the risk."

That night as the four of us lay on our bunks in the compartment, winding slowly through the vast country, Roselle sang the new national anthem as she drifted off to sleep: *Nkosi Sikelel' iAfrica*.

I remembered the first time I'd heard it in the dusty community hall thirty years before, and as I joined in singing with Roselle, I felt I had come home.

* * *

It was exciting to be lying between clean cotton sheets in a comfortable berth on a train chugging through the African night. We were lulled by the gentle movement of the wheels on the track.

I woke in the morning feeling rested. We tidied up, showered and dressed, then all four of us set off for the dining car.

"Oooh! Bacon and eggs," cried Roselle, and her face lit up at the unaccustomed luxury of a full English breakfast.

"We're going to meet our aunt when we get to Cape Town," explained Faye as we ate. "She's paid for this journey. Our mother is in a nursing home. She had an operation but they gave her too much anaesthetic and it damaged her brain, so she's got dementia. Roselle is going to stay with our aunt for a while." Again, I wondered about Roselle and Faye's life. Would Roselle's dream of becoming an air hostess ever come to fruition? Would she achieve a place at University? I pondered on these thoughts as I gazed out of the window.

Black smoke belched out from the stacks on the massive locomotives as the train snaked its way around the rugged hills of the Great Karoo desert. We passed rolling farms, mountain ranges and fertile wine-lands until we entered the broad citrus-growing valleys of the Cape. I stood in the corridor glued to the window as the landscape scrolled by.

Eventually we saw Table Mountain in the distance, majestic in the bright sunlight with its "table cloth" of cloud obscuring the summit. Twenty minutes later, with much heaving and straining, a horrible screeching of brakes and the smell of burning, the train inched into Cape Town station.

Would we be as welcome here as we had been in Jo'burg? Or would Capetonians reject our ideas and send us packing?

We were met by Anne Oglethorpe, the director of the Quaker Peace Centre. She had been waiting more than two hours and was flustered, her grey hair ruffled by the persistent sea breeze.

"I'm afraid the train is very late," she said, "which is not unusual, of course. So I won't have time to show you round the Centre today. But I'll get you to your meeting."

We hurriedly said goodbye to our travelling companions and set off with Anne.

Our appointment was with Jonathan Muthige, a good-looking young theatre practitioner who was using drama techniques with people in the informal settlements, creating improvised plays with stories of conflict. We met him in his cramped office. He was smartly dressed in chinos and an open-neck shirt.

"I'm not happy with these plays," he said. "I want to use drama where everyone participates to try to deal with what's going on in their lives. People should be on their feet and *doing*, not just being an audience sitting back watching."

Jonathan had dreams of trying to tackle the violence and conflict that was endemic in the townships. We talked for a long time. We told him of the experience Theresa and I had of using Forum Theatre, and how we hoped to run workshops in South Africa. Forum Theatre is a form of interactive theatre where actors present a short play or scene in which the protagonist does not achieve his or her goal and there is no clear solution to the problem presented in the play. Audience members call out STOP! if they wish to change the action and make a suggestion for how the play could move towards a satisfactory, peaceful, conclusion. The actors then attempt to do what is suggested, but will ensure that a resolution to the conflict is not achieved. People from the audience are invited to join the actors on stage to assume a role within the drama and attempt to change the outcome by making new choices.

Johnathan was excited by these ideas and said, "I think you should come to Cape Town and set up here. We could work together." We promised to think about this as we said goodbye.

Afterwards, we made our way to the suburb of Mowbray where we had been offered cheap accommodation at the Cape Town Quaker Meeting House. This was a single-storey Cape Dutch building, just across the road from the Peace Centre, run down and in need of a lick of paint. But it had an imposing front door approached by wide stone steps, and pink bougainvillea tumbled over the curving portico.

We were ushered in by a dark-skinned woman with a glowing smile.

"Good afternoon," she said, "my name is Frances Barnett. I live here as caretaker for the building."

We sat with her in the kitchen having a cup of tea and she introduced us to her little boy, Max. Theresa asked her what her African name was.

"My mother never gave me a Xhosa name. She thought I would have a better chance in life with just an English name. My skin was fairly light when I was young and she hoped I might pass for coloured."

"And did you?"

"No. And anyway I didn't want to." Then she added proudly, "I am a Xhosa."

We had already discovered that names, skin colour, race, language and accent were frequently jumbled up in South Africa. We had met "black" people with English-sounding names, whose first language was Afrikaans, and who turned out to be "coloured". Race was flexible here: many people had either been forced by the apartheid authorities to change their official designation, or had themselves applied to change.

An individual making a personal application for a different classification invariably wished to join a race with a paler pigmentation. When considering whether someone should be categorised as white, coloured or black, one of the tests used to determine the outcome was the ludicrous pencil test. This involved inserting a pencil into an individual's hair: if the pencil didn't slide out, that person was designated black.

Many relatives were split apart by this pernicious test as the hair of different family members varied in texture. Parents, husbands, wives and siblings were forced to live in different areas and had to apply for official permits to visit each other.

In 1985, Mrs Helen Suzman, the MP for Houghton and sole liberal voice in Parliament, demonstrated the absurdity of the 1950 Population Registration Act. She asked how many South Africans had officially become members of a different race group. The answer was almost eight hundred:

518 coloureds became white
14 whites became coloured
7 Chinese became white
2 whites became Chinese
3 Malays became white
1 white became an Indian
50 Indians became coloured
57 coloureds became Indian
17 Indians became Malay
4 coloureds became Chinese
1 Malay became Chinese
89 blacks became coloured
5 coloureds became black

After giving her the answer, a Government Minister asked her, "Mrs Suzman, why must you ask such embarrassing questions?" To which she'd replied, "It's not the question that's embarrassing, Minister. It's the answer."

The Act wasn't repealed until 1991.

Because we were in the Cape during the Easter holiday period there weren't many people at work available for us to talk to, but when we met the staff at the Quaker Peace Centre they were as encouraging as Jonathan had been. As Thabo Makgoba had suggested to me in London, although there were people in South Africa who were experts in the field of conflict-resolution, and others who were experienced theatre practitioners, as yet we had found no one who seemed to have the particular mix of skills that Theresa and I had. Maybe this would be where we would find a niche.

I was humbled by people's enthusiasm for our ideas. So far no one we'd talked to had suggested or implied in any way that we were interlopers. They seemed to be open to two foreign women coming to their country to set up workshops in their communities. Why were they so welcoming – and especially to me, a Brit? The relationship between South Africa and Britain had not always been comfortable. The Anglo-Boer Wars of 1880 and 1899 had created a rift between the two countries, and more recently Margaret Thatcher had demonstrated her contempt for Nelson Mandela, labelling him a terrorist. She had also condemned the economic sanctions Desmond Tutu had called for.

On Easter Monday, Theresa and I took the Trans-Karoo Express back to Johannesburg and spent most of the hours on the train quietly thinking, writing and reading. We would be staying at the Quaker Meeting House once we were back in Jo'burg, and there were more meetings planned. But for now, we could reflect.

* * *

I had been given an introduction to a man called Nick Hayward, a coloured South African who was working in the communities around Bethal, a town one hundred and fifty-five kilometres east of Johannesburg. It was a traditional Afrikaans area where racism was endemic. We hired a car and drove out to meet Nick in front of the Kentucky Fried Chicken in the centre of the *dorp*. Black, white and coloured people walked dejectedly along the hot, litter-strewn pavements past sleazy shop fronts. We could sense tension in the air. The whole place was unappealing and felt slightly threatening.

At his office Nick introduced us to Themba Dube, a tall young Zulu who was working for him as a volunteer. Together they were trying – against resentment and powerful opposition from the local Afrikaans population – to persuade the black and coloured residents to register to vote. The community elections were to be held the following November, and Themba had thousands of leaflets to distribute.

He drove us to the township outside Bethal to meet two women named Belina and Thandi, who were running a school for children with mental and physical disabilities. We travelled over uneven dirt roads with deeply gouged-out dongas each side, past hundreds of tin shacks. Each had its own small plot of dried earth, where a few straggly maize plants struggled to survive.

"Some of the houses in the formal part of the township are serviced," said Themba, "but the municipality cut off all the electricity and water to try to force people to pay their rent."

"What about those who can't afford to pay?" I asked. "Is there any unemployment benefit?"

"There is nothing for people without work," replied Nick. "That's why there are so many criminals."

"What happens if they don't want to turn to crime?" I

persisted.

"They have relatives who live in the country," Themba said vaguely and I wondered, not for the first time, how people survived.

We arrived at Belina's shack, situated not in the serviced township, but on the edge of the informal settlement – the "location". She and her friend, Thandi, who had come from her own home, were waiting to greet us. Thandi was about forty years old, with a round, open face and smiling eyes, while Belina was older, perhaps fifty-five, and was lined and worried-looking. Both had brightly coloured *doeks* wound around their heads and Belina wore an apron over her thin cotton frock. There was no electricity or drainage, but she showed us with pride the water tap connected to a hose-pipe that disappeared through the open window, rigged up for her above a tin basin placed on a shelf.

The shack was about three metres square, and although it was made of corrugated iron and hardboard with just a strip of lino on the beaten earth, it was spotlessly clean and tidy. There were two rooms: in the first was a table covered with a plastic cloth, two upright chairs, and an enamelled metal kitchen cabinet with saucepans, mugs and plates. A few packets of food – rice, tea and mealie-meal – were stacked on a small set of shelves. The walls were covered in pages torn from magazines which created lively wallpaper. Through a doorway I glimpsed a narrow bed with a pink candlewick bedspread neatly covering it.

Belina and Thandi led us across a wide expanse of dried, brown grass to the "school" which consisted of two shacks made of tin sheeting. They stood half a mile from the township under the blistering sun. Green and white paint was flaking off the outside walls. The floors were bare earth mottled with worm-casts, and the few small plastic chairs were broken and unusable. Rain had come in through the roof and dripped onto a table which held pictures the children had made, making the paint run. The glass in the one window was cracked, and a large photograph, printed on cardboard, of a smiling Nelson Mandela was wedged on its side, covering the gap. His face was warped and disfigured with rain. Twenty-two children, all with different disabilities and needs, attended the school. Six adults worked as teachers, all unqualified and unpaid.

I asked Thandi if she had a disabled child of her own and wondered if this was why she'd started the school.

"No. I have two sons, but they are both okay. I used to watch the special children playing in the rubbish dump while the other kids were at school, and I decided to do something."

"But why?"

"Because I love them."

I choked back tears.

The purpose of our visit was to hand over five hundred rand (about fifty pounds), but it was a pitifully small amount in the face of such need. The money had been donated by the teachers at the comprehensive school in England where I worked. The head teacher had generously given me an extended Easter break.

Saying goodbye, Belina gave us a curtsey. She bobbed her knees and tilted her head to one side, bringing her hands up towards her face in a gesture almost like prayer. Theresa and I tried to convey that curtseying was definitely not what we wanted, but to no avail – the habit of deferring to white people was too ingrained.

As we left, Belina said, "Thank you, madam, thank you."

Back in Bethal, Theresa went to a telephone booth in the Post Office to confirm our flights for the following day. I stood outside, leaning against the car chatting with Themba.

"Please tell me what your name, 'Themba', means in English," I said.

"Themba means hope," he replied.

"But that's *my* name," I said, and we shook hands with delight, like a long-lost brother and sister, using the three-way African handshake.

Theresa came dashing out of the Post Office.

"We have to leave this evening," she blurted out.

"What?"

"We've got to get back to Jo'burg right away" She took a deep breath. "The airline cancelled our booking because we hadn't confirmed. I managed to persuade them to put us back on the flight – but it's tonight, not tomorrow. We must leave now if we're going to make it."

We hurriedly said goodbye to my new "brother" and set off through the dusty streets of Bethal, weaving our way through the grid system of roads until we were out on the four-lane highway and heading at speed for Johannesburg.

It was an uncomfortable and abrupt departure, with no opportunity to say goodbye to our new friends. I felt bereft as I boarded the plane.

* * *

Back in the UK, Theresa and I went our separate ways, she to her flat in London, I to my house in Sussex. We arranged to meet again in a few weeks' time once we'd both had a chance to digest our experiences in South Africa. The welcome we'd been given had been encouraging, and everyone we'd met had asked us to go back. But was this really feasible? Both Theresa and I had work in the UK and it wouldn't be an easy matter to leave for any length of time. Had we set up unrealistic expectations – both for ourselves and for the people we'd met in South Africa?

Late in May, Theresa came to Sussex and we went for a long walk by the river Arun, near my home. The pink campions and cow parsley nodded as we passed, and the swallows, newly arrived from Africa, wheeled above our heads. The river was deep and peaceful, eddying slowly as the tide turned. Elderflower and hawthorn bushes filled the air with their pungent scent.

"What do you think?" I asked, after some time walking in

silence, "Should we try to go back?"

"Yes, I think we should. Everyone asked us to. They liked what we were suggesting."

"The problem is how we're going to manage it. We'll need to raise money. No one would be able to pay for the workshops, and we can't live on fresh air."

"True, but there's money around for projects in South Africa at the moment."

After supper that evening, we sat one each side of my small pine kitchen table and made a list of "What Has To Be Done".

"If we're going to start fundraising for a proper project, we need to choose a name, a logo, a colour, and find some high-profile people to put on our letter-head," I said.

We thought for a bit, and then Theresa came up with a suggestion.

"How about calling it *The State of Flux Theatre Company*?"

"That's brilliant – South Africa *is* in a state of flux: everything is changing all the time. And flux is something you use to join different things together, too, so it's like connection."

But then Theresa changed her mind. "Actually, maybe it's not such a good idea: for a Zulu or a Xhosa the word 'flux' would probably be unpronounceable with the 'x' at the end."

"I expect you're right," I said, "and if you're not careful, it can sound pretty rude in English. Come to think of it, it's also a nasty bodily discharge."

We stayed in my kitchen coming up with all sorts of ideas, each one less appropriate than the last. Eventually, giggling, I suggested *Facilitation, Arbitration, Reconciliation and Training*. Theresa countered with *Conflict Resolution Always Possible*.

At this point we stopped, and I took a breath. "I know," I said, "let's call it the *Themba Project*. Remember meeting Themba in Bethal? He told me Themba means 'hope'."

"Now that's a *really* good idea," Theresa said.

"Okay. The Themba Project it is. Now a logo – what can that

be?"

We sat in silence for a while, pondering, and then I asked Theresa, "That jade you always wear around your neck – doesn't that have a meaning?"

It was a swirl of beautiful grey-green stone, hung on a leather thong.

She gently untied the cord and removed the jade.

"Yes, let's base our logo on this," she said. Then she added, "The word the Māori have for jade is *pounamu* and it's always been precious to them. It has sacred powers. Now it's valued by the *Pakehas*, too, the white New Zealanders."

Theresa placed the stone on a piece of paper. I picked up a pencil and drew round it: it was a simple spiral.

"It's the symbol of new life and growth and strength," she said, "and to the Māori it conveys the idea of perpetual movement. It's based on the unfurling silver fern."

"I'll send this sketch to my brother and ask him to draw it properly for us," I said.

The summer of 1995 was a drought year in Sussex, and as I trudged back and forth from the house to the vegetable patch with buckets of water saved from my shower, I began to plan how I could spend some months in South Africa the following year. I was teaching drama and business studies in a comprehensive school, and Theresa worked in prisons as part of HM Prison Inspectorate. She was also lecturing in the drama therapy department of Roehampton College. We would both have to approach our respective employers and ask them to give us time off.

I potted up some tiny hollyhock plants grown from the seeds I'd taken from the garden at St Benedict's convent in Johannesburg. Together with a jam-jar for the money, I put them on the footpath by the river with a notice: HOLLYHOCKS. TO RAISE MONEY FOR RECONCILIATION WORK IN SOUTH AFRICA. 25p. By the end of the day there was enough money to buy stamps to post our first appeal letters.

A few days later, after Theresa had returned to London, I sat down to work out a comprehensive fundraising plan together with a draft budget and a letter to people who might agree to become patrons of the new Themba Project.

As I worked, I suddenly realised with a shock that although we'd discussed with everyone we'd met in South Africa the idea of running interactive drama workshops for conflict resolution, the one thing Theresa and I hadn't talked about was the detail of what we were actually going to *do*. What would happen in the workshops? How would they be structured? Where would the participants come from? What did we hope would be the outcomes? And maybe most important of all: how well would the two of us work together as a team? We had taken a great deal for granted. Although we had both been trained at the Institute of Drama Therapy, were trainers with the Alternatives to Violence Project, and were both drama practitioners, we had never actually run a workshop together.

Theresa came back to Sussex in August and we began to plan in earnest. Once again we sat in the kitchen with the door to the garden wide open and the rose-scented summer air drifting in.

We decided that the workshops would all have the same

basic structure, adapted according to whatever group we were working with. Each one would begin with welcomes and a short introduction to the day. Then, after the guidelines had been agreed, we'd run some getting-to-know-you games, and different drama activities and exercises.

We would use Forum Theatre devised by Augusto Boal from Brazil; the same process we had explained to Jonathan Muthige when we'd met him in Cape Town. After the initial exercises and games, people would get into small groups and work on a short improvised play with a specific conflict at its core. Each group would show their piece to the rest of the participants, and then we would choose one play to explore with everyone, using an interactive theatre process. People would take on different roles within the drama and come up with their own ideas about how to resolve the conflict.

Because Quakers were supporting us both financially and spiritually, we asked if we could run a pilot workshop with Friends at my Quaker Meeting, the Blue Idol in West Sussex. This would give us an opportunity to see if our ideas were realistic.

In February 1996, thirteen members from the Meeting gathered to experience what was to become the Themba Project, exploring through drama how conflicts could be resolved. The feedback the Quakers gave us that day was extremely positive, and Theresa and I realised we did indeed have a workable structure – *and* would be able to work happily together.

When we arrived in Johannesburg two months later, however, the people who came to our workshops and the stories we explored were very, very different.

Chapter 6

Johannesburg, 1996

April 12 1996. I landed at Jo'burg airport, and went once again to stay with the Sisters at St Benedict's. The school in England where I was teaching had agreed that I could take the whole of the summer term off, and it was with a mixture of excitement and relief that I settled back into the rhythms of convent life. The Sisters made me feel very welcome, and they were glad to be involved in the Themba Project as it began to take shape. But my stay with them was touched with sadness. Sister Jane, who had been the mother of the convent, had died a few months earlier of a brain haemorrhage. It was she who had planted the garden, filled with roses and hollyhocks, and I enjoyed its peace and that of the Sisters as they moved calmly through the convent, engaged in their work.

I knew, however, that it wouldn't be feasible for Theresa and me to stay there for the whole of the South African winter. We needed a place to rent for the next four months, and a car to get about in. The latter I bought on the recommendation of a friend of the Sisters, the Rev Horace McBride, who was the manager at St Peter's, the ecumenical centre across the road. Mr McBride, a coloured South African, had an Indian brother-in-law who ran a second-hand car business. When I rang Horace to ask if he could help me, he answered the phone with these words:

"Jesus Loves You."

"Pardon?"

"Jesus Loves You."

"Oh, thank you very much."

"Don't mention it."

When I brought the car, a vivid yellow Mondeo, back to St Benedict's, Sister Patricia promptly (and aptly) named it "The

Yellow Peril".

The house I found to rent was in Yeoville, a run-down but lively area of Johannesburg. The infamous Rocky Street ran straight through Yeoville, with cafés, nightclubs and drinking dens, and music blaring out from the clubs each night. Illegal drugs were openly for sale in doorways. There was an arcade where traders hawked their wares, and along the side of the road were dress shops and a dingy Shoprite supermarket. Makeshift barbers operated on the pavements, their customers sitting on plastic chairs under small, tent-like structures which they erected each day. Electric flexes for the shavers ran perilously across the pavement to power sockets in the shops. The area was noisy, grimy, dangerous – and exciting.

I took the Yellow Peril to the Automobile Association (AA) and asked them to check it. It turned out to be a complete disaster because it failed almost every test. The CV joints were nearly worn through, the brakes were dodgy and the tyres needed replacing. It was much too big and heavy for me to drive so I had to prop myself up on cushions, but then my feet couldn't get to the pedals. I felt foolish and embarrassed about having bought it, and replaced it at an auction with a small City Golf in sensible blue.

One Saturday morning I heard shouting from outside in the street, and hammering on the gate. I went to investigate. "Come quick, madam," a young man shouted, "there's a mugging. He's in the street. He's bleeding."

I grabbed my house keys and hurried out. On the kerb sat a young man with blood oozing across his shoulders and pouring down his arms. His vest was slashed, and I could see gashes across his back and in his neck. The flesh was pale pink under his dark brown skin, and brilliant red blood pumped out, dripping into the gutter. I sat down next to him and wanted to put my arm around him, but there was no way I could hold him without getting myself covered in blood.

HIV, HIV, HIV – the thought ran through my head – *he might have HIV.*

A crowd gathered. Someone rang for an ambulance. People stood around repeating the story of how they'd seen the man lurching down the street. Another guy had jumped out from behind one of the trees that lined the road, stabbed him repeatedly, and ran away. We heard a siren and soon the injured man had been patched up and driven off.

I bought a number of pairs of latex gloves after that, and never went anywhere without them.

* * *

The purpose of the workshops Theresa and I planned to give was to help people deal with the conflict they encountered in their lives. But I began to realise I had begun to absorb the all-pervading atmosphere of violence myself.

I'd met a number of people (mostly white or coloured) who had become so paralysed by fear that they were afraid to leave their homes. They were victims of the concept of the *swaart gevaar* – the "black threat". They'd heard about frightening incidents, seen the television and read the papers. They had friends who'd been mugged, raped, hijacked and murdered. Their dread wasn't paranoia: there was a very real danger that the same could happen to them. But it was the *fear* that paralysed.

I sank deep into this fear myself after about three weeks. Almost everyone I knew warned me what could happen if I walked in *that* street, drove down *that* road, shopped for food after 6.00 pm, or walked anywhere alone. Anxiety gripped me and held me fast. Wherever I went I imagined that I would be stabbed, mugged or hijacked. I couldn't bring myself to contemplate rape. I always made sure I had money in my shoe (*But they make you take your shoes, off, anyway,* someone said) and checked that no one was following me (*They come up behind you and throttle you*). I worried over which was safer: to leave the car engine running while I jumped out to open the security gates at my house, or to turn off the engine and take the keys with me (*They shoot you when they hijack your car so you can't identify them*). Always the ubiquitous *They*.

Along with the debilitating fear, I began to feel homesick, so I phoned some English friends, the Farmers, who were now living in Swaziland.

"Come and visit," said Bill Farmer. "We'll have apple crumble with custard, and there's a roaring fire."

I needed no persuading. Winter had set in, and in Johannesburg it is not a kind season. The days are clear and sunny, but it's very cold at night and frost is not uncommon.

I set off from Jo'burg a few days later and on the way visited my "brother" Themba in his tiny, bare office in Bethal. We greeted each other with a hug.

"Howz'it, Themba?"

He sounded dispirited. "Eish, it's hard, man. I'm trying to help the farm-workers. Their employers treat them badly and won't pay them properly."

"What can you do?"

"I'm trying to teach the workers their rights, but they're not confident. Even though we've had the local elections, the people still feel they can't stand up to their bosses."

He sat in his chair looking morose. I decided to give him my news.

"I've got something to tell you which might cheer you up, Themba. Theresa and I have decided to call our work The Themba Project. We've named it after you."

He looked across at me, and a broad smile spread across his face. "Hey, man – that's *lekker*!"

The following morning, I left the lush, fertile Crocodile River valley with its orange groves, palm trees and brilliant purple and white bougainvillea, and climbed steadily into the mountains.

The drive south towards Swaziland was breathtakingly beautiful. As I entered the tiny kingdom through the Jeppe's Reef northern border post, the air was crisp and the atmosphere changed. Immediately through the gates I knew I was in "real" Africa. Women sat at each side of the pot-holed road nursing babies and selling avocados, aubergines, oranges, pineapples and pawpaws. Towers of logs stood like sentinels along the edge of the road, the vendors sitting behind them keeping watch. The wood looked precarious and ready to teeter to the ground. The smoky, biscuity aroma of roasting mealies rose into the air as they cooked on grills placed over fires in old oil drums. It was a far cry from the high-rise buildings, pollution and diesel smell of central Johannesburg.

I drove south through lovely mountains with smooth, grassy flanks, and stopped at a wide river to eat my sandwich. Water rushed boisterously over boulders so I didn't hear the children approaching. Out of nowhere they appeared: half a dozen boys and girls, all barefoot and raggedly dressed. They looked at my food, their big brown eyes widening. What should I do? I couldn't go on eating in front of these waifs. They stood still in a semi-circle in front of me and stared.

"Do you speak English?" I asked.

They gazed at me.

"All right, you can have the *naartjies*, but you must share them. I don't have enough to give you one each."

I held out the three small oranges. The tallest boy stepped forward and, with great care, took them from me. He split them in half and handed them to the others. They grinned and ran off, and in a moment had disappeared. I finished my hard-boiled egg and sandwich and continued on my journey. I looked out for the children, but they were nowhere to be seen. Where had they come from? There were no buildings in sight, no shacks or houses. The children had been swallowed up by the mountains.

The Farmers lived in a big house in the main town, Mbabane.

It was comforting to sit by their log fire in the evening, listening to their CD of the Soweto String Quartet, sipping wine and indulging in an "English" supper (which included, as promised, apple crumble and custard). We were joined for the meal by the Principal of the nearby Waterford Kamhlaba United World College and his wife, Janet. The College was perched high above the town, halfway up a mountain, and Janet taught drama there. When I told her about the Themba Project, she invited me to run a workshop for conflict resolution with some of her students.

"There's enough conflict up at the college to keep you busy," she said, "but I don't think I'll be able to organise a workshop with the staff – even though they need it most. No one would come. So I'll just ask you to do something with some of the pupils."

After breakfast the next day I drove up the hill to meet a dozen or so of Janet's students. They were fourteen to sixteen years old, and came from many different countries in the world. Janet watched me and made notes as I worked.

After the young people had left for their next class, Janet said, "I wish they were as absorbed as that in my lessons. How do you do it?"

"I don't know," I replied. "Maybe it's because I'm a visitor, and they were being polite."

"They're not usually so cooperative. I want you to explain more about how you teach."

I felt embarrassed and didn't know how to respond.

Janet changed the subject. "Come and have lunch and I'll tell you about Waterford. Do you know about the United World College movement?"

"I heard of it for the first time last night."

We wandered across the campus and a little way down the hill to the Principal's house. It was large, airy and well-furnished, with cream-coloured sofas and pale wood tables. I leant against the kitchen counter as Janet prepared a salad.

"The movement began in 1962," she said. "Kurt Hahn was the founder, and his idea was that if you bring young people from different countries and cultures to be educated together, they would learn to respect each other and this would lead to a more peaceful world."

"Sounds like a good idea."

"Waterford started because of apartheid," Janet went on. "It wasn't a United World College to begin with. Michael Stern, who'd been a head teacher in England, was asked by Trevor Huddleston to come to South Africa to run a school for boys from different ethnic groups. But of course when he tried, the authorities closed the school down. After that happened three times he gave up and came here, and raised the money to buy this mountainside."

"But why is it called Waterford?" I asked.

"It was a farm before it became a school. The guy who sold Michael the land was an Irishman, and he'd called his farm Waterford."

"And Kamhlaba?" I asked, trying to get my tongue round the unfamiliar word.

"Oh, that was granted to the college by the last King of Swaziland, King Sobhuza II. It means *We are all of one earth*."

Over lunch Janet told me more about the school and I recounted some of my experiences of teaching drama in the UK. If I'd known then that I would one day apply for a job at the college, I would have asked her a lot more questions.

* * *

I returned to Johannesburg after my trip to Swaziland and learnt to live with the day-to-day anxiety and the feeling that I had to constantly watch my back. Over the next few weeks I worked on making contacts in different parts of the country, and also ran a few workshops on my own in Johannesburg. However, I missed having Theresa with me as co-facilitator; she was still in England, finalising some work in London. I drove across vast swathes of South Africa; over mountains, alongside rivers, through deserts, across farmland and to towns and villages. I had been warned it was too dangerous to travel on my own, but how else was I to meet with people in the different organisations who wanted to book the Themba Project? I decided I was not going to be intimidated by the doom-mongers. Instead, I relished the opportunity to visit different parts of the country. I loved the sense of freedom as I drove along almost deserted highways and saw the landscape and sky changing as I went.

On 16 June, the twentieth anniversary of the Soweto uprising of 1976, I was taken to a vast, cold community hall in Khayelitsha, a sprawling township just outside Cape Town, which Theresa and I had passed the previous year. I had been invited to join in the celebrations for National Youth Day. Hundreds of people of all ages, from very small children to ancient men and elderly women, were singing and dancing. They were mostly dressed shabbily in old overcoats, with woollen beanies on their heads. Some of the men carried knobkerries, and many of the women had babies strapped to their backs. This public holiday marked the day when Hector Pieterson, a twelve-year-old schoolboy, was shot dead by police. He, together with hundreds of other children, had been protesting in Soweto against a recently passed law which stated that the medium of instruction in all state-run schools would henceforth be Afrikaans. This was regarded as the language of the oppressor, and the decree was totally unacceptable to the students – and to their teachers, many of whom could not speak Afrikaans. As the pupils, most of them in school uniform, marched through the streets near their school, the police fired on them. Over the following days one hundred and seventy-six people, mostly children, were killed, and a thousand injured. This spontaneous uprising spread across South Africa, bringing more deaths and injuries. Ultimately the

Government backed down and English was once again allowed as the language for teaching in the township schools.

* * *

I was returning to Johannesburg after yet another meeting when I realised it was growing dark. I hadn't booked a B&B or hotel to break the long journey because I'd expected to find a place along the way. I had forgotten, not for the first time, what an enormous country I was travelling through. Dusk doesn't last long in Africa and I was beginning to worry when, out of the gloom, I saw a bright orange HOTEL sign. With relief, I turned in and stopped. I was at a place called Jamestown.

The large wooden door to the hotel stood open. In the shadowy, echoing entrance hall, I found two small children, a boy and a girl, hardly more than four or five years old, both with white-blonde hair and brilliant blue eyes. They looked up at me.

"Could you find your Mummy and ask her if she has a room for the night?"

There was no response. They gazed at me uncomprehendingly. I tried again. "Would you go and get your Mummy or Daddy for me?"

The infants stood mute. They looked like children from the *Midwich Cuckoos*, and obviously hadn't understood a word I'd said. They were clearly Afrikaners and it appeared that they spoke no English.

A harassed-looking woman arrived, wiping her hands on her apron. She was probably only thirty, but her worried expression and lank brown hair gave her the appearance of someone older. She was skinny, and her spindly legs stuck out from beneath cut-off jeans. She shooed the children away and turned to me. "Ag, sorry. We're not used to guests. Do you want a room?" She spoke in halting English with a strong Afrikaans accent.

"Yes please," I said. I was reluctant to stay because the place had an air of dejection and seemed vaguely threatening, but it was now pitch dark outside and I didn't want to drive on in the night.

"Do you want a meal?" the woman asked.

"Yes please." I said again. "*Dankie*."

"I can do chicken or beef. Which do you want?"

"Chicken, *asseblief*," I replied. "Please."

I thought I detected a slight frown pass over the women's brow and was about to ask her which would be easiest, when she said, "I'll show you where you can sleep."

The room was on the ground floor down a dark, dingy corridor. There was a very low double bed with a grey-green cover, one upright chair and a chipped, cream-painted wardrobe. The room was bitterly cold, and smelt musty and damp.

"The bar upstairs is open if you want a drink," said the landlady. "I'll go and do your meal."

She left me and I looked around, in vain, for some form of heating. I started down the corridor in search of a heater and when I saw a one-bar electric fire in an unoccupied room, I picked it up and carried it back. The flex was badly frayed, and as I plugged it in to the wall socket, I wondered whether it would start a conflagration in the night and burn down the building.

The bed had only a couple of threadbare blankets, so I set off again and removed bedding from another room and took it back with me. Then I climbed the wide wooden stairs to find a drink.

I could hear rowdy laughter and loud male voices. I reached the top step and opened the door. As I walked over to the bar, the talking and laughing stopped and six pairs of eyes followed me in silence. No one seemed to be serving, though all the men had glasses or bottles in their hands. A big, red-faced bear of a man, with a shock of sandy hair and enormous paunch, heaved himself reluctantly up from his stool and squeezed round to the other side of the bar.

"What do you want?" he said in English.

"Um ... Could I have a ..." I was about to ask for a glass of wine, but decided that in this company it was probably not a good idea.

"Can I have a beer, please? A Castle Lager?"

The conversation among the men resumed quietly in Afrikaans. I asked the man who'd served me if I could pay, but he looked nonplussed and shrugged. As the men continued talking, with occasional glances in my direction, I began to feel like an alien from another planet. The longer I sat there the more uncomfortable I felt.

The landlady reappeared: my meal was waiting for me in the dining room. As I ate the dry, stringy chicken, tinned peas and soggy chips, she explained that she'd had to get the stove alight before she could cook. I realised, too late, that if I'd chosen beef she would have lit the *braai* (barbecue) and cooking would have been easier for her.

As I chewed the meat, the landlady, whose name was Annike, stood over me watching. I asked her to sit with me, and after glancing nervously over her shoulder, she did so.

"Is this your hotel?" I asked.

"Yes." Then she stopped and thought for a moment. "Well – I don't know. I think so. My husband left so I suppose it's mine now."

"Were those your children? The little ones I saw when I arrived?"

"Ja – they're mine. I've got a couple of others – boys – but they're away."

"Away?"

"Yes. The school is far so they have to board. I see them only in holidays. I don't have money to visit. I can't afford a car, so they go on the bus. It takes all day." She sounded bleak and lonely.

"Those men in the bar upstairs," I ventured, "do they all live around here?"

"They're farmers. They come in most nights. They can be loud and – how do you say, *irriterende* – annoying, but I have to put up with it. We don't get many people wanting to stay."

The noise from upstairs had increased in volume and as I went along the corridor to bed, I could hear the men arguing loudly with each other. It sounded as if they were getting more and more inebriated, and some were now singing lustily. There was no lock on the door of my room, so I wedged the chair under the handle and prayed for an undisturbed night.

The one-bar fire had taken the chill off, but it was still horribly cold and the bedding was damp. The blankets had the sour, foetid smell of unwashed towels that have been left too long in an airless cupboard. I burrowed into bed fully dressed, turned off the light, and fell fast asleep.

It seemed like hours later when I was woken by thunderous banging, and shouts and yells in Afrikaans. The men were leaving, and as they went, they were thumping on all the doors of the rooms along the corridor. I was scared. In their drunken state, who knew what they were capable of? I was just one English woman in a god-forsaken part of the country. If they wanted to take revenge for the Boer War, I was a perfect target. There was only a rickety chair pushed up against the flimsy door handle between me and them. As they got closer to my room, I could think of no way to protect myself if they bashed the door down. I lay curled up in bed, cold, shivering, and frightened.

They crashed their fists against the wall, and I knew they were standing right outside my door – I could hear their heavy breathing. They roared and yelled, and I didn't need to know Afrikaans to understand their threats. Then, from a distance, I heard a woman's voice shouting, and I guessed Annike was telling them to clear off. The banging stopped, the voices died away, and the men retreated with heavy footsteps.

It was a long time before I fell asleep again.

The next morning I was up before seven o'clock and had a

wash in freezing water in the hand-basin. I walked down the corridor and found the back door. The only thing that was keeping it closed was an old wooden spoon slotted through two metal hoops designed for a padlock. It would have been easy for the men to return in the night, wrench the door open and come back into the building. I shuddered when I thought what could have happened.

It was not yet light outside, and my car was covered in thick ice. Back in the hotel there was no sign of Annike, or the children, or any of the men. I hung around, went outside again and put my suitcase in the car, and walked back into the building. Still there was no one around. I returned to the car and scraped the ice off the windscreen with my credit card.

At eight o'clock I decided to set off, leaving some money on the table. Once on the road, away from the hotel from hell and with a warmed-up car, I began to feel better. Just forty minutes later I arrived at Aliwal North, where a bright, modern motel showed signs of life. I went straight to the dining room and ordered a slap-up Afrikaner breakfast: eggs, bacon, mushrooms, tomatoes, fried bread, toast, jam and coffee. I should have travelled on a little further the previous night.

I checked the map and noticed that my journey was about to take me past the turn-off to one of the Concentration Camp Memorials. Most people in England only know about the concentration camps of Nazi Germany and are unaware that it was in fact the British who invented them during the Boer War. They were created to incarcerate the women and children of the Afrikaner farmers who had left their families and gone away to fight. A number of black servants were imprisoned there too – those who had refused to leave their masters. Conditions were barbaric, with inmates herded like cattle into kraals. The sun beat down, there was no shade, and the prisoners died of heat, hunger, thirst and sunstroke. Food rations were minimal, and treatment harsh. More than twenty-two thousand Boer children died in those concentration camps, as well as four thousand mothers and over a thousand men – those who were too old or unwell to fight.

The memorial was constructed of huge triangular blocks of grey stone, pointing sharply up into the blue sky. One of the slabs was engraved with the names and ages of the children who had died there. Some had been less than two years old. Against one wall was a carved relief in granite of an emaciated woman, a child kneeling at her feet. A bunch of fresh white roses had recently been placed on the base of the plinth. Who had left them there? Although the conflict had been a century before, memories lingered. I stood with my head bowed and was close to tears as I read the names of the mothers and children who had died in the camp. It was a terrible reminder of the brutality of war, and of the uncomfortable relationship English-speaking South Africans and Afrikaners continued to share.

I travelled on to Johannesburg contemplating how the many diverse population groups in South Africa were attempting to come to terms with their very different histories.

Chapter 7

South Africa, July 1996

A few days after my experience at the "hotel from hell", I went with the Sisters to one of the hearings of the Truth and Reconciliation Commission (TRC) being held in the Methodist Central Church in the heart of Jo'burg. When we entered, Archbishop Desmond Tutu was on the stage, surrounded by other commissioners. They were listening to the testimony of Nombulelo Makhubo, the mother of Mbuyiso, the boy who had picked up the body of twelve-year-old Hector Pieterson during the 1976 student uprising in Soweto. The photograph of Mbuyiso running towards the camera with Hector in his arms, Hector's sister by his side, became one of the iconic images of the struggle against apartheid. Mrs Makhubo told the commission that her son had fled after being harassed by the security police when the photo was published in newspapers around the world. She had received one letter from him, posted in Nigeria in 1978, but had heard nothing since. She had no idea where her boy was, or even whether he was still alive.

"The Arch", as Desmond Tutu was affectionately known, stopped the proceedings when emotions ran too high and gave everyone a breather. He saw the Sisters and me enter the hall, called a temporary halt, and came down from the stage to greet us. It was humbling to be in the presence of such a man.

"Are you alright, Desmond?" asked Sister Maureen.

"No, I'm not at all alright," he responded. He gave each of us a big hug. There were tears in his eyes.

"I hope you're praying for me?" he asked.

"Of course we are," said Sister Maureen. "What do you think?"

"Good thing, too," replied The Arch, "I need all the help I can get."

We stayed at the hearing for the whole day and heard some unbearable testimonies. Terrible things had been done by both sides during the struggle against apartheid.

The next morning I read in the paper that we had been there on one of the "worst" days so far.

* * *

I was invited to visit the informal settlement of Diepsloot, one hour to the north of Johannesburg, to see a performance by a group of teenagers. I drove through some of the smartest and most expensive northern suburbs – Houghton, Rosebank, Sandton, Morningside. The houses were grand with massive electric gates, razor wire on top of high walls, wide drives, gardens with huge trees and swimming pools. I branched off the main road onto the R511 where the surroundings became steadily less salubrious. The desperately poor township of Diepsloot was only forty-three kilometres outside Jo'burg, but it might as well have been on another planet.

Thousands of shacks extended away to the horizon, with dirt tracks running between them. People drifted along, apparently aimlessly. Piles of rubbish spilled out of plastic bags, and dogs and pigeons rummaged among them. Women sat by the roadside at makeshift wooden counters selling peanuts and small packets of orange-coloured crisps. Babies played in the dirt. A few men wandered up and down peddling cans of Coca Cola and orange Fanta from nests of ice in plastic buckets. Occasionally a passer-by would stop and buy a drink.

It was a crisp, sunny morning, and the performance I'd come to watch took place out of doors on the dusty ground. The play told an all-too-common story: first a girl is abused by her father. She asks a teacher for help, but he turns her away telling her not to be disgusting. So she goes to the police, but they taunt her and call her an *isifebe* (a slag) and attempt to kiss her and touch her breasts. The audience enjoyed this scene in particular and laughed and clapped raucously. The girl tells her mother about the abuse and is thrown out of the house. She wanders away and eventually finds other homeless children, and they become friends.

The play ended with all the youngsters standing in a line, their right fists raised, singing *Nkosi Sikelel' iAfrika*. It seemed to imply that everything was fine now in the New South Africa – which it plainly wasn't.

From the passionate way she performed her part, I had the impression that the girl playing the main protagonist was acting out her own story. After the performance, I went behind the rudimentary scenery screens to have a chat with her. She was standing by herself wearing the tight pink T-shirt and grubby white mini-skirt she'd worn in the play. She looked shell-shocked and forlorn. I walked up to her with my hands outstretched and she fell into my arms. I gave her a hug and she clung to me, even though she had no idea who I was. She would have seen me earlier in the audience – the only white person there.

"That was very powerful acting," I said as I drew away.

She looked down at her feet, her breath coming in sharp gasps.

"Thank you."

"What's your name?" I asked.

"Vusile."

"It's a very sad story," I continued.

"It's my story," she muttered. "It's what happened to me."

"I thought maybe it was," I said. "I'm sorry Vusile." I paused for a moment, then I put my arm around her and asked, "How does it feel – acting it out with lots of people watching?"

She shrugged and said nothing. I could feel anger rising in me. This child, who was probably no more than thirteen years old, had just told her story of violent sexual abuse to an audience of sniggering men and women. No one was supporting her, no one appeared to realise how vulnerable she was. I couldn't help wondering how many other young girls had been abused in this way and had been ignored when they'd tried to tell their story.

* * *

I was relieved when Theresa joined me in Jo'burg. I felt as if I had been carrying the Themba Project alone on my shoulders. I still seethed every time I thought of Vusile and I felt powerless in the face of all South Africa's woes. It would be good to have someone to share all this with. I hoped Theresa would be happy with the workshops I'd arranged.

One of the first was in the township of Thokoza. Richard Qongo, the leader of the Freedom Artists who'd invited us, warned us that the people living in this area had suffered some of the worst violence during the run-up to the first democratic election. Different factions supported either the IFP (the Inkatha Freedom Party, Mangosuthu Buthelezi's movement) or the ANC (African National Congress, the party led by Nelson Mandela). People living on one side of the main street had been terrorised by those on the other, and there had been brutal killings and even "necklacings". Many had fled their homes, and now the houses were occupied by others, usually of a different political persuasion. Tension was rife.

Richard had phoned me with directions to the Municipal Hall in Khumalo Street. He told me that since hardly any whites visited Thokoza, people living in the township would assume Theresa and I were doctors or social workers, so we would be relatively safe. "But if you drive into Soweto, you'll probably be seen as tourists and are more likely to be attacked," he laughed. I knew that the worst of the violence had taken place on this very street, and conflicts still simmered.

We arrived at ten o'clock in the morning at the smart, new

hall. It was built of yellow bricks, with a corrugated iron roof painted green. Someone had already opened up and arranged the plastic chairs in rows, but there was no one about. The place smelt clean, with a whiff of disinfectant. At one end of the room there was a laminated kitchen table on which someone had placed a hand-written sign: "Themba Workshop – Today".

Theresa and I set about reorganising the room, making a circle of the chairs. We waited, but no one came. We wandered outside to the car park which was surrounded by a high chain-link fence. Standing in the sunshine, we watched people walking up and down the busy street. They glanced over at us, but didn't seem curious. After half an hour, a car screeched through the gate and stopped. A tall, thin young man in jeans and a royal blue workman's jacket jumped out, extended his hand and apologised.

"Eish, man, I'm sorry. You're Kim and Theresa, hey? I'm Richard. People are coming for the workshop. Everyone's delayed, but they'll be here."

We waited a bit longer but no one else arrived.

Suddenly Richard said, "I'll take you to the school. There are some children practising there. They said they'd like you to visit."

"What if people come for the workshop while we're not here?" Theresa asked. "Won't they think nothing is happening and go away again?"

"It'll be OK," said Richard.

We took him at his word and piled into his car. He drove fast through the township, but when we arrived at the school, it seemed deserted. It was a Saturday and there was no one in the reception office, and there appeared to be no children or teachers. We walked down a long corridor past empty schoolrooms until we heard muffled singing in the distance. Richard flung open a door, and a wonderful sound burst forth. Twenty girls danced and sang in harmony, their faces shining with bright smiles.

They were about twelve or thirteen years old. One wore a gym-slip, but most were in jeans and sweaters. They stamped their feet and their bodies swayed in unison as they sang.

When the song came to an end, the children crowded around me and Theresa, hugging us, laughing, and thanking us for coming.

We returned to the hall in Khumalo Street, but there was still no sign of anyone. The chairs that Theresa and I had arranged in a circle had, however, mysteriously been put back into theatre-style rows. The room was chilly, and we shivered in our green Themba T-shirts. About half an hour later people began drifting in, and eventually thirteen members of the Freedom Artists had assembled.

We ran the workshop we'd planned. After some warm-up exercises, we introduced the interactive theatre process and people formed themselves into groups and created plays based on some of the conflicts they had experienced. Then in the second half they tried out different ways of solving the problems non-violently. Towards the end, we gathered in a circle and I asked for feedback. Richard said, "I can see how this sort of interactive theatre can help people tackle some of the conflicts we have here. We'll try to use this in our own work."

Then we held a ceremony. We called each participant up individually to shake hands and receive a green Themba certificate. All the Freedom Artists beamed with pride. Because of the paucity of education, South Africans valued diplomas for any sort of learning activity. There was a desperate shortage of jobs, and people needed evidence to show they had achieved some training, however informal or unaccredited.

As we left Thokoza, I wondered how the other workshops I had booked would compare to the one we'd just run for the young Freedom Artists. Would we succeed with all the groups we were due to meet?

* * *

The beautiful Magaliesberg Mountains were a couple of hours' drive north of Johannesburg. Theresa and I had been invited here to a conference organised by The Community Dispute Resolution Trust (CDRT) to run a workshop at an international gathering of conflict-resolution experts. Here we met three people from Cape Town who were working in non-government organisations trying to reduce the level of violence in the country: Andrew, Ghalib and Razaan. We very soon became firm friends.

Although Theresa and I had now run a number of workshops in Jo'burg and received feedback as to their value, it was nevertheless intimidating to be at an international gathering of professional non-violence practitioners from different parts of the world. Would they be able to set aside their expertise and play? Some of the papers at the conference were given by esteemed academics, and we weren't sure if they would be able to relax enough to participate.

We needn't have worried. We proved to be a welcome relief from the sometimes dry lecture-style presentations the delegates attended. Everyone commented on how effective and enjoyable our workshops were. Warm up drama exercises and games were followed by participants working on improvised plays from their own real-life experiences of conflict.

A few days after the conference was over, Theresa and I travelled to Durban in KwaZulu Natal. We were about four hours into our journey when I turned to Theresa and said, "I need a hair-cut. And I feel like having it bleached. Like Annie Lennox. What do you think?"

"I want to get mine done, too," she said. "I want it short – get rid of this French pleat."

We arrived at the city of Pietermaritzburg and stopped at a general store to buy a snack.

"Could you tell us if there is a ladies' hairdressing salon near here?" I asked the woman behind the counter.

"There's Luigi's round the corner," she replied, "but he's usually fully booked."

"It's worth a try," I said.

When we arrived at Luigi's, he said, with a heavy Italian accent, "My lady, she jus' cancel. She suppose' come today, but she no show. She phone. I do you both, now-now, if you want."

I asked him if he knew what Annie Lennox looked like. He did. Theresa and I sat in the salon for the rest of the afternoon, giggling like a couple of silly teenagers, getting our hair done. While the bleach was cooking on my head, Luigi re-styled Theresa's hair into a fashionably asymmetric "Vidal Sassoon" bob. She looked very much younger. When the bleach had taken and my hair trimmed, I looked better, too – but not exactly an Annie Lennox look-alike. This light-hearted interlude was a welcome, although brief, relief from the stress of living and working in Johannesburg, where we were often exhausted and anxious.

It was less than fifty more miles to Durban. We arrived on 6 August, Hiroshima Day, and went to the Japanese Gardens to pay our respects. We strolled in the sunshine, crossed the little red bridge, and looked down at the water lilies. I watched the white ducks swimming contentedly on the lake and contemplated the terrible destruction that had taken place in Japan fifty-one years earlier. It was a sombre reminder of the challenges of finding nonviolent answers to conflict.

One of the most powerful and emotionally-charged workshops of the whole four months took place in Pietermaritzburg a few days later on 9 August: South African Women's Day. The event had been arranged by Family and Marriage in South Africa (FAMSA), and all the women who came had experienced some form of domestic violence. They'd been attending support groups run by a sister organisation called Women in Need, and were learning to become facilitators to run activities for other abused women. All were white or Asian – there were no black Africans. We were told that black women rarely disclosed the mistreatment they suffered in their homes.

We worked in the hall of a building that had originally been a prestigious private school for girls. Once it must have been elegant, with arched doorways, large windows, cloisters of warm stone and a sun-filled quadrangle. Now it was dilapidated. It smelt damp and stale, and was very much in need of a lick of paint. A number of non-government organisations were housed there, all focussed on helping the country drag itself out of the mire of apartheid.

The women arrived in ones and twos looking a little nervous. Although they were familiar with the building, and most of them knew each other, they hesitated at the door.

"Come in," Theresa called, "come and find a chair."

They huddled together in small groups, chatting and glancing over at me and Theresa. They were in their thirties and forties, and most wore jeans with silk blouses in a variety of gorgeous colours: turquoise, purple, scarlet and gold. They were like beautiful exotic birds. We moved the chairs into a circle, scraping them across the splintered parquet floor.

We began with each woman saying something about her name: Sushi, Maya, Neta, Sonya, Irma, Avril, Halima, Bibi, Tamara, Valerie, Jasmine, Rita, Shakira.

Because it was such a significant day for South African women, Theresa and I had planned an activity which we used just this one time.

We placed a table in the middle of the circle with a large piece of flip-chart paper on it, together with felt pens in a rainbow of colours. Theresa asked each participant to come forward one by one and write the name of a woman they wanted to honour or remember, a foremother who at some point in their lives had helped them and given them strength. They could speak the name out loud and say why she was significant, or they could stand silently at the table while they thought about her and wrote her name.

"On this special day, South African Women's Day, it's important for us to remember with respect and love those women who have supported and cared for us," Theresa said.

One by one the women approached the table, many choking back tears as they spoke about the sister, mother, aunt or friend who had helped them through a difficult time. The woman who was the director of FAMSA and who had invited us to come and run this workshop, was named three times. She stood very straight, hands clasped tightly across her stomach, with her head up and her eyes glistening with tears.

When everyone had honoured the special woman in their lives, there was a deep silence in the room. The air was thick, and we stood still and quiet in the circle. Some of the women smiled, their eyes bright and moist, while others looked down to the floor, faces flushed.

Theresa gathered up the piece of paper and fixed it to the wall.

After lunch we arranged the women into three groups. We asked them to create short plays illustrating a time when they had experienced conflict or violence. All the plays had scenarios based on the abuse of power in the family. The one which was chosen for everyone to work on together was a story of adultery, with the wife, played by Sushi, being undecided about what to do. The husband was abusive, and there were children involved. The solution they arrived at was not a happy-ever-after one, but they'd had the opportunity to look anew at ways of dealing with the violent situation.

As we were nearing the end of our time together, I asked everyone to stand in a circle to create a "rainstorm". This began in silence. We rubbed our palms together to make a soft swishing sound. The "rain" began, pitter-patter, with the clicking of fingers. It increased as we slapped our hands against the front of our thighs. Finally, the thunder came with loud stamping on the floor. Then the sounds were made backwards as the "storm" subsided until there was calm. Everyone stood still in the circle, holding a moment of silence.

Then we broke into soft laughter.

At the very end we all stood in a tight circle and I taught them the song which I'd learnt at the Greenham Common Peace Camp in the 1980s: *We Are Gentle Angry Women:*

We are gentle, angry women, and we are singing, singing for our lives

We are gentle, angry women, and we are singing, singing for our lives ...

We are gentle, powerful women, and we are singing, singing for our lives,

We are gentle, powerful women, and we are singing, singing for our lives ...

After further work in KwaZulu Natal, Theresa and I drove back to Johannesburg where we ran a two-day, residential Alternatives to Violence workshop at St Benedict's. One of the participants was Manya Gittel, a woman who was an expert in Forum Theatre. She would one day become instrumental in the development of the Themba Project. Two others were Jabulani Mashinini and Judy Connors, both from an NGO called Transfer of African Knowledge (TALK). Although we had no idea of it at the time, we would later work closely with them.

* * *

On 19 August Theresa and I flew to Cape Town where we were greeted by the friends we'd met at the international conference in the Magaliesburg Mountains in July. They were bubbling with excitement.

"Guess who's in Cape Town?" asked Andrew.

We looked blank.

"The Dalai Lama!" said Razaan.

"What? *The* Dalai Lama?"

"Ja," joined in Ghalib, "The Dalai Lama has come to give the Desmond Tutu Peace Lecture tomorrow at the City Hall – and we're all going."

The next day we queued up outside the City Hall with over a thousand other people waiting to get in for the lecture. The balcony at the front of the building was where Nelson Mandela had spoken after he had been released from twenty-seven years' incarceration. He'd ended his speech with the same words he had spoken from the dock in 1964 just before being sentenced to jail for life:

I have fought against white domination, and I have fought against black domination. I have cherished the ideal of a democratic and free society in which all persons live together in harmony and with equal opportunities. It is an ideal which I hope to live for and to achieve, but if needs be, it is an ideal for which I am prepared to die.

We were some of the last people to get in – the huge chamber was already packed. People were sitting on the stairs, on each other's laps, standing on benches at the back, and hanging precariously from ornate ledges protruding from the side walls. We squeezed into the few remaining seats.

Onto the stage came a choir of African women singing (rather incongruously) a Mozart oratorio. Next, about thirty local dignitaries walked in, some dressed formally in dark suits, others in colourful traditional attire. After a pause the Dalai Lama arrived, clad in maroon and gold robes, followed by Desmond Tutu in his dark blue cassock and white surplice. The audience clapped, cheered and whistled. The Dalai Lama came forward slowly to the lectern at the front of the stage.

He was smiling broadly. By his side was a dapper young Tibetan in a smart grey suit, white shirt and tie. They stood together for a moment or two, perfectly still, while we all quietened down. Then the Dalai Lama began to speak – in Tibetan. Everyone in the audience leaned forward and listened reverentially, not understanding a word. The young man translated, sentence by laborious sentence, into English. Most of what he said seemed to be thanking people for inviting him.

After about three minutes, the Dalai Lama stopped, looked up, grinned and said, "Would you prefer me to continue in English?" The audience roared with laughter and yelled, "Yebo, yebo!"

Once everyone had settled down, the lecture began in earnest and again we all leant forward to listen. Suddenly there was a violent crash from the rear of the hall. It sounded as though a bomb had gone off, and for a moment there was a stunned silence. Someone yelled from the back of the auditorium, "It's okay – a bench fell over." Desmond Tutu and the Dalai Lama burst into fits of giggles. The audience followed suit until the whole place was filled with more than a thousand people laughing hysterically, with these two deeply spiritual religious leaders chuckling and hooting like a couple of schoolboys. After the Dalai Lama had regained his composure, he resumed. He spoke about the violence meted out by the Chinese onto the Tibetan population, and how they had resisted non-violently. He also told us about his flight from Tibet to northern India. Although it was a privilege to be in the presence of such an intensely spiritual man, the recurring theme of violence was yet another reminder of how much work there was to be done.

At the end of the evening, we all stood to sing *Nkosi Sikelel' iAfrika*. The South African national anthem uses five of the most widely spoken of the country's official languages: different verses are sung in isiZulu, isiXhosa, Sesotho, Afrikaans and English. When we arrived at the Afrikaans section, the white woman who was standing next to me said through gritted teeth, "I can't sing it. I just can't sing it."

Afrikaans was still regarded by many as the language of the oppressor.

* * *

Theresa and I were booked to run a workshop with members of the Quaker Peace Centre which we'd visited the previous year. The Centre had recently undergone changes of staff and there was uncertainty and anxiety about the future, and some conflict. The director, Anne Oglethorpe, was retiring, to be replaced by Jeremy Routledge, a local Quaker. Both were at the workshop.

We had been asked to try to help people understand the organisation and their place in it. We were in a bright, echoing hall, with a white-tiled floor and high, narrow windows reaching up to the ceiling. After our usual preliminary exercises and drama games we asked everyone to help set up the chairs in a large rectangle.

"We're going to imagine this is a public swimming pool," said Theresa, indicating the arrangement of chairs. "What do you think there would be here?"

"Changing rooms," someone called out.

"An entrance where you have to pay your money."

"Diving boards."

"The deep end and the shallow end."

"The place where non-swimmers can watch."

The group agreed where everything in the "swimming pool" would be situated and then Theresa explained, "I want you to imagine that this swimming pool represents the Quaker Peace Centre. It's a metaphor. Can you decide where you would place yourself? For example, are you on the diving board, or on the side? Are you in the deep end or the shallow end? When you've worked out the position which represents where you think you are in the Centre, please move to that spot. Please do this in silence."

Everyone stood still contemplating the "swimming pool". They looked a little hesitant and embarrassed. Then one by one they began to place themselves within the image. One man stood on the edge of the pool nervously preparing to jump in. A young woman went and lay on the floor in the deep end and flailed about as if she was drowning. Anne headed for the exit, while Jeremy stood hesitating at the entrance. A man sat down on the bottom of the shallow end, sloshing his feet around. He ignored the looks of annoyance from some of his colleagues who were sitting on the edge of the pool dipping their toes into the water.

When they had all found their places, Theresa said, "Please would you think about what it's like to be in this position in the Peace Centre. Talk with the person nearest to you and discuss how you feel."

After a little while Theresa spoke again. "Would you now move, in silence, to where you would *like* to be in the pool. Remember this is a symbol for the Quaker Peace Centre."

Almost all the participants went to a new place. The drowning woman "swam" away from the deep end and stopped flailing her arms when she was no longer "out of her depth". The man languishing in the shallow end got out and stood behind the chairs making a clear statement that he wished to leave. Anne moved away from the exit and sat down outside the group. Jeremy took up his position on the diving board, ready to plunge in.

Theresa said, "I'd like you to turn to the person nearest to you, and talk with them about your responses to this exercise. What has it shown you about your role in the Quaker Peace Centre?"

Later, during the evaluation, all the participants said the swimming pool activity had been illuminating and had helped them understand some of the tensions within the organisation. The criticism, however, was that as a metaphor it was not particularly suited to black people: generally speaking, Africans didn't frequent public baths, and many never learnt to swim. The exercise provoked some uncomfortable discussion about the inequalities in the country, as well as conflict within the organisation. It proved to be a turning point for the Peace Centre, for they began to work more harmoniously together from that day.

The workshop I was looking forward to most was booked to take place on Robben Island, within the prison where Nelson Mandela had been an inmate. Although it no longer housed political prisoners, it was still a penitentiary for men with criminal convictions.

At seven o'clock on the morning we were due to sail across, the phone beside my bed in the guesthouse rang. I was half asleep.

"Could I speak to Kim, please?"

"Speaking."

"Good morning. This is the governor here."

"Governor?"

"Robben Island. I don't know if you've noticed, but during the night a storm has come up."

"I heard the wind – it was howling."

"The sea-swell is too dangerous for you to make the crossing."

"What?"

"I'm sorry, but we'll have to cancel the workshop."

My heart stopped. I knew there would never be another chance. There were plans to turn the prison on Robben Island into a museum. I was desperately disappointed.

I could only imagine the sadness and frustration the wives of prisoners must have experienced when the swell was too high for them to make the crossing. They would have travelled for days across South Africa to visit their husbands. When the boats were stuck in harbour, the women were forced to return home because their authorisation for travel was date-limited.

They would have been arrested if they'd outstayed their pass. Sometimes the women saw their husbands only once a year because the boat which would carry them over was cancelled due to bad weather.

As Theresa and I took off from Cape Town airport the next day, I could just make out the island through the grey mist and rain. It looked tantalisingly close to the mainland. I didn't know if I would ever have another opportunity to go there, and as the plane circled over the sea before heading north, I was deeply depressed and unhappy.

When we flew back to the UK a few weeks later, I had no idea when – or if – I would ever return to South Africa.

Chapter 8

South Africa, July 1997

I should have been excited about being back in South Africa, but my diary states clearly, *I DON'T WANT TO BE HERE.* I was exhausted after three very demanding terms teaching and directing plays at the comprehensive school where I worked, and I wanted to stay in England and rest for the whole of the summer holidays.

It was winter in Johannesburg and very cold at night. I stayed with my friend Jennifer, whom I'd originally met through the Quakers. She had an open fire in her sitting room which she lit for me each evening, but I still needed my thermal vest, thick shirt, warm trousers and sweater. I envied my friends and family in England sunning themselves in sleeveless tops. I missed my house in Sussex, my garden, the river, the gentleness of the English summer, and especially my children. I had just made contact again with the man I had been engaged to when I was seventeen, and we'd had a very brief, and beautiful, revival of our love affair. I wanted to be at home in England not here in cold, brittle Johannesburg.

The Labour landslide on 1 May was something to celebrate. I looked forward to experiencing Britain under the new Government and felt disloyal leaving the country just when (New) Labour was getting its feet under the table.

But here I was, and there was work to be done, and I would only be away for a couple of months. I had a week before Theresa arrived, and needed to act fast to set up meetings and book workshops.

Despite wanting to be in the UK, I was – perversely – continuing to explore ways to return to South Africa semi-permanently. I had never believed it was appropriate for Theresa and me to "helicopter in and helicopter out", running workshops in townships and then disappearing back into our comfortable lives in the northern hemisphere. I'd seen other people do this and had always mistrusted their motives.

A number of organisations had asked us to come back and set up the Themba Project on a long-term footing. One option was to amalgamate or link in some way with the Transfer of African Knowledge (TALK). Liz Botha had set up TALK in 1990 to help South Africans bridge cultural divides and to teach indigenous languages. Jabulani Mashinini, who was a Zulu speaker, and Judy Connors, whose first language was English, had joined her. Jabu had started his life in the slums of Soweto and was still a boy when he began hawking old clothes from pavements. He was helped by a man who gave him a suitcase, and he began slogging around the streets of more affluent suburbs peddling second-hand clothes door-to-door. Later he progressed to selling fruit and vegetables from the back of a bicycle, and then to the sidewalk of the main street in Yeoville. Here he was discovered by Liz. Unlike most white women, Liz would buy vegetables from the men and women on the street rather than from the supermarket; she would spread her custom, going from one trader to the next to buy fresh produce. Liz met Jabu and would converse with him in isiZulu. She recognised that he had intelligence and drive and invited him to become a "buddy" at TALK. Liz began to train Jabu in the art of teaching, and he eventually became a full-time trainer.

One of the things I loved about South Africa was the way that unplanned and unexpected opportunities sometimes appeared for people to help them work their way out of poverty. It required intelligence, determination and above all luck, but when those three elements combined, there were possibilities. Of course, only a minority were blessed in this way, but Jabu Mashinini was among the fortunate.

Liz arranged for us all to visit a rural area in KwaZulu

Natal. The Anglican Bishop there had asked her to explore the possibility of a joint project to benefit the local community. We set off to drive to Emanzi, a village near Ladysmith, where we stayed at the Zama homestead: Gogo Zama had once worked as a maid for Liz's family in Jo'burg. Gogo is a term used for a grandmother, or a respected, older woman.

The small collection of dwellings was scattered over scrubland strewn with smooth brown boulders. A few thorn bushes and stunted Marula trees were dotted here and there. Some of the homes were traditional circular rondavels made of mud with thatched roofs, others were oblong, built of breeze blocks and corrugated iron. There was no electricity, mains drainage, or running water, and just one pit latrine, partly concealed with sheets of tin on three sides. Besides Gogo Zama, the matriarch, there were six women, two young men, a boy of thirteen, two girls who looked about twelve, five very young children, and four babies. Two of Gogo's daughters worked in town and were the sole providers for the family.

We arrived in two cars, laden with chickens and vegetables. The women cooked supper on stoves which burned wood and coal. That evening, after our meal, the children came to the rondavel where we were to sleep, and performed for us. They were ragged and barefoot, and as they danced they sang. I went outside and sat on the step of the hut to watch the sun go down, listening to the lovely, spontaneous harmonies. The cooking smells from the kitchen mingled with wood smoke and the sweet earth-scent of Africa. My heart ached and I remembered again why South Africa drew me back.

I wondered how feasible it would be for TALK and Themba to work together in this rural area. Earlier in the day we'd broken our journey from Johannesburg at the Bishop's small brick-built house by St Chad's Church. His wife had opened the door, smoothing down her apron and tugging at the skirt which was far too tight for her. Her feet were encased in pink fluffy slippers.

"Good afternoon, Sisi," said Liz, "is the Bishop in?"

"He's gone to a meeting. He said you would call."

"Shall we come back later?"

"No. Come tomorrow. He should be here then."

Although I was beginning to get used to the way in which arrangements were changed, people were late, and appointments broken, I still found it frustrating. It seemed to be endemic in South Africa, and a huge amount of time was wasted waiting for things to happen. We said we'd return the following morning.

When we met him, the Bishop seemed to think that a local government land reclamation scheme would soon make a real improvement to the lives of the people in his community. But I was unclear how TALK or Themba would fit into this. I was concerned that Liz seemed unaware that people might not take kindly to two white foreign women arriving in the area to set up a project, but I didn't feel able to voice my doubts.

After our meeting with the Bishop we went to the Wimpy in the town for a much-needed dose of caffeine. As we sipped our drinks, I wondered about the benefits of development. When electricity arrived in the villages, people would acquire televisions and be exposed to the pernicious materialism of the American soaps. But who was I to condemn this? Why should people in rural communities in Africa be deprived of access to the rest of the world? I mused on this some more during the journey back to Johannesburg. Theresa, Liz, Jabu, Judy and I talked for a long time, but reached no decision about whether TALK and Themba might have a future together.

On our return to Jo'burg, Theresa and I were invited by a member of staff at the Centre for Policy Studies (CPS) to run a workshop, and we asked Jabu to join us as a third (trainee) facilitator. The CPS was an off-shoot of the University of Witswatersrand, and we'd been told, unofficially, that the organisation was in a mess. We'd received a fax from one of the staff, part of which read:

> ... *essentially it seems that the nasty South African problem has raised its pervasive head here too, and (backbiting) accusations of (real or imagined, I dunno) racism are flying around all over. I really think that for once in the CPS's existence the problem mustn't be intellectualised ... At the moment seething rumours fly and anger bubbles and flares, but nobody ever confronts one another.*

Theresa, Jabu and I attended a meeting with the directors of the CPS to explain our experiential method of working through drama to help people resolve conflicts. Our plan for the day was accepted, but when it came to actually running the workshop, we were in for some surprises.

Because the Centre was weighted in favour of academics and researchers, we believed that working in silence for a number of exercises would be appropriate. We knew there would be people from all sections of the organisation, from the director to the cooks and cleaners, with a variety of South African languages as mother tongue. We wanted to ensure that they all had an equal opportunity to contribute to the day.

The workshop took place in a wide, airy reception area. We began with a number of activities designed to help all the staff work together, something they were obviously unaccustomed to. We ran listening exercises and getting-to-know-you games, mixing people up so they were working with colleagues with whom they would normally have little contact. Slowly people began to relax, and the atmosphere in the room shifted from suspicion to cooperation.

However, when Theresa introduced the main exercise with the instruction that there be no talking at all, the participants looked at us, and at each other, in dismay. We had taken away the most important skill the senior people in the room possessed: their ability to articulate. By removing the power of speech, we had empowered those lower down the hierarchy, and they were able to work on an equal footing with everyone else.

At the end of the day we asked everyone to fill in an evaluation form. All but two responses were extremely positive. The director was furious, however. Although he had agreed in advance to the format of the workshop, he had been denied his ability to communicate through language. He appeared to be very unhappy at having to work with the rest of his staff in a cooperative manner which attempted to make everyone equal. As we were tidying up he rudely brushed past Theresa with a thunderous expression on his face.

"Satisfied now?" he growled.

* * *

A few days later we flew to Cape Town to run more workshops. I, though, was feeling dissatisfied and unhappy, partly because of the terrible weather: it rained almost continuously and the wind howled. I heard on the radio that the temperature in England was thirty degrees, the hottest August since records began. Here I was, in the middle of a bitterly cold and rainy winter, and lonely.

Part of the problem was that we didn't have enough to do in Cape Town because a number of workshops I'd booked were subsequently cancelled with no time to arrange others. If the weather had been better, we could have enjoyed a short break, with walks along the beach. Instead we set up meetings with different people to discuss how we could move the Themba Project forward. We'd had enough feedback to know that what we had created was of value, but we didn't feel it was appropriate for a Brit and a Kiwi to continue the work. We knew it was unlikely we would find one individual who happened to have the same mix of experience and skill that Theresa and I had, but we hoped we might find a couple.

Finally, the weather let up and I was able – at last – to cross the bay to Robben Island. The prison had already been turned into a museum. I travelled on an ex-prison boat together with a party of coloured school children, some Indian South Africans, a group of black Americans, and a few white couples and individuals. We were taken around the island by two female guides, one white, one Indian. The white woman told us that there had once been a thriving village with a primary school with fifty children. Now there were only seven.

"We're waiting for a new influx of people to come and live here once the new peace centre has opened," she said.

Everywhere I looked there were empty houses, run down and tatty. Paint was peeling off walls both at the jail and in the surrounding abandoned homes.

"Whenever a woman in the village had a baby," went on the guide, "a bell would ring and a flag was raised on the church tower. Pink for a girl, and blue for a boy. So everyone knew the sex of the baby."

Everyone – except the prisoners. I'd read that they didn't see a single child in twenty-three years. But just once, in all that time, Ahmed Kathrada, who was jailed along with Mandela, said he'd heard a child laughing on the other side of the razor-wire-topped wall.

The irony of Robben Island was the enormous notice over the gate at the entrance to the prison: *We Serve With Pride*. It was meant to refer to the warders, but the political prisoners appropriated it for themselves: they were serving their sentences with pride.

Along with the other people from the boat, I joined the tour of the island, the village and the jail. We crowded around the grey cell that had been Mandela's. Prisoner number 46664. Mandela was over six-foot tall, and the cell was only a foot or so longer. He had exercised each morning in that tiny space, making sure that his body, along with his mind and spirit, stayed strong and active.

There had been some lively conversation among the visitors on the way over, but on the journey back to the mainland everyone was silent and thoughtful. Nelson Mandela had been in prison for twenty-seven years, and now he was President of this extraordinary country. Many of his colleagues in Government had been incarcerated by the previous regime, and yet, rather than overthrowing the old order, the new politicians were attempting to forge links and work cooperatively. Only time would tell how successful they would be.

* * *

I was sure it was right to find South Africans to run Themba, because it was inappropriate for me and Theresa to continue to travel back and forth from England. When we met Tessa Edlmann and Genni Blunden at a workshop Theresa and I were running in Cape Town, the answer seemed to present itself. Tessa was a drama practitioner, and Genni a businesswoman and strategist. They were both experts in the field of conflict resolution and had already been exploring the possibility of working together and setting up a project to help reduce conflict and violence. Tessa was tall, with a strong-boned, handsome face and a mass of dark, wavy hair. Genni was shorter and rounder, her straight, dark hair scooped behind her ears. Both were in their mid-thirties. Genni and her husband, Johannes, were planning to move away from Cape Town to the Eastern Cape, and Tessa and Genni hoped to set up a conflict-resolution programme there.

Theresa and I talked with them about the possibility of them taking over the Themba Project. They were enthusiastic, but cautious. Themba already had a name, a history and a reputation. It was supported by Quakers in the UK and in South Africa, as well as by several high-profile sponsors. There was nearly one thousand pounds which would be handed over to whoever took on the Project, money raised from donations for the specific purpose of helping reduce violence and conflict through interactive drama and participatory workshops.

If Themba, with its unique mixture of drama and conflict resolution, was truly valuable, local people needed to take it on if it was to survive. But however rational I tried to be, Themba was my "baby" and I felt reluctant to give it up.

On 1 September, Genni and Tessa came to see Theresa and me off at Cape Town airport.

"If we do take over Themba from you, we'd want to use the logo and the name to honour the work you have already done," Genni said.

"I don't want it to be an onerous burden for you both," I replied. "If you decide you want to run with it, you must feel free to move forward in your own way."

I believed that Tessa and Genni were exactly the right people to undertake the Project. Although I grieved, there was a sense of lightness.

Tessa said, "I'll send a fax in a week or so, when we've decided. Is that all right?"

"Of course."

As Theresa and I flew north, I thought about my relationship with South Africa. I was sure it wasn't yet over. How or when I would return I didn't know, but I sensed that somehow I would be back.

Part Three

1998–2001

Live adventurously. When choices arise, do you take the way that offers the fullest opportunity for the use of your gifts in the service of God and the community? Are you working to bring about a just and compassionate society which allows everyone to develop their capacities ...?

Religious Society of Friends, Advices and Queries. Numbers 27 and 33

Chapter 9

Swaziland, 1998–2000

I'd been content with my job as Head of Drama at a comprehensive school in Sussex when in April 1998 my Swaziland friends, the Farmers, told me about a job at Waterford Kamhlaba College. I wondered whether this might be the stepping-stone I'd longed for to take me back to South Africa.

The post was for the Head of Theatre Arts, but there was no proper job description so I didn't really know what I was applying for. Then, when I was asked to meet two men at the Paddington Bear stall at Paddington Station for an interview, I nearly withdrew my application because it seemed a bizarre place for such a meeting.

I'd felt conspicuous standing at the shop. I pretended to be looking at the bears, but this soon wore thin and the stall-holder began to look at me suspiciously. Two tall men approached, walking towards me shoulder-to-shoulder. One was in a grey suit and the other wore a linen jacket and lightweight trousers.

"Hello, you must be Kim. Come on, let's find a pub."

Deon Glover and Colin Jenkins introduced themselves. For a short time in the 1970s Deon had been Principal of Waterford Kamhlaba College. He and his companion were both on the Governing Council of the United World College movement, and had travelled to London from a UWC conference in Cardiff.

The interview took place in a bar off one of the station platforms. The men drank pints of bitter while I sipped my Perrier water.

"Well, this all seems satisfactory," said Deon, after I'd answered a few questions.

I waited as he turned the pages of my CV.

"Oh, just one thing, though," he said, "have you ever been

arrested for child abuse?"

"Child abuse?"

I wondered what had prompted this, and began to feel uneasy.

"Um … no… not for child abuse, no."

"Ah ha! So, you have been arrested?"

"Well, yes, but that was when I sat down in front of the Houses of Parliament – protesting about the Gulf War. In 1991."

"Oh, in that case you'll do fine at Waterford," he said, folding up my CV, and that was the end of the interview.

It was so unprofessional that when the telephone call came offering me the job, I very nearly turned it down.

But I didn't.

* * *

Arriving in Swaziland at the beginning of September 1998, I got off to a shaky start. Janet, the wife of the previous Principal had been teaching drama, but there was no actual Theatre Arts department to be head of. There were no facilities, no budget, few books and no designated space in which to teach. In addition, I had nowhere to live because the cottage I had been assigned was still occupied by people who, though they were no longer on the staff, had not yet moved out. I was worried, too, about my own children back in England. Although they were now in their twenties, they were still young, and maybe they needed me. My son had reacted badly when I'd said goodbye to him as I was leaving the UK, and I recognised that this was his way of showing how upset he was. My daughter had appeared fine, but she was a bit older, and didn't express her feelings so obviously. Was I a terrible mother for leaving them? Their father was in Sussex and would be able to help if need be, but I would be thousands of miles away, perhaps for as long as three years. Had I damaged our relationship irreparably by coming here?

Then, to add to my anxiety, in November a bomb exploded

at the Prime Minister's residence, killing a guard and injuring nine passers-by. Bombs were unheard of in Swaziland, despite the growing unrest within the country. People were shocked and horrified: bombs were considered "un-Swazi," cowardly, not traditional. Tradition was everything in the kingdom, but many in the population were beginning to demand democracy, recognition of trade unions, and workers' rights. King Mswati III was the last absolute monarch in Africa, and head of the Swazi family. He wasn't in any hurry to concede to the wishes of his people. To date, he had eight or nine wives and enjoyed a lavish lifestyle while his largely rural subjects lived in poverty. The incidence of HIV and AIDS was high and the state hospital was unable to cope with the demand for treatment.

The only bright moment in my first term was when Lord Richard Attenborough and his wife, Sheila, came to the college with the founder, Michael Stern. Richard was on the Governing Council and was the vice-president of the United World College Movement. He and Michael addressed the staff and the students. They were inspiring, speaking about the foundations of the college and the vital importance of education. I shared their passion for learning and decided that, despite my misgivings, I would stay on and try to make the best of things.

* * *

It was May 1999 when I received an email from South Africa telling me that Tessa and Genni, who had taken on the mantle of the Themba Project from Theresa and me in 1997, had decided they were no longer able to continue. Genni and her husband were moving to Pretoria, Tessa was planning to go to America. They asked if I would meet with them to decide the best way forward.

By coincidence – one of many coincidences that seemed to surround and uphold the Themba Project – Theresa was due to come out from the UK to visit me and have a holiday in Swaziland. The four of us met for a weekend's *indaba* (meeting) in August at The Good Shepherd retreat centre near the Magaliesburg Mountains north of Johannesburg, to decide what should be done. Themba had a reputation, a little money, and had achieved good work in its time. Now it appeared to be coming to an end. We deliberated for two days, taking walks in the hills, talking quietly in one of the meeting rooms at the centre, and cooking and eating together.

Although none of us was in a position to take on the work, we all sensed that the Themba adventure was not yet over. Towards the end of the weekend we came up with a metaphor: we agreed Themba was a "book". Some chapters had already been written, but maybe there were more to write. We agreed to put the "book" on a shelf, and if any one of us wanted to take it down in the future and write more chapters we could do so, as long as we had the agreement of the others. I had no inkling that I would be the one to do the "writing".

* * *

I'd met a splendid woman in Swaziland called Jenny Thorne, and she soon became a very dear friend. She lived in the Malkerns Valley between the towns of Mbabane and Manzini. She was tall, and moved like a gazelle. Her strong, lively face was haloed by a mass of chestnut curls, gently transforming into grey, and her brown eyes seemed always crinkled in a smile. She was one of the very few people I've met in this world who always saw the best in everyone. She had a wicked sense of humour and could mimic people wonderfully, but it was never done with malice. She ranged around her farmhouse home in long wide skirts or old denim shorts. I envied her beautiful long legs.

Jenny had started a small roadside business with local women, making woven tablemats and rugs from the grass that grew in the mountains. By the time I knew her, the enterprise had grown and there were now seven hundred Swazi women across the country, cutting grass, dying it, and weaving exquisite artefacts for the home. These were exported and sold in places like Liberties of London, and in New York. The women earned money, independent of their husbands, and were able to pay for their children's schooling, uniforms and books.

Although Jenny had been born in England, she had lived in Africa for much of her life. She was invaluable in helping me understand the country.

One day we were sitting on the *stoep* outside her house, sipping tea and looking towards her cactus garden. It was a beautiful day and the sun shimmered off the dark green spikes of the pineapple plants growing in serried rows in the distance. We were discussing the political situation in Swaziland.

Jenny said, "You do understand there is no real democracy here, don't you?"

"I'm beginning to discover that," I replied.

"Trade unions are forbidden," she went on, "and the position of women is terrible."

"How?"

"Swazi women have to do exactly what their husbands tell them. By law they are only minors – the same as children."

Jenny and I had dreams of helping to empower women in Swaziland. We wanted to set up a radical theatre group to explore some of the issues. Maybe this would become the new Themba Project.

* * *

It was nine o'clock in the morning when the phone rang. I was in my garden hanging up the laundry on the whirligig washing line.

The garden fell steeply down from the house and the rotary

line was near the bottom of the slope close to the path which meandered out of the college and down the mountain towards the town. This road was in constant use by everyone: students, teachers, maintenance staff, gardeners, parents, delivery men and the college drivers. I was always careful to hang my knickers and bras on the inside of the whirligig so they weren't in full view of passers-by.

I threw down the basket of washing, dashed up the grass into the house, and grabbed the phone.

"Hello."

"Hi, Kim. It's Thabo."

Thabo Makgoba, who I'd first met in the crypt of St Martin in the Fields in London, was the priest-in-charge at the Church of Christ the King in Sophiatown, Johannesburg, and he was also co-director of the new Trevor Huddleston Memorial Centre next door.

"Oh, Thabo. Sorry – I was just doing the laundry."

There was a pause. It was unusual for a white woman to wash her own clothes. My insistence on doing domestic chores myself had not been appreciated when I'd first arrived in Swaziland because it meant I was depriving someone of an income. So now I had Nellie to clean the house, and Victor who helped in the garden, but my discomfort at having other people fulfil the ordinary household tasks of my everyday life stayed with me the whole time I was in southern Africa.

"What can I do for you, Thabo?"

"Some of the people at the Church have asked me to find out if you'd be willing to come over to Jo'burg and run some workshops with the youth. We'd like you to do some drama with them looking at HIV and AIDS."

My stomach churned with excitement. I took a deep breath.

"I'd love to," I said. "Very much indeed. When do you want me to come?"

I was grinning to myself as I put the phone down; this might

105

be just the opportunity I had hoped for and I was thrilled to have been asked. I went back into the garden and looked out across the valley to the distant mountains. It was a lovely August morning, the bright winter sun already warming the air. A light mist still hung above the town of Mbabane nestled in the valley below, giving the foothills a dreamlike appearance. Would the workshop I'd been asked to run in Jo'burg turn out to be the opening to allow me to move to South Africa? Although Swaziland was an incredibly beautiful country, and the people were warm and generous-hearted, the lack of democracy, the treatment of women, the King's absolute rule and the fact that the death penalty was still in existence (but thankfully never used) meant that I found living there extremely challenging.

A few weeks later, I was in the hall next to the Church of Christ the King in Sophiatown, working with a dozen young people, helping them to devise a play about HIV.

"The idea is that we create a play which presents a particular problem to do with HIV and AIDS. It needs to be unfinished, unresolved, so that after it's been performed, the audience – sorry, congregation – are invited to make suggestions about how the story can move on. Then you, the actors, take some of those ideas and act them out, and try to reach an ending for the play that everyone is happy with."

I was only able to speak English which was, for every other person in the room, their second or third language. I tried to talk simply so that everyone would understand, but I felt awkward. I knew it was unusual for a woman of my years to talk openly about things like HIV, which necessarily meant discussing sex. There was my skin colour, too, and with it came the vast arc of cosmic guilt associated with colonialism, oppression and apartheid.

We rehearsed in the church hall, a huge space with a cold, tiled floor, a wide stage at one end and white plastic chairs strewn haphazardly about. When Sunday came and the play was performed in the church, the actors were hampered by the pulpit on one side and the lectern on the other. The congregation sat in rows enclosed in heavy wooden pews. Nevertheless, we continued undeterred, with me acting as the facilitator between the actors and the audience. The play had a simple storyline showing the stigma associated with going for an HIV test, with one of the characters refusing to go, even when his friend tried to convince him.

Despite the constraints, we succeeded in getting people to contribute to the outcome of the story, and the young man was persuaded to go for a test. When the service was over, a number of worshippers came to tell me they'd enjoyed the play and, most importantly, had learnt something about HIV and AIDS.

I returned to Swaziland after the service and continued with my job at the college. Although Thabo and others at the church seemed pleased with what the young people had achieved, it didn't feel as if this was going to be the opportunity for me to work in South Africa.

It turned out I was wrong.

* * *

The students at Waterford Kamhlaba College helped me to believe my work was worthwhile. They were challenging, stimulating and highly intelligent. The older scholars, who came from countries all over the world, studied for the International Baccalaureate. Those studying the Theatre Arts course regularly staged "studio" productions – though there was no actual drama studio – and every year I produced one or two short plays with the senior students, as well as a major play or musical with pupils from every year group. I became more and more involved in the life of the college, and soon I was directing Shakespeare's *The Tempest*.

The cast came from all corners of the globe: Prospero was

Nigerian, Caliban Venezuelan, and Miranda was a Puerto Rican. I set the play in Swaziland, even though the country was surrounded by land rather than sea. Richard and Sheila Attenborough came to see the production and Richard was moved to tears when Odiri as Prospero delivered, in his deep mellifluous voice, the lines: *Our revels now are ended. These our actors, as I foretold you, are all melted into air, into thin air ... We are such stuff as dreams are made on, and our little life is rounded with a sleep.*

I now had a group of experienced senior drama students, and felt it was time for them and me to branch out and use our skills in the wider community of Swaziland. Part of the requirement of the International Baccalaureate was that every student, together with a member of staff, had to engage in Community Service, or "commserve" as it was nicknamed.

The commserve I devised took place across the other side of Swaziland on the border with Mozambique to the east, in the tiny mountain community of Shewula. I had been invited to discuss with the villagers the idea of using drama for social issues and it seemed to me that this would make an ideal commserve activity. The issues turned out to be HIV and AIDS, teenage pregnancy, drugs, and overgrazing by cattle. A Swazi man's wealth and standing in the community was measured by the number of cows he owned, so any matter involving livestock was of very great importance.

Nomsa Mabila was the dynamic young Swazi woman from Shewula who had asked for a drama practitioner to help the community explore these concerns. She had an open, smiling face, and wore western clothes with ease, with a necklace of Swazi beads. When I arrived in Shewula with five students, she greeted us warmly. We went to a small, half-built brick building with an earth floor and openings in the bare breeze-block walls where, one day, there would be windows and a door. On three sides were wooden benches and plastic chairs, and on these sat, very quietly and still, some ancient men. They leaned forward with their hands placed one on top of the other on their knobkerries. Their chins rested on the backs of their hands, their fingernails encrusted with earth. Most of the men had grey hair, and their eyes were rheumy and bloodshot. As the sun poured relentlessly through the half-completed roof, they deliberated in low voices about whether I and my students should be allowed to run drama workshops in the village.

Nomsa showed deference to these old men, bobbing a half-curtsey to the one who seemed to be the leader. When invited by a gesture from him, she sat down in an empty chair and indicated for me to sit. A long meandering conversation then took place in siSwati. I couldn't understand much of it, but I watched and listened as opinion flowed back and forth. After about an hour, it appeared that the consultation with the old men was concluded, and Nomsa stood up. I shook hands with each man in turn, using the traditional three-way African handshake, thanking them in the little siSwati that I'd learnt: *Siyabonga, siyabonga kakhulu.*

We left the hut and trooped across the scrubby grass. Once we were some distance away, Nomsa turned, smiled widely at me and the students, and gave me a big hug.

"They agreed you can come," she said. "They want me to report to them every month, but they have agreed. That's wonderful!"

We piled into the college combi and drove the short distance up a dirt road to a school. Like most southern African primary schools, it consisted of a few single-storey brick buildings arranged around a playground which was simply a square of earth. We were greeted by some very small pre-school children who were practising a traditional Swazi *sibhaca* dance. They were semi-naked, in costumes of beads and strips of cotton. The youngest child, who was an accomplished dancer, looked less than three years old.

After the performance, the children scuttled away, and

together with some of the villagers we moved into the school hall. After an hour's drama activities we sat down to talk about what the community hoped to achieve. Nomsa's language skills were excellent, and she moved easily between siSwati and English so we could all understand what was being said.

"There's this project: the Peace Parks Project," said Nomsa. "The idea is that the boundaries between Zimbabwe, Mozambique and Swaziland will come down, and we – and the animals – will be able to cross the borders freely."

This was news to me. I hadn't heard anything about a cross-frontier project; all I had been asked to do was run some drama sessions.

"How does this involve us?"

"We are to work on some plays with issues that affect our community. There are people down the other side of the mountain in Mozambique who are doing the same. Then we'll show our plays to each other, and learn about what we have in common."

I wondered how much this would benefit the people of Shewula, the majority of whom lived in poverty. Surely they had more pressing needs, like growing enough food and building serviceable homes? Nevertheless, I was glad they had decided they wanted me and my students to help with this project. I would gain an insight into rural Swazi life, and be able to get away occasionally from the hot-house atmosphere of the college on the other side of the country.

With the help of an Italian NGO in Mbabane, the Shewula villagers had embarked on constructing a small eco-tourism camp on a high point of the flat-topped Lubombo Mountains. My students and I went to Shewula about once a month, and I usually stayed in one of the eco-camp's rondavels. After our day's work I would sit on one of the smooth, warm rocks near the top of the mountain and watch the sun set. Flaming orange, scarlet and vermillion would intensify over the river, the bush and the distant sugar cane fields, until the golden ball was swallowed into the horizon. There would be a pause when the heavens shimmered a pale shade of green before becoming violet, purple and grey. Then the stars appeared, one by one, in the blackening sky. It was breath-taking to experience such beauty searing through this land of poverty, inequality and AIDS.

The commserve students, the Swazis and I continued to work on the plays, and by the end of term the village actors had become confident enough to form themselves into The Shewula Theatre Group. One Saturday morning we arranged some benches in a circle in the dust outside the primary school fence and set up "theatre-in-the-round" under the shade of a spreading thorn tree. It was a blazingly hot day.

The seats were soon occupied, and latecomers sat around haphazardly on the ground. The AIDS story was the most powerful and included a death scene. The audience laughed in embarrassment and recognition as the play unfolded, and they gasped in horror as they watched the young man "dying" melodramatically of AIDS. It was a story they were all too familiar with. When we came to "Foruming" the play, people were keen to join in and take over the roles to try to find a conclusion. One by one they jumped up to enter the story.

Ultimately everyone recognised that the way to avoid contracting HIV was to use a condom, or abstain from sex. Although this was the message we were keen to convey, it was not one that fitted well with Swazi culture or the Swazi way of life. There was a rumour going around that *the Americans have put HIV in the condoms so more blacks will die.* How was one to refute this with people who had no reason to disbelieve it, and with little access to accurate information?

Condoms were problematic, too: they cost money, and the majority of the population was extremely poor. A South African charity had sent thousands of free condoms to Swaziland, but they had been *stapled* to the information card in the packet so they were worse than useless. Another batch of complimentary condoms had been delivered from a Chinese organisation, but these were much too small.

Abstaining from sex was not considered a serious option. Nor was the notion of having only one partner: after all, the King was the role model for Swazi men and he had as many wives, fiancées and girlfriends as he liked. Polygamy is lawful in Swaziland.

The most distressing aspect of the spread of AIDS was the myth that if you had HIV you could cure yourself by having sex with a virgin. More and more girls, and some boys, were raped by infected men so they could be "cured". So the disease spread among younger and younger children because men wanted to make sure it was a virgin they were having sex with. Heartbreakingly, even very small children and babies were raped and became infected.

* * *

Once the commserve was over, I continued to visit Shewula. I spent the evenings chatting with Nomsa and her friends as we cooked the communal evening meal in the *lapa*. As we chopped the vegetables and stirred the pots, she told me that a number of people in the village had relatives who were seriously ill, or who had died. In the mornings I would amble through the nature reserve, thinking about HIV and wondering what, if anything, I could do to help reduce the spread of the virus.

One day, Nomsa told me that the local Chief would soon be getting married again. She said she could arrange an invitation for me to attend the customary wedding.

We stood among the throng of Swazis who were dressed in traditional attire. Both men and women were clad in cloths patterned in black, red and white wrapped around their bodies. The older women wore black, tightly-pleated skirts under these cloths, and they'd done their hair up in what they called a beehive style. The men were bare-chested, sported goat-skin aprons and carried wooden sticks and shields of cow hide. The villagers surrounded a circular area, swaying rhythmically singing in harmony, waiting for the proceedings to begin. The men kicked their legs high, their feet coming down in unison, with a heavy stamp making the ground shudder. They banged their knobkerries loudly on the beaten earth and the vibration pulsed through my chest as dust rose into the hot air.

Nomsa stood beside me. "Those are the Chief's two wives," she murmured, indicating two large women who sat on wooden stools on the far side of the compound. They both wore red and white patterned *tishweshwe* cloths wrapped around their breasts and waists, under which were black, pleated skirts. They leant back against a fence of entwined strips of wood, waiting for the entrance of the Chief.

Suddenly, with a rattle and a clatter, a rusty old banger roared into the circle. Children dived for safety as the car screeched around a few times, then came to an abrupt halt. It stopped in front of the wives.

The Chief climbed out of the driver's seat, lurching a little and appeared to be drunk. He gesticulated menacingly with his knobkerrie and growled at a dozen small children who were peeking from between their mothers' legs. The children scattered, squealing as they ran. Some of the people from the village pushed the vehicle away, the crowd parting to allow it through. The men drummed on the car roof, adding to the general noise and excitement.

The Chief sat down on a low stool between two of his ministers, his massive belly ballooning over his thighs. He wore a beaded band around his head, with one red feather sticking upright from the back and two more tucked in front of his ears. Another band of beads crossed over his naked chest, positioned diagonally from his right shoulder past his sagging breasts to his waist.

We heard high-pitched ululating. From a hundred yards away, two lines of young women approached the area, walking slowly and swaying in unison. The people moved aside for them, and the sound increased in volume as the girls progressed towards us. They came up from the river, bare-breasted, clad in traditional skimpy skirts made of brightly-coloured beads. The bride was the last in line. She had strips of black cloth covering her face, and her body was draped in beaded material. On her head she balanced a battered leather suitcase, and under each arm she carried a grass mat.

"That's all her worldly possessions," Nomsa whispered.

The two lines of women separated, forming a semi-circle in front of the crowd, and the bride came forward to her new husband. The contrast between the two seated wives, the Chief, his ministers and this young woman was striking. Although her face was partly concealed I could see she was very pretty and probably no more than eighteen years old. I dreaded to think what life held for her.

* * *

The Shewula Theatre Group asked if I would help gather stories from local people, in order for them to create a community play about the history of the area. An old Swazi called Constantine, who was losing his sight, said he wanted to tell us the story of the Shewula "nation" so Nomsa arranged for him to come up to the *lapa* one evening. I brought my tape recorder and a Swazi drama student from college, Mysh Dlamini, who would translate if needed. My friend Jenny drove us up the mountain in her big four-by-four.

When Constantine arrived he was reeling and appeared very drunk. He was accompanied by the headmaster of the local school, who was even more inebriated. They staggered up the hill, supporting each other as they wobbled towards us. The two men swayed as they lowered themselves gingerly down onto a wooden bench, arms around each other's shoulders, each with a gourd of beer in his hands. The headmaster was roaring incoherently and kept shouting and interrupting Constantine as he attempted to read us the account he'd written out on scraps of paper.

I set up my microphone, but Constantine was either too blind or too drunk to read his notes. He looked at me blankly, his bloodshot eyes expressionless, apparently incapable of answering my questions.

The headmaster meanwhile had moved to a corner, and was quietly filling up his gourd with more of the beer from the plastic container they had brought with them.

It was after midnight before the two men staggered, farting and belching, as they slid down the hill into the night. They bellowed at the stars as they went, and we could hear their racket as it faded in the distance. The dogs in the village woke with a cacophony of yelps and barks.

* * *

The cottage I had been assigned on the Waterford campus was near one of the main gates. In my garden was an enormous avocado tree which overhung the road that wound past my house towards the other staff cottages, the maintenance department and the laundry. When the "avos" were ripe, the workers picked up the fallen ones from the grass under the tree. The women sometimes persuaded the maintenance men to climb up, and the laundry ladies ridiculed them when they couldn't reach the best fruit. They shouted risqué jokes in siSwati which I couldn't understand, but I knew were rude by the ribald laughter.

One afternoon the head of catering knocked on my door. I liked him – he had a kind, gentle face, and always gave me a cheery smile.

"Can I use your phone?" he asked. "Someone was supposed to come to the gate to give me a lift home, but he hasn't pitched."

"Of course," I said, and gave him the handset.

He dialled the number, and as he waited for an answer, he said in a matter-of-fact tone of voice, "I buried my son at the weekend."

"What?" I wasn't sure I'd heard correctly.

"I buried my son at the weekend," he repeated.

I was shocked; not so much by the fact that his son had died, but by the straightforward way he'd told me. I didn't know what to say. I guessed that his son had died of AIDS, but there was a taboo about mentioning the virus.

"There are too many young people dying these days," I said, hoping this innocuous remark might open the door for him to say more if he wanted to.

He spoke to the person on the other end of the line, put the phone down and turned to me.

"Yes. It's AIDS," he sighed.

I was surprised by the way he said this, almost as if it was an inevitability. It was unusual for a Swazi to be so frank about the virus. The stigma surrounding AIDS was so great that even when the symptoms were obvious, people pretended nothing unusual was happening. AIDS exposed the two great taboos: sex and death.

"I have six grown children," he went on, "and I think I will outlive them all. There are ten grandchildren, and I expect my wife and I will soon be looking after every one of them." He looked sad and resigned.

HIV/AIDS was everywhere, but no one was talking about it. No doubt there were people at the college who had contracted HIV, but there was a wall of silence. I wanted to talk to Laurence, the Principal, to ask what Waterford might do. First, however, I had to work out how to broach the subject.

Chapter 10

Swaziland, 2001

A student from my tutor group came to see me one morning. She stood at the door of my office, hesitating. She glanced behind her to make sure no one else was around then came in and closed the door. She said nervously, "My friend asked me to speak to you. She doesn't know what to do." I looked up from my desk.

"She's been raped by her ex-boyfriend. He's a Swazi in town."

I wasn't sure how to proceed. "You'd better sit down," I said. "Tell me what happened."

"We were all in a bar. He came up to her and they had a nice conversation. He was upset about her breaking it off, but he seemed OK. She went with him to his room, just to talk and stay friends."

"Go on."

"Then she realised he'd had too much to drink, but before she could get out, he got her on the bed and raped her."

"Did he use a condom?"

"No he didn't." She paused for a moment, then said, "She's afraid he might be HIV positive."

"Tell her to come and see me at my house," I said. "As soon as she can."

I walked down the hill to my cottage and waited. When Marie (not her real name) arrived about half an hour later it was obvious she'd been crying. Her face was flushed, her cheeks smeared with tears, and her long blonde hair was a tangled mess.

"I'm so sorry about this, Marie." She looked down at the floor.

I guessed what she needed from me was practical help rather than sympathy.

I asked when the rape had happened. I knew that the first seventy-two hours after unprotected sex was the crucial time:

117

if antiretroviral medication was given during that period, HIV might be stopped from infecting the body.

"Two nights ago."

This was not good news.

"Have you seen a doctor?"

"No – I didn't want to go to the college doctor in case this gets out."

I asked her for more details, then said, "I'll go to a doctor in town and ask for the medication. Then we'll have to get you tested as soon as we can."

She looked up with hope in her eyes. I asked her, "Were you a virgin before this happened?"

"Why do you want to know?"

"If you were a virgin when he raped you, then there could be small tears in the vagina which could let in the virus, but if you'd already had sex, the chance of that is a bit less."

Marie looked embarrassed, and hung her head. "No I wasn't a virgin."

"That's good," I said.

She gave me a wan smile.

I went to see one of the doctors in town. She was nearly eighty years old and I wasn't sure she would be up to date with the latest information about HIV. But I thought it would be best to go to a lady doctor in case she needed to see Marie. I told her the whole story.

"Silly girl," said the doctor.

"Sorry? What?"

"Silly girl. Shouldn't have got herself into that position. How do you know it was rape? You said it was her ex-boyfriend."

"Yes, but that's hardly the point. The young man might well be HIV positive, which means we need to get antiretrovirals into Marie as soon as we possibly can."

"Oh she'll probably be all right," said the doctor. "The chances are the boy isn't infected. Anyway, those drugs are powerful –

they make you feel dreadfully ill. I don't recommend them to anybody."

I could feel resentment and anger boiling up inside me. How could this woman, this *doctor*, be so obtuse, so ignorant? Wasn't she aware that one in five young Swazi men were thought to have the virus? I steeled myself to remain calm.

"Marie has asked me to get a prescription for her for the medication. I would be grateful if you would write the script for me now, so I can get down to the pharmacy immediately."

Very unwillingly, the doctor reached for her pad.

"Thank you," I said as I leant forward to take the paper.

"Of course, she won't know if she's got the virus for another three months. You do know that, don't you?"

"Yes," I replied through gritted teeth.

"Does this girl know what symptoms there could be? Fluey feeling, cough, mouth ulcers, upset stomach?"

"Yes," I said, "I'll make sure she knows what to look out for."

I almost snatched the script from the doctor's hand and drove straight to the chemist.

When I explained the situation to the pharmacist, he said Marie would need to have a test straight away and another in three months' time.

"Yes," I said. "I'll take her to Jo'burg as soon as I can. But my first priority is to get the drugs into her as soon as possible."

"Quite right," he said, and I felt my sense of urgency had been justified.

I took Marie to Jo'burg for the first blood test, and an anxious three months followed. She chose not to report the rape, and when we went again, we discovered she was not, after all, HIV positive. She sobbed with relief when she was given the result. I cradled her in my arms and felt vindicated as she looked up and gave me a small smile. "Thank you," she whispered.

* * *

My concern about HIV and AIDS was growing. I thought that Waterford could play a part in helping to reduce the spread of the virus, even if only among the community of the college. I decided to speak to the Principal, and arranged an appointment with him in his office.

I was nervous, but also determined to open up the issue. "I've come to talk to you about HIV and AIDS," I said. "Do you think we should have an HIV policy for the school?"

Laurence looked surprised by my question. "Go on," he said.

"The son of head of catering has just died, and he has told me he thinks he will outlive all his six children. One of my students has recently been raped by a local Swazi. Some of the older students are almost certainly engaging in sex, and the laundry ladies and the maintenance men surely are. Plus, there are all the cleaners and gardeners who come onto campus every day. And then there are the teachers. What are we doing to protect them all?"

Laurence waited.

"Surely, at the very least, we should have a condom dispensing machine on site," I continued. "And it would need to be put where everyone can use it without any fear of gossip."

"I doubt if the Governing Council or the parents would like that," Laurence said.

"But if we can show them that having condoms available doesn't increase sexual activity with the students, surely they will agree? After all, we are only trying to protect people."

Laurence thought for a moment. "You're right. We should be doing something. I'll look into it."

"Thank you," I said.

"In the meantime, maybe you could draw up a draft HIV policy and let me see it? We'll work on it together. I'll do some research and find out whether there are other colleges who have condom machines."

"Great."

"Actually, I'm sure I've read some research somewhere," said Laurence, "about schools and colleges and the incidence of sexual activity. I think it said that providing condoms didn't increase the amount of sex students were having. I'll dig it out."

"If we put a condom machine on site," I said, "it'll have to be designed in such a way so people can only take them out one or two at a time. Otherwise handfuls will be taken and then sold on the roadside in town."

"Good point."

I left Laurence's office feeling more optimistic.

After numerous discussions with teachers, governors, students and parents, the HIV policy was finally approved. I organised an AIDS Week and invited everyone from the college community to get involved, as well as representatives from local NGOs. There were discussion groups and speakers. Special lessons were introduced by the maths, history and geography teachers, covering AIDS statistics, development of the disease and prevalence country by country. Students put on a benefit concert for the AIDS charity in town, and the Community Service department developed a new commserve specifically working with people who were HIV positive.

The one place which was visited by every single person in the college was the big, steamy laundry. There were no washing machines in the different student hostels, so all pupils took their dirty clothes to the ladies who washed and scrubbed and ironed all day. Many of the teachers used the laundry, too. The place was a social hub where all the non-teaching staff would gather to chat over lunch. Everyone had a legitimate reason to visit. We installed the specially designed condom dispensing machine there. How many people in the college community used it, I don't know – the whole point was that it would be easy to access without it being obvious.

* * *

The students at Waterford were enthusiastic and eager to learn. There were no discipline problems and the senior scholars were creative and exciting to teach. I had only taught up to A level before so my own practice developed as I worked through the International Baccalaureate theatre arts syllabus with the older students.

I was given free rein to choose what plays I wanted to direct. My first production with the IB students was Steven Berkoff's *Metamorphosis*. I chose this play, adapted from the story by Kafka, because one of my students, Mikal, a skinny, gangly, "stick insect" from Norway, was ideal for the part of Gregor Samsa, who wakes up one morning transformed into a gigantic beetle. The play is highly stylised, with white face make-up and formal, abstract mime and movements.

I also directed *Yerma*, by Federico Garcia Lorca; *Cats* (the musical by Andrew Lloyd Webber from the poems by T.S. Eliot); and *Mountain Language* by Harold Pinter.

In the midst of all this, I had another call from Thabo Makgoba in Johannesburg.

"Hi, Kim. Can you come and do another weekend? The youth want to do more drama with you and make a new play."

So, in July I was again in Sophiatown working with youngsters from the Church of Christ the King. This time the theme of the play they devised was how to avoid catching the virus. It was considered un-African for young people to talk about sex in front of adults, but the actors knew it was important to openly address ways of preventing the spread of HIV, and this necessarily included mentioning condoms. We succeeded in getting members of the audience involved in the play. This time we moved it a stage further, and some of the congregation left the safety of their pews and took roles within the drama to help the story come to a satisfactory resolution.

After the service was over, there was a gathering in the car park with tea and cakes. The children who'd been in Sunday school ran up and down enjoying the sunshine. The actors and I got into a huddle and had a de-brief discussion. We were all pleased with what had been achieved: we had raised a number of issues to do with HIV and AIDS, and had confronted prejudice and stigma through the medium of drama. They were beginning to understand the power of interactive theatre, and were eager to do more.

A member of the congregation came over, carrying a cup of tea for me. He was involved in the development of the new Trevor Huddleston Memorial Centre which was situated in a bungalow just across the car park.

"What do you think of the idea of turning the sort of thing you've done this morning into a full-scale project at the Centre?" he asked. "Would you consider that?"

For a moment I was speechless and hesitated, my mind whirring. Was this the opportunity I'd been hoping for – to live and work in South Africa?

"Oh – I – I don't know ..." I stopped and thought for a moment, then quickly added, "I'd love to, if I can. Thank you very much."

I was elated. If I could take up this invitation, I would move to South Africa and start a project at the Centre, working with young people, using drama to help prevent the spread of HIV. Was the universe about to take me in a new direction?

I found Thabo and asked him if this was an official request. He said that it was.

* * *

The journey from Johannesburg to Swaziland takes about four hours. That afternoon, as I manoeuvred my Suzuki Escudo through the maze of streets, busy even on a Sunday, thoughts and ideas jumbled in my head. Once I was out of the city and onto the dual carriageway heading east, my mind was racing with possibilities.

Soon the flat plateau of the East Rand gave way to the undulating hills of Mpumalanga, with cattle grazing in the distance and a few shacks and rondavels dotted over the veld. After I'd turned off the main highway, I passed through the town of Carolina, and the landscape changed once more, becoming rocky and rugged. Vast plantations of pine trees spread out over the hills and valleys. Enormous rocks were scattered across the grassy flanks of the mountains, as if thrown haphazardly by a pre-historic giant.

My mind became more focussed the closer I came to the Oshoek/Ngwenya border. I talked aloud to myself, thinking how a project like this might work. I made lists in my head about what would have to be done to set the whole thing up, and my ideas began to crystallise into the beginning of a plan.

Then I remembered Themba. We had put the "book" on the shelf with a number of "chapters" already written. Maybe this was the moment to take it down and start writing more.

As I approached the border post the outline of a proposal was fully formed in my head, but before I could get home to scribble down my ideas, I had to face snail-like officialdom, along with a seething mass of humanity all jostling to get through immigration and customs. Sunday evenings were always busy as people came back home to Swaziland after a weekend's *jol* in South Africa. I queued up in the ramshackle one-storey building together with men and women in Swazi traditional dress, children bound to their mothers' backs with thick blankets held on tight with enormous safety pins. The babies' toes peeked out from under the wrapping each side of wide buttocks. Labourers and government officials stood alongside each other, the men pushing and elbowing their way to get to the front.

I hated being shoved to one side by some self-important man, but I lacked the confidence to assert my right to be seen in order. If I protested, I would be regarded as yet another whingeing whitey, but as a good feminist I felt I was letting my sisters down if I didn't object. I queued for nearly an hour before I was able to get to the grille, but eventually I was outside again, away from the crush of bodies.

I'd been driving with the sun at my back all the way, and while I'd waited to get my passport stamped the sunset had come and gone, and the brief African dusk was over. The moon appeared over the mountains, brilliant in the darkening sky, and it felt like a good omen. I drove back to my little house on the college campus as the stars came out, and by the time I arrived home, the Southern Cross was visible high in the firmament.

* * *

If this new Themba Project was going to be a full-scale undertaking, we would need to raise a great deal of money, and that would mean asking important people to lend their names in order to impress potential funders. Lord and Lady Attenborough, Richard and Sheila, were staying at the college for a few days: another of the coincidences that made me feel as though I was maybe walking hand in hand with the universe.

As I was head of the theatre arts department and Richard was an actor and film director, it was natural that he and I had become friends. He took a genuine interest in the work I was doing and had come to watch my productions of *The Tempest* and *Cats*. We were both on the Governing Council of the college – me as staff representative, and Richard as a Trustee and Deputy President of the United World College Movement.

I sought him out the next day. He was sitting at the desk in the Principal's office.

"Richard, I have a very big favour to ask you," I said.

I guessed he thought it was something to do with my department, so I hurried on.

"I've been invited to move to Johannesburg, to work at the

125

Trevor Huddleston Memorial Centre. They want me to set up a project with young people using interactive theatre. To try to reduce the spread of HIV."

I took a deep breath and looked at Richard. He stared back at me. I sat down on a chair, feeling a little like a student about to be given the results of a test.

"If I do start this programme," I said, "I'm going to need to raise a lot of money. I wondered if you and Sheila would agree to be my first patrons and let me use your names when I start looking for funds. I'm not asking you for any money – just your names."

There was a silence while Richard took all this in. Eventually he spoke, his voice trembling.

"But Kim darling, I don't want you to leave the college." His eyes filled with tears.

I explained that my three-year contract was coming to an end, and that I was not planning to stay on anyway. Richard found a hankie and wiped his cheeks, and I recalled that a few evenings earlier he'd been in tears as he'd spoken to students and staff about his film *Gandhi* winning so many Oscars.

"It should have been Steven, you know – *E.T.* was such a wonderful film," he'd said.

Richard cried easily, particularly when he felt a wrong had been done.

We talked about the two weekends I'd already run in Sophiatown, and the invitation for me to go back and work permanently at the Trevor Huddleston Centre. I told him that I'd been in South Africa as an actress thirty years earlier and had returned in '96 and '97 with the Themba Project. "This work at the Centre would be a development of Themba," I continued. "I'll ask my colleague, Theresa, if she'll come and join me in Jo'burg and we'll re-start the Project. But with a new focus – HIV prevention among young people."

He listened attentively. Then he stood up, walked around the desk, looked down at me and said, "Yes, darling, *of course* you can use our names. And *of course* we'll be patrons."

I stood too, and asked, "Hadn't we better ask Sheila first, before committing her as well?"

"Oh, Sheila will be happy about it," he replied. He paused for a moment, then added, "And one day I'll hold a dinner in London for you, too." He gave me a huge smile and a great big hug.

I didn't know how to find the words to thank him. Now it was me who had tears in my eyes.

Richard Attenborough had directed the film *Cry Freedom,* about the death of the freedom fighter Steve Biko while in South African police custody in 1977, and the flight to safety of Donald Woods and his family. Richard was a passionate advocate for human rights and once told me that his great dream was to direct a film about Thomas Paine, the activist, campaigner and author of *The Rights of Man.* It was an ambition he was never able to fulfil.

After my meeting with Richard, I walked back to my office behind the stage of the assembly hall and sat down. I held my head in my hands with my elbows resting on the desk. I asked myself, not for the first time, whether I believed in God or some sort of higher power. It seemed too much of a coincidence that just when I needed the support of Very Important People, Richard and Sheila happened to be right here. Was this just chance, or was the universe operating in some inexplicable way to help this project come to fruition?

I had often asked myself about God. God, if there was such a thing, was like a presence which I experienced all around me, accepting me, loving me. I sensed God in that dawn-breaking breath of wind which comes before the sun. I felt God as I sat by the river near my home in England, watching the sunset; in the morning, as I hung out the washing in the garden, with a gentle breeze blowing; in the evening, when I brought the laundry inside again, smelling of fresh grass and sunshine. I saw God in the eyes of friends, in their smiles. When I experienced a sense of rightness about how I was living my life, I thought I knew God. So was God, or whatever name one wanted to use, active now?

I'd had a number of experiences of the numinous at different times in my life. The first was as a child of six, lying on a threadbare blanket in the yard at the back of our house in south London. The sun's rays streamed into my skinny little body and I'd repeated to myself, like a mantra, *I am a sun worshipper, I am a sun worshipper* ... I felt I was being raised up into the sun and subsumed into it.

There was the occasion when, as an adult, I'd melted into the whole of teeming life as I'd manoeuvred my Morris Minor around the busy Vauxhall Bridge Road junction in London. My molecules seemed to have dispersed and become diffused among all the other particles in the immediate vicinity – in my car, the road, the other vehicles and drivers, the railway bridge, the tall office buildings. It had been a dangerous moment as I tried to remain in control of the car – but joyful, too. It seemed as if I, as a separate entity, had dissolved and become absorbed into all other living and non-living things.

I'd sensed God's hand on my head as a physical sensation at the Clearness Meeting the Quakers had held for me when I was working through my ideas which eventually become the original Themba Project. The meeting had lasted two hours, and at the end we'd sat for a while in silence, absorbing everything that had been said. No decision had been arrived at, but the Friends had listened and asked questions, so my thoughts had clarified and my mind felt easy.

I didn't know if I *believed* in God. It was rather as if I *experienced* something which could, for want of another name, be called God.

Was God at work now?

Chapter 11

Swaziland, 2001

For my last production at Waterford I wanted to direct the ancient Greek tragedy *Oedipus Rex*. The play was apt for Swaziland for two reasons: the main protagonist is a King, and his people are all suffering from a plague. Mysh Dlamini was an unusually talented young actor. Despite being only eighteen, I was sure he would be capable of rising to the challenge of the main role.

After three months of rehearsal, the play was performed at the The House on Fire. This space, which had been created by Jiggs Thorne, the son of my friend Jenny, was a semi-out-of-doors "Afro-Shakespearean" amphitheatre with outlandish, bizarre carvings and exotic statues. It was in the valley a few miles out from the college, past the town of Mbabane, and it provided a perfect arena for the production. Towards the end of the play, as the huge metal doors in the centre of the stage swung open, a red spotlight lit Oedipus from behind. Mysh came forward through a haze of dense smoke, with his eyes apparently gouged out, and his face, chest and hands covered in blood. There was an audible intake of breath from the audience as people realised the full horror of what Oedipus had done. As the last lines were spoken and the actors came forward for their curtain call, the audience was on its feet, cheering and applauding.

As the term drew to a close, we were due to take the play back to Waterford, this time to be performed in front of one of the college buildings which fortuitously was adorned with "Greek" pillars. But our plans were nearly cancelled: a much-loved teacher, Hennie Van Vuuren, died suddenly one afternoon of a massive heart attack. Everyone was in a state of shock – Hennie had always seemed so strong, both physically and spiritually. Students stood mutely outside their hostel, or walked around the grounds stunned and disbelieving. Some pupils wept, others kicked at the walls of buildings. We were all asking ourselves the same question: "Why Hennie? Why Hennie, of all people?"

I wondered whether the next performances of *Oedipus* should be abandoned, but the cast and I decided that Hennie would have been mortified if the play was called off.

On the first night, Mysh, playing Oedipus, made his entrance on the roof of the building, about twenty feet above the audience, silhouetted in his pale robes against the darkening sky. Old oil drums filled with fire encircled the playing area and flames licked up into the night. Mysh's opening speech included the lines:

> *In the city I hear prayers for the dying,*
> *And the sound of weeping. The air is laden*
> *With incense and tears ...*

As he said these words, a shooting star arced through the black sky and fell behind him. A whisper was heard, gathering momentum as it travelled through the audience: "Look, that's Hennie. It's Hennie. He's saying goodbye."

The term ended. The production was packed up and the costumes put away. The students left for their homes, taking with them the burden of Hennie's death.

I handed in my notice and began preparations to leave Waterford.

Before I moved forward with the new Project I wrote to the three original Themba women telling them about the invitation from Thabo Makgoba to set up a programme at the Trevor Huddleston Centre. They enthusiastically endorsed what I was proposing to do, and Theresa said she would try to join me in Johannesburg.

* * *

The evening before the start of my final term at Waterford, I walked up the hill from my cottage to attend a concert in the assembly hall. I detected an unusual and disturbing atmosphere. Instead of the usual boisterous noise of students greeting each other after the long holiday, the place was eerily quiet, with a few scattered, muted conversations. I turned to one of my colleagues and asked him what was going on.

"Haven't you heard?" he asked. "Two planes have crashed into the World Trade Center. It's been non-stop on the TV all day." The date was 11 September, 2001.

Somehow, I managed to sit through the concert. It ended in silence as we sent prayers to America. Then I went home, turned on the television and watched the horror alone in my room.

It was a dreadful beginning to a very difficult term. The bombing of Afghanistan coincided with students, and even staff, pitted against each other over a number of petty issues. Accusations of racism and xenophobia were flying about. It felt as if Waterford was a microcosm of what was happening in the rest of the world.

I tried to act as an honest broker between students and staff and spent hours listening to arguments from both sides, attempting to steer them away from confrontation. But I began to feel I was losing friends among my colleagues as I appeared to be siding with the students. It was a horrible atmosphere in which to work.

One weekend, to get away from the claustrophobic life at college and also to say goodbye, I drove over to Shewula. It was a relief to be on the other side of the country, up in the clear air of the Lubombo Mountains. When I arrived, the women were engaged in a community meeting to discuss *umcwasho*, a traditional practice which had just been imposed by the King. Colourful woollen tassels were to be worn around the necks of unmarried teenage girls. It was a sign that they had vowed to abstain from sex for five years. Whether this had any effect on the spread of HIV I never knew, but whatever the outcome, it seemed to me grossly unfair that it was the girls, and not the young men, who were expected to agree to the no-sex commitment. Swaziland was – and is – an extremely patriarchal society.

That afternoon I was invited to attend the graduation of a dozen newly-trained *sangomas* – traditional healers. Nomsa took me to the special compound where the ceremony was taking place. As we neared the enclosure we could hear the drums beating. Although I was the only non-Swazi there, I felt completely at home. One by one, each graduate approached the circle of spectators. They were bare-chested and bare-breasted with just a cloth wrapped around their middles. They crawled on their hands and knees over the dry, sandy ground, towards a huge tub set in the earth under a Marula tree. The pot was filled with a cloudy liquid with some unidentifiable bits and pieces floating in it. The graduates knelt and lapped up the mixture with their tongues – like dogs at a water bowl. Then they turned away and vomited onto the earth. I guessed it was a sort of purification.

Next, all the *sangomas* who had been mentoring the students ran off into the bush, each one bearing a three-foot-long rod with a blown-up sheep's bladder, like a small balloon, tied on one end.

Nomsa said, "They'll hide those sticks, then the new *sangomas* will go to search for them. If they find the right one and come back with it, that'll mean they've used their magic powers to find it. They'll have passed the final test."

We stood around under the hot sun as the drumming grew in speed and volume. I noticed a gathering of old men in a hollow in the ground sitting in a circle contentedly smoking *dagga*. The sweet, pungent aroma wafted towards me, and I was reminded of the time I'd first smelt marijuana at the Glastonbury Festival in the late 1970s.

Soon the teachers came back, without the canes, and the graduates dashed off to discover them. They returned one by one, and hurtled into the circle, holding their stick with the bladder attached high in the air. As each new *sangoma* arrived, the noise of the crowd increased, with singing, stamping, ululating and shouting. People from the crowd leapt forward and danced with the successful candidates as the drums throbbed. The excitement grew. All but one of the bladders had now been found. The drumming quietened as we anticipated the return of the final graduate.

Amid a great swell of noise, the last of the new *sangomas* dashed through the throng, leaping and jumping and bearing the bladder aloft. It was a magnificent piece of theatre. The drums thundered, the spectators erupted, and a melee of people – teachers, *sangomas*, men, women and children all joined in dancing, stamping, singing, ululating and celebrating.

It was my last visit to Shewula.

* * *

I'd written a detailed fundraising document for the Themba HIV & AIDS Project and sent it to Tricia, the friend who'd originally introduced me to Thabo Makgoba, and who had helped set up an NGO in Britain called the Bishop Simeon Trust. The BST was named after the South African Bishop Simeon Nkoane who had been an ardent opponent of apartheid. Tricia worked on my proposal and delivered it to Comic Relief. She was a majestic and determined woman, and had raised thousands of pounds to help educate young South Africans who were too poor to go to school.

After the proposal was sent off, all we could do was wait. I carried on with work at Waterford, and continued my preparations to leave the college.

The weeks passed.

As the term wore on I began to think I must be completely crazy. I had put down a deposit and signed a rental agreement for a house in Johannesburg, organised the relocation of all my belongings, and even obtained a passport for my cat. But there was no word from Comic Relief or from any of the other potential funders Tricia and I had sent proposals to. How could I go to South Africa and set up this Project if there was no money for it? The Quakers have an expression: *Live Adventurously.* I wasn't sure whether I was being adventurous or foolhardy.

In late October, when I was getting dressed to go to a concert by the Soweto String Quartet at the House on Fire, a phone call came through from London: Comic Relief liked the proposal and would fund the work.

With a huge sense of relief, I dashed to town, bought champagne, and drove to Jenny's house to celebrate.

All would be well.

Part Four

2002–2007

Theatre is a form of knowledge. It should and can also be a way of transforming society. Theatre can help us build our future, rather than just waiting for it.
Augusto Boal, *Games for Actors and Non-Actors*

Chapter 12

Sophiatown, Johannesburg, January 2002

I sat at an empty desk on the morning of Thursday, 10 January 2002, staring at a blank wall in the back room of the Trevor Huddleston Memorial Centre. I wondered what on earth I was going to do now. I felt like a beached whale, remote from everything I had ever known. How could I possibly implement this Project I'd had the audacity to envisage? Ma Bompas, the cleaner at the Centre, sang to herself in the kitchen as she washed up at the stainless steel sink. I could hear her putting away the cups and saucers, slamming drawers and clattering about as she tidied up from a meeting the day before.

It was the height of summer and the scrubby grass at the back of the building was brown and shrivelled. I stared out of the window and knew with absolute certainty that I was an imposter and would soon be exposed. I didn't know anything about the lives of young South Africans, I was completely unaware of how to raise money locally, and I was ignorant about HIV and AIDS. The one thing I was certain of was how to create interactive theatre, but I knew that on its own wouldn't be enough. I felt out of my depth and very apprehensive.

I listened to the ever-present Johannesburg sound of the hadeda ibises screeching their distinctive *haa-haa-haa-de-daah* call, and flapping their vast wings overhead as they flew above the bungalow and swirled over the church car park.

After a few gloomy minutes I came to my senses and reminded myself that I *had* written the HIV and AIDS policy at Waterford, *had* worked as a professional fundraiser in the UK, and *had* raised a great deal of money in the past (albeit not in South Africa). I had also learnt something about the lives of young people in this part of the world while living and working in Swaziland. But none of that took away my insecurity and self-doubt.

Although I had been introduced to Busi, the Centre's admin assistant, and Ma Bompas, I knew no one else, and I felt very alone.

I joined Ma B in the kitchen and asked if I could make myself a cup of coffee. I didn't know where anything was kept, and despite her apparent friendliness, Ma B exuded an aura that told me unmistakeably that I was an intruder. She was a big woman, with a wide bust over which she wore a faded apron with a somewhat suggestive picture of a maize cob emblazoned on the front. While she banged about opening cupboards and taking down mugs and coffee, I found myself trying to justify my presence there.

Ma B in the kitchen of the Trevor Huddleston Memorial Centre

"Were you in the church when I came and did those plays with the young people?" I ventured.

"Not that I remember," she said.

I tried again. "Do you think Thabo will be coming to the Centre today?"

"*Father* Thabo doesn't come very often. He's busy with the church and the university."

She made it clear that by not saying "Father" I had implied an inappropriate familiarity, but the word would have stuck in my throat if I'd used it. Thabo was my friend, not my priest.

Down the corridor past the kitchen were two rooms that had once been bedrooms. I thought it likely that the office I had been allocated had once belonged to a little girl. The walls were a lurid pink and there was a dark fuchsia carpet, worn and stained in places, with the indentations of long-forgotten furniture still visible.

Whenever I am presented with a problem, I write a list. This one was headed: "What Has To Be Done":

Buy stationery, flipchart paper and stand. Buy kokies (felt pens)
Get another desk and chair (Theresa)
Buy second-hand filing cabinet
Get phone line into office
Talk to Manya Gittel
Meet with Thabo
Find venues for auditions
Plan auditions
Discover how to advertise auditions
Recruit young people
Find out about booking the church hall for training
Plan training
Talk to/fax Theresa
Buy 2 mugs (office)

I needed advice on where to advertise the auditions. They would have to be held close to where the young people were living rather than expecting them to travel to Sophiatown. This meant finding venues in the townships. When Thabo came to the Centre I asked him for his ideas. He suggested I use church halls in Soweto and Alexandra. He said most of the churches ran youth groups, and he gave me the names of contacts.

* * *

A white woman alone in a car – especially one with a Swazi registration – was a rare sight in the townships, and I didn't know my way. Although I had been given directions, I was nervous as I drove into Soweto. I knew that violence was endemic, and there was a possibility that I would be threatened or, at the very least, unwelcome. I half-expected my car to be high-jacked and me dumped on the roadside.

I was relieved I'd managed the journey safely when I reached the entrance to the Ipelegeng Centre, next door to St Paul's Jabavu church. I explained my mission to the man at the big iron gates and he let me through. There were a number of brick-built buildings around a dusty courtyard, and the semi-circular wall of the huge church loomed to one side. The Centre ran courses and training for young people. I parked, locked my car, and followed signs to Reception.

A tired-looking young woman behind a grille looked up.

"*Sawubona, Sisi,*" I said. "Hello, sister."

I'd learnt some siSwati while living in Swaziland, and a little isiZulu when I'd worked in the original Themba Project in 1997. Jabu Mashinini had been my *umfundisi* (teacher). The two languages had a great deal in common. I'd even been given my own Zulu name, Thokozile, which meant be happy, be thankful, rejoice. *Sawubona* literally translated meant "I see you".

No doubt I had pronounced the word atrociously but at least I had tried. I continued in English, but the greeting had aroused the woman's interest and she looked friendlier.

"I wonder if you can help me? I'd like to find out about

booking one of your spaces for drama auditions."

The woman looked interested.

"We're starting a new project in Sophiatown, at the Trevor Huddleston Centre, and I need to recruit young people to come and join us."

"Ah, Father Thabo," she said.

"Yes, that's right."

She showed me into a large hall with narrow windows high up near the ceiling. The wooden floor was dirty and splintered, and the walls, originally painted white, were scratched and marked from years of use. It was about the right size to run a drama workshop for forty or fifty people. I booked it for 7 and 8 February.

Next, I needed to find a venue in Alexandra Township to the north-east of Jo'burg. Thabo had suggested the brand-new Church of St Michael and All Angels, run by Father Sam. It had a nearly-completed community centre attached. Alex was a much smaller township than Soweto, and I felt more at home there. But this was the first time I'd driven in on my own, and once again I was apprehensive. I felt I was being watched as I drove through the over-crowded streets.

The church, when I was shown in by the secretary, was already well furnished, with new, highly polished pews, a pulpit and a grand altar. It was vast, almost circular, with large stained glass windows set high up in the walls. The sun flooded in, splashing a myriad of colours across the stone floor. I guessed the church could house more than a thousand worshippers under its pitched roof. I booked it for 14 and 15 February.

Back at the Centre, I phoned Manya Gittel.

"Hi, Manya, it's Kim."

"Kim?"

"Yes. We met when I was in Jo'burg in '96. You were at the Alternatives to Violence Project workshop Theresa and I ran at St Benedict's. Do you remember?"

"Suss, man, of course I remember," she replied. "Howz'it?"

I explained why I was back in Jo'burg, and told her a little about the Project. Manya had years of experience of using Forum Theatre, and had even worked with Augusto Boal when he'd visited South Africa.

"I'm phoning because I wondered if you'd like to help me run auditions for young people in the townships."

She agreed to meet me.

A few days later, after I'd bought stationery and had even organised a telephone extension into the pink bedroom, Manya drove over to Sophiatown. She was a tall, rangy woman in her thirties, with thick brown hair and an outlandish, slightly hippyish style of dress. She was keen to be involved.

"Theresa will be coming out from the UK soon," I said. "But I need to get on with finding young people straight away and get things started."

Manya listened closely as I told her more about the Project.

"I don't think it's possible for me to run the auditions on my own," I said. "One person needs to lead an exercise while the other observes. Then we'd swap over."

Manya was enthusiastic and had lots of useful ideas. She suggested we include a young woman she knew called Lebo Mashile.

I began to feel my confidence returning.

* * *

On the morning of Thursday, 7 February, I woke with my stomach feeling hollow and uneasy and worries scurrying in my head. What if no one turned up for the audition? What if people came, but refused to join in, and the whole thing was a fiasco? What if someone had double-booked the hall in Soweto? Lying in bed thinking about the day ahead, I visualised everything that could go wrong. At the same time, I was keyed up and excited.

I had given up a safe, secure job in Swaziland and come to Johannesburg to establish something new and innovative. Today was just the beginning: I had no idea where it would lead.

I was conscious that the whole idea of the Project was predicated upon all the diverse experiences I'd had in my life: drama teacher, theatre practitioner, workshop facilitator, Alternatives to Violence trainer, fundraiser, project manager, journalist, public relations officer, staff manager. Because of this, the onus for its success or failure rested squarely on my shoulders. It was an awesome responsibility.

Manya and I had designed the audition workshops so that even those young people who were not chosen would at least learn something about HIV and AIDS and find out how to keep themselves safe from the virus. I had often held auditions for the plays I'd directed, but this was different: I was offering those who were selected the chance to become involved in an exciting new programme which would give them skills and opportunities, and which might, just might, save lives.

We were looking for young people between the ages of seventeen and twenty-five to train to become "actor-educators" – peer educators using interactive theatre. They would be unemployed and not in school or college, and it was therefore likely they would suffer from low self-esteem. We were aware they would be vulnerable to rejection, and many of them were inevitably going to be turned down at the end of the workshop. This was an aspect of any audition that I always disliked – the fact that some people didn't get picked.

When Manya, Lebo and I arrived at the Ipelegeng Centre in Soweto, there was already a motley queue of about fifty young people waiting for us in the corridor. They had learnt about the auditions from leaflets I'd left at a number of churches and youth groups in the area, and from an advertisement I'd placed in *The Sowetan* newspaper. We set up the flipchart stand on one side of the hall, arranged the chairs in a circle in the middle, and put a table by the door with registration forms, name labels and pens ready.

Then I opened the door.

As the young people filed in, registered and wrote their name badges, I had a strong sense of something significant beginning, but I had no premonition about how life-changing this would be for some of them. I watched them hanging around the hall keeping as close to the walls as possible waiting for the workshop to begin. They were probably as apprehensive as I was.

I took a deep breath.

"Good morning, everyone. Thank you for coming today. Won't you come and sit on these chairs, please?"

I noticed with a smile that I had used the South African "won't you" rather than the English "would you". I was already becoming acclimatised.

They shuffled towards the circle and sat down. Some of the young men stretched their legs out in front of them, tipping their chairs and leaning back, suggesting they were unconcerned. One linked his hands behind his head, eyes directed at the ceiling, body slouching in the chair, apparently in an attempt to show how relaxed he was. The girls sat more primly, eyeing each other. I spotted one young woman who was unsuitably dressed for a drama workshop, in a tight red skirt which she smoothed down nervously over her thighs. She looked embarrassed. She had obviously dressed up for the occasion and now found herself out of place among the others, most of whom were in old jeans and T-shirts.

I realised that for these young people the day offered them the prospect of doing something new and different with their lives. I wondered whether they had come because they had an interest in drama, or because they were concerned about the spread of HIV. More likely they were here because they hoped it might be a way of earning some cash, or simply because they had nothing better to do. Their days stretched endlessly, idling around the townships with no money, no jobs, no training and no hope for the future. The promise of the "New South Africa" was taking a long time to be fulfilled.

Once we were all settled, I spoke to the group.

"Good morning. My name is Kim, and I'd like to introduce you to Manya, and to Lebo."

I looked at the young people sitting in the circle. They were leaning forward, listening carefully.

"While one of us leads an exercise, the other two will observe, so don't worry if you see us making notes. At the end of the morning we'll choose some of you to come for a second selection workshop. That will be in Sophiatown in two weeks' time."

I watched their faces. Some already looked resigned to failure, a few feigned a lack of concern, but I was glad to see the majority appeared lively and enthusiastic.

"OK. Let's get started."

Both Manya and Lebo were South Africans – one who spoke Afrikaans, and one a Zulu. Together we made a good team, although I was very aware of my colour, my English accent and my maturity. Lebo was a very beautiful young woman, about the same age as the people in the hall. She was able to relate to them in a way that I could not, even though she spoke no indigenous African language. She had been born in the United States after her parents had fled when apartheid was at its height, and had recently returned to her homeland. She was a budding actress and performance poet.

After the name games, some "getting to know you" activities and drama exercises, we split the young people into groups and asked them to prepare short improvised plays on any subject related to HIV and AIDS. I watched as they began to work together and it became obvious that a few of them had no idea how to cooperate. After they had planned and rehearsed, each group performed their play to the rest of us.

One play was about stigma, with a story of a young man who

tried to tell his parents he was HIV positive. Their reaction was to violently throw him out of the house. The father was performed horribly realistically by a tall, self-assured young man. I guessed he belonged to one of the many township theatre groups. The girl with the short, tight skirt played the mother – somewhat unconvincingly. Her voice was quiet and she appeared to lack confidence. Other plays told stories of rejection by a boyfriend or girlfriend, ignorance of how HIV was contracted, embarrassment at a hospital, teachers who displayed prejudice, siblings who were ill, and unexplained death. There was even one play set at the side of a grave with the actors miming shovelling in the earth.

Watching the young people discussing, preparing and performing, we noticed that those who were confident actors were sometimes the least able to work cooperatively. We were looking for folk who would be sensitive towards each other, could listen and concentrate, collaborate and follow instructions, and didn't dominate others. Acting ability would be useful, but at this stage it was far from being the most important quality.

Even the youngest of these young people had suffered the indignities of the "Bantu Education Act," which had only been repealed in 1994. The Act had enshrined the expectation that the black population would be *hewers of wood and drawers of water*, and the curriculum was designed to discourage abstract thinking, creativity and an enquiring mind. Hendrik Verwoerd, who was Minister for Native Affairs in 1954 had (in)famously said, *There is no place for him (the Bantu) in the European community above the level of certain forms of labour ... What is the use of teaching the Bantu child mathematics when it cannot use it in practice? That is quite absurd. Education must train people in accordance with their opportunities in life, according to the sphere in which they live.*

Black schooling had received just one-tenth of the resources allocated to white education. Teachers were poorly trained, and misdemeanours by pupils were punished by the cane. We were asking a lot from the young people in the hall, and it was noticeable that some of them were unable to follow even the simplest instructions.

The results were encouraging, however. One particular young man, Bongani, stood out from the rest. He seemed to have an inner strength, and it was evident he had acted before. I saw that he worked generously with others in his group, always finding opportunities to help them shine. He was tall, with a strong jaw, and he wore a beanie on his head throughout the session. When I looked through the names and addresses on the registration forms, I saw that he had travelled all the way from Tembisa, a vast, sprawling township across the other side of Johannesburg, near the airport. He had demonstrated extraordinary determination to arrive at the audition on time because three or four combi-taxis would have been needed to get him to Soweto. He would have left his home very early indeed – probably with no breakfast.

Bongani

Mary was another of the young people who showed real promise. She had an attractive, smiling face and worked sensitively with her group. She could act, too, and her voice was strong. Her registration form showed she lived nearby.

Towards the end of the morning, after we'd seen all the improvised plays and applauded each one enthusiastically, I was struck by the very different atmosphere in the hall. The young people were lively, animated and excited. But now came the moment of reckoning. I showed the group how to play the *Pattern Ball* game which they then continued on their own, while Manya, Lebo and I got into a huddle and went through the observation forms. We quickly made three piles: Yes, No and Maybe. Then we went through the "maybes" and discussed who should be moved to the "yes" or the "no". We returned to the group, and called out their names.

Manya stuck a small yellow sticker on the chests of more than half the people in the room, while I attached a green sticker on the others. Then we asked each group to move to different ends of the hall. Manya and Lebo went with the "yellows" and I walked over to the "greens".

"Please don't shout or cheer," I said in a low voice to my group, "but we would like you all to come to the Trevor Huddleston Centre the week after next for a further selection workshop."

I watched their faces, suffused with suppressed excitement. "This doesn't mean that we'll be able to keep you all: we can only take a dozen or so people this time round, and we'll be holding further auditions here and in Alex. But we are interested in you. You have some of the qualities we're looking for."

The young people were grinning and looking around at each other to see who else was "in" with them.

"The next workshop will be in Sophiatown and will last all day, starting at ten o'clock in the morning."

Some of them looked perplexed. I knew that it would indicate real commitment if they actually managed to get themselves to

Sophiatown from Soweto. It was a long and complicated journey needing a minimum of two mini-cab taxis.

"Can you all get there? And on time? One of the things we're looking for is the ability to be punctual. So this is all part of the selection process." They nodded enthusiastically and I handed out directions to the Trevor Huddleston Centre. They left the hall jubilant, and I could hear joyful whooping in the corridor.

I crossed over to join the other group. By the look on their faces, most of them had already guessed they were the "rejects". There is nothing one can say in these circumstances to make people feel better.

"It's been a difficult choice, and I'm sorry to have to tell you that we won't be asking you to come to Sophiatown this time around. But we will be recruiting again later in the year and you could try again then."

It didn't make any difference. The mood was sad and melancholy. The tight-skirted girl looked desperately disappointed, and I thought I could see tears in her eyes. One young man stood up and silently walked away with as much dignity as he could muster. Nobody complained or appeared angry. It was as if they knew their lack of success was inevitable. I felt terrible.

In the afternoon we repeated the workshop, but with a smaller group. Once again, we discovered some young people who had potential to join the Project.

Manya, Lebo and I returned to Sophiatown with the names of twenty people out of the eighty that we'd seen. The next day we repeated the process, and discovered another fifteen who we invited to come to the second selection round.

I was excited that the Themba Project had actually begun. And very pleased that we'd found thirty-five people who we'd invited back. But I was haunted by the faces of those we had turned away. I reminded myself that we had planned the auditions so that everyone attending would learn about HIV and AIDS and how to keep themselves safe from the virus. This made me feel a little better.

The following week, in Alexandra, we ran three more auditions over two days and found thirty more people who we invited to come to Sophiatown.

The final full day's selection workshop was held in the hall at the Church of Christ the King a few days later. This was to be the rehearsal space for the development of the Themba HIV & AIDS Project. It was important for the young people to discover what their journeys entailed – how long it would take them, and the cost of their fares.

Out of the three hundred or so young people we'd auditioned in all, we invited eighteen to join the Project: Montana, Mary, Sabelo, Seipati, Tshepo, Obey, Thato, Precious, Sibusiso, Stanley, Kedi, Zodwa, Jordan, Floyd, Bongani, JR, Basetsana and Refiloe.

We were on our way – there was now no going back. I felt excited, but anxious, too. What would the following weeks and months bring when these young people were trained to become actor-educators in the Themba HIV & AIDS Project?

I had no idea of the extent to which being part of Themba would change all our lives.

Chapter 13

Johannesburg, February 2002

It was thirty-eight years since I'd toured South Africa with the Cambridge Theatre Company, and during that time, living in England, the desire to return had never left me. But now that I was back in Johannesburg, I asked myself why I had so often longed to be here. The city was dangerous and polluted, with an incredibly high crime rate. It felt like a gold-rush city still.

People lived in closed-off complexes behind high walls, and security guards paraded the streets. There were beggars at most of the *robots* (traffic lights) and I kept a supply of *naartjies* (small oranges) and apples in my car rather than give cash to the homeless people.

There was one particular set of robots where barefoot urchins of about eight or nine years old hung around, openly sniffing glue from plastic bags. They begged for money from the drivers who stopped at the lights. The boys' eyes were red and watery and they had pus-filled, bleeding sores round their mouths. Their bodies were powdered with the pale dust from the gold-mine dumps which surrounded Johannesburg, and their shorts and T-shirts were ragged. They lived in discarded concrete tubes left over from road-works nearby, and when – if – they grew up they would no doubt become *tsotsis* and join one of the many criminal gangs. I felt guilty whether I gave them something or not: I had my comfortable rented home, enough money to buy food and petrol and to go to the movies or out for a meal if I wanted to.

"Ag madam, I am hungreeeee," these children would whine as they came up to my car while I waited for the lights to change. They all had the same practised dejected expression on their faces, and they gestured as if putting food into their mouths. Or they would hold up their hands, one placed on top of the other, both palms turned upwards, begging for money. When I gave them apples or naartjies rather than cash, their eyes squinted at me malevolently and I would speed away as fast as I could.

In the northern suburbs of Johannesburg the wealthy owned vast, sprawling mansions, with air-conditioning, manicured gardens, tennis courts, private swimming pools and armies of servants (or, as they were called in these democratic days, "domestic workers"). High walls were topped with rolls of razor wire, with burglar alarms, electric fences and automatic gates. The informal settlements which had sprung up around the edges of the townships had no running water, no electricity, no services of any kind. Here people lived in cramped, makeshift shacks, freezing cold in winter and blazing hot in summer. The ditches, *dongas* and earth tracks between the dwellings were clogged with litter.

The disparity between the rich and the poor was grotesque.

The house I was renting was in an area called Melville, slightly to the west of Johannesburg city centre with its high-rise office blocks and New York-style skyline. By contrast, Melville's old-fashioned high street was full of little antique shops, cafés, restaurants, grocers, hairdressers, beauticians and art galleries. The pavements were occupied by Zimbabwean refugees making small model animals, necklaces and earrings from wire and beads, which they sold to tourists. The area was deemed safe but it was impossible for me to walk home down my tree-lined street in the evening in case I was attacked. This was not paranoia – there had been too many cases of assaults on unsuspecting holidaymakers in that part of town to dare to walk at dusk, and even in daylight I never felt entirely safe. When I met friends for supper in the main road (7th Street) only five minutes' walk from my house, I would get in my car and drive up.

The low-level anxiety was constant – I was always looking over my shoulder.

But there were compensations: unlike the reticence of the English, South Africans were never afraid to speak their minds, and lively discussions over good local wine were frequent. One Sunday, I decided to walk to the house of my landlord, Lucas, with his mail. It was a lovely summer afternoon, and Lukas lived only about ten minutes' away. Clare, my lodger, came with me. I was glad to have her company as I didn't want to walk alone, even on a bright sunny day.

When we got there, Lukas was in his garden with some friends enjoying a *braai* (barbecue).

"Come in, come in!" he cried. "We're having a braai – you must join us."

Lukas brushed from his forehead a curl which had loosened from his pitch-black hair, and I wondered – not for the first time – whether he used self-tan or make-up to achieve his golden skin tone. I was sure his hair was dyed, and possibly even artificially set, in its thick black shiny waves. Lukas looked like the stereotypical hero from a *Mills and Boon* story, and his high spirits were infectious. Anton stood beside him, tanned and boyish, and Lukas reached over and languidly laid an arm across his shoulder and repeated his invitation. "No, really man, you must stay – we insist."

The sun was shining, the garden was surrounded by tall evergreens providing pleasant shade, Lukas and Anton's guests were all mildly drunk, and the smell of braai-ing meat was irresistible. We stayed for the whole afternoon, and to begin with I enjoyed the animated conversation.

"Mbeki will never be a popular President."

"But the economy is growing."

"Ja, but that's not enough to make him well-liked."

"And look what he's been saying about HIV and AIDS. He *ought* to know what he's talking about – it was his responsibility when he was Mandela's deputy. But he seems to want to steer clear of the whole issue now."

"It does look like that, ja."

"Yes, but he's got a lot to live up to, hey? Taking over from Mandela was always going to be an impossible job."

"That's true, man. But he's not got what it takes. He's like all the rest: arrogant, too clever by half, and probably lining his own pockets."

"You think so?"

"Suss, man, he is an economist …"

"Economist? Where did he learn to be an economist? Not in South Africa, for sure …"

"He could have gone to Fort Hare. That's where the blacks went, isn't it?"

"I suppose. But I never heard he went there."

I wanted to join in the conversation and tell them that Thabo Mbeki had in fact been a student at the University of Sussex while he'd been in exile, but I decided to hold my tongue and see where the discussion would lead. I was interested to learn how much people would reveal, so I waited to see what transpired.

Despite the disparaging tone of much of the conversation, it soon became apparent that everyone at the braai had a grudging respect for Nelson Mandela – even though only a few short years before they would have regarded him as a terrorist. It was difficult, if not impossible, in these "enlightened" days to find any white person admitting to having supported the apartheid regime.

As the afternoon wore on and the wine and beer flowed the discussion veered dangerously close to racism. Lounging around in garden chairs people began on the well-worn topic of the domestic worker problem.

"My girl … ag, sorry, I'm not supposed to say 'girl' any more, am I? Well, I found her the other day cleaning the toilet with washing-up liquid! I mean! There were bubbles all over the floor, man. I asked her, I said, 'What are you doing, hey?' and she said, 'Sorry, ma'am, but the toilet cleaner is fineeeshed.'"

"Ag, shame, man. But ja, it's the same in the shops. Why can't these people order more stock *before* something runs out? They don't seem to have any idea of forward-planning."

Clare and I glanced at each other at the abhorrent expression *these people*. She raised an eyebrow questioningly. She had only been in South Africa a few weeks, but she'd already begun to pick up the unspoken, unpleasantly patronising attitude many whites still showed towards black people.

We left the braai soon after this.

With all the inconveniences and underlying racism, I often pondered what it was that made me want to stay. It was a far cry from my easy, safe existence in Sussex, but I was enjoying living and learning in a new country. I also seemed to have developed a sense of mission: something to do with righting wrongs. First there had been the conflict resolution and non-violence work with the original Themba Project, and now there was the HIV prevention programme with young people. Maybe in both cases I was trying to counteract the injustice I'd felt as a child. I felt an affinity with the young people in South Africa who had been given little opportunity to learn, or to use their brains. I wanted them to have a second chance too.

* * *

The summer sun was already hot as I left the house, backed my car out of the garage and drove to Sophiatown. It was only a fifteen-minute journey via Melville with its pretty streets, across the bridge over the Westdene Dam and along the dilapidated main road. I noticed how quickly, in Johannesburg, the character of one suburb changed, abruptly and sometimes dramatically, to another.

Outside Westdene's scruffy shops, semi-conscious men lay on the patchy grass which lined the pavements Some were sleeping off the drinking of the night before, propped up against broken lampposts nursing their *bobelases* (hangovers). As I approached Sophiatown, the area became more suburban, with ugly 1950s bungalows surrounded by low walls or wrought-iron fences, with a good array of gnomes and a few straggly plants in pots in the paved-over gardens.

Sophiatown was steeped in history: Ray Street, where the Trevor Huddleston Memorial Centre was situated, was part of a grid pattern of roads which had kept their names since the 1950s forced removals of the original residents: Meyer Street, Edith Street, Toby Street, Victoria Road. Weeds grew out of the cracks in the pavement slabs, and the place had a run-down feel to it.

I parked and went into the Centre to greet Ma Bompas and Busi. They were chatting about the Mars space probe and bemoaning its cost.

"Eh, wena. Why put all that money into something that does no good for the rest of us?" said Ma B.

"Yebo, Ma," replied Busi, "but I expect Mr Bush thinks it'll make his people love him."

"Huh," responded Ma B. "It'll take more than a trip to the moon for that."

I wanted to join them in their chat, but I was too keyed up. It was the first day of training for the young people we'd selected to join the Project. I went through to the Themba office to collect what I needed for the day.

The sun slanted through the spiky leaves of the tall fir trees that skirted the car park, and as I walked across the warming tarmac towards the church hall, I thought about what lay ahead. Would my ideas for the Project work out? Would the young people we'd selected respond well to the training, and what sort of effect would being part of Themba have on their lives? Would they even turn up? How long would the money last, and what would happen to us all if it came to an end? Most important, would we succeed in reducing the spread of HIV – and save lives?

I reflected again on my audacity, and the same question continued to haunt me: who was I to think I had anything useful to offer?

Nonetheless, we had eighteen recruits, and funding from Comic Relief. I couldn't turn back now. I took a deep breath, entered the cavernous hall and looked around, blinking my eyes in the cool, dark air.

There they were: the young people we'd selected at the audition workshops. They were sitting about in ones and twos, waiting to begin.

"*Sanibonani*. Good morning, everyone."

Expectant faces turned to me. "*Sawubona, Ma.*"

My nerve nearly failed me, but summoning up as much confidence as I could muster, I held a sheet of sticky labels high above my head. "OK, before we get started: name badges."

We wrote on the labels, and stuck them on our chests. They were beautiful names: Montana, Mary, Sabelo, Tshepo, Obey, Thato, Sibusiso, Stanley, Kedi, Zodwa, Jordan, Floyd, JR, Basetsana, Refiloe, Precious, Seipati and Bongani.

They had all come.

"Right, we'll begin with some of the games and exercises you did when you were in the selection workshops. So, let's start with *The Sun Shines On* ... Do you remember?"

At mid-morning, after I'd led a number of different games and exercises, we went to the church hall kitchen where I'd provided coffee, tea, sugar, milk and biscuits. I leant against the counter and watched with a mixture of dismay and amusement as JR heaped three huge spoonsful of sugar into her mug.

"What's the matter?" she asked.

"It's just ... sorry ... but that seems an awful lot of sugar," I said.

JR grinned and shrugged her shoulders.

Most of them stirred similar amounts into their tea or coffee. Some had brought loaves of thick-sliced white bread and they made sandwiches with bright pink *polony*. It looked like a very unhealthy diet, but it was cheap and filling.

After the break, I ran an actor's warm-up. The young people learnt to stand and relax in the neutral position, breathe deeply and use their voices and their bodies. I could see that the physical fitness of most of them would need to improve if they were to achieve the stamina required for the work ahead. Many were getting short of breath and beginning to slow down.

By the end of the morning everyone was hot and puffed and needed a rest. We stopped for lunch.

Some of the participants walked to the pavement vendors on the main street to buy *bunny chow* – half a white loaf with the middle scooped out and filled with curry. Others went into the car park for a cigarette and a chat, while some took plastic boxes out of their bags with greasy pieces of cooked chicken and rice, which they ate with their fingers. Some had nothing to eat, so I went to the Centre and brought over more biscuits and some apples.

Back in my office I sat at my desk eating my salad.

In the afternoon I asked everyone to sit in a circle while I explained the Themba HIV & AIDS Project and its mission to help reduce the spread of HIV. As I looked around at the faces of the young people, I wondered what was going through their minds. Some would have direct experience of family members with HIV or AIDS. Some might be HIV positive themselves. I wondered if all this talk of acting seemed irrelevant to them.

"I'll teach you a technique called Forum Theatre, which is a type of interactive theatre devised by a man called Augusto Boal from Brazil. He engaged with factory employees to try to improve their conditions of work. The people in his audiences worked with the actors to find their own solutions to the stories in the plays." I paused for a moment in case anyone wanted to ask a question, but they were all leaning forward and listening intently, their eyes shining.

"Although we are not looking at issues around employment, the process will work for us, too. We'll start by training you as actors, and we'll help you create plays about HIV and AIDS which will have characters and stories that are true to life. Then we'll teach you how to use Forum Theatre."

"When do you think we'll be ready to start showing these plays?" Bongani asked.

"I don't know. It will depend on how we get on."

Then Refiloe spoke: "Will we get paid for this?"

There was an immediate change of mood. I had suspected that money would be a concern, and I sensed that the others were relieved, but a little embarrassed, that Refiloe had had the courage to ask the question.

"No, you won't get paid a wage, but we will give you travel expenses. Once I've raised more money I hope we can give you a stipend. But it won't be like a proper job. You will be trainees, not employees, coming here three days a week, learning about HIV and AIDS, creating plays, and practising interactive theatre. When we're ready we'll take the plays into schools."

I looked around the group and I wished I was in a position to pay them. But it was true that to begin with they would be learning and would benefit from the training. I was ashamed that I was to be paid from the Comic Relief grant to lead the Project while the young people would receive so little. Some of them would be the sole supporters of their families.

I had no idea then how much of an issue money would become as time went on.

We ended the day with an evaluation go-round called *Thumb-thing*. We stood in a tight circle, stretched our right arms into the middle with our hands in a fist and our thumbs pointing up, and each said a word or phrase to sum up how the day had been for of us. These included: *exciting, different, fun, challenging, tiring, it was unusual*, and *I enjoyed myself*.

We all turned our hands sideways, slotted our thumbs into

the clenched fist of the person on our left, and made a circle of our connected hands. Then, with a great cry of *Bayethe!* we flung our arms into the air and scattered backwards.

It was the end of Themba's first day.

"Hambani kahle," I said. "Go well, everyone."

They replied with the traditional response as they made their way out of the hall: *"Sala kahle,* stay well."

Circle of Themba hands

The following morning when I arrived at the Centre, I was greeted by an irate Ma Bompas.

"Those children," she exclaimed, "those children."

"Children? What children?" I asked.

"Eish. Those children who are in my kitchen yesterday. It's all in a mess and a muddle."

"Do you mean the church hall kitchen, Ma B?"

"Yes, *my* kitchen," she replied.

"They're hardly children, Ma B. Most of them are over twenty, and Stanley must be coming up for thirty."

I waited for a reaction, but she just stood there looking at me, arms crossed over her impressive bosom.

"And we tidied up before we left," I continued. "I made sure everything was put away. *And* I brought the Themba tea and coffee back here to the office."

"Nothing is in the right place," she responded, her face screwed up in annoyance, "and the floor was dirty too. And the tea-towels have been used."

"If you're that bothered," I replied, "I'll buy drying-up cloths for Themba and we'll use only those. And maybe you'd like to come over next week and tell us exactly where you want things put in the cupboards?"

I wasn't going to be intimidated by Ma B, despite her being a South African *and* black, *and* a former resident of Sophiatown. "And as for the floor – yes, we did stand on it."

Ma B let out a humph of annoyance. Then she said, "And the chairs weren't put back properly in the hall, either."

I walked into my office. After all, it was Ma B's job to clear up and to do the cleaning, and I knew we had left the hall tidy. Maybe this was her way of getting at me because she disapproved of the Project. I knew she hadn't been party to the decision to invite me to the Centre.

Her disparaging attitude to the Themba trainees surprised me because the "youth" in South Africa were generally held in high esteem – certainly more so than young people in the UK. The African National Congress Youth League was a powerful political force and had been in the forefront of the struggle for freedom and democracy.

I returned to the kitchen.

"Ma B, I would like you to refer to the Themba participants as 'young people', please. They are *not* children."

"They're children to me," she replied.

"They may be to you, but to themselves and to the Project

and to me, they are young people. They must be treated with respect."

She humph-ed again and I wondered if I had broken a cultural precept or some unnamed invisible rule by insisting that the trainees *not* be referred to as children.

As it turned out, Ma B was to be the least of my worries.

Chapter 14

Sophiatown, March–April 2002

The young people came to Themba for training three days each week, and I worked Mondays and Fridays in the little pink office at the back of the bungalow where the Trevor Huddleston Centre was housed.

I sat down at my desk, took a sheet of paper from the drawer, and began the laborious task of drawing up a fundraising strategy. Money was a constant anxiety: we never had enough to cover all our expenses, and I spent many sleepless nights fretting. The Comic Relief grant was generous and without it the Project would never have begun, but I needed to raise considerably more money if we were to survive. I had no grant-making contacts or fundraising experience in South Africa so it was a challenging task. I didn't want to rely solely on funds from the UK.

Theresa came to South Africa after the Project had officially started – she had been delayed in the UK by the birth of her first grandchild. When she arrived, she set to work on number-crunching, thinking through how many hours of training we'd need to provide before we had something resembling a theatre company, and how many people we'd train as facilitators. I watched her as she bent her skinny back over the task, shoulder blades protruding, hunched over her desk with her head down, her fine grey hair flopping over her face. Theresa had a bubbling inner energy, while on the surface she remained calm. I was glad she had come.

We sat in the Themba office and talked for hours, hammering out the beginning of a business plan. The following week, together with the young people, we agreed the guidelines we would all adhere to while working at Themba:

Show respect for each other's differences

Be punctual at the beginning of sessions and performances, and at the end of breaks

Finish at the agreed time

Communicate with Themba if we are unable to attend or have been delayed

Only leave cell phones on when this has been agreed by the group

Not to be under the influence of drugs and/or alcohol during our work with Themba

Be as open as we are able to be with each other

Listen to each other

Support and be sensitive to each other

These "rules" proved to be invaluable later, when we needed them as a benchmark against which to measure the behaviour of some of the trainees.

Theresa had more detailed knowledge of HIV than I had. She took on the task of teaching the young people how the virus was contracted and the way it spread through the body. The common indicators were mouth ulcers, skin rashes, yeast infections, diarrhoea, sweating, persistent dry cough, stomach cramps, weight loss and 'flu-like symptoms. She also clarified what behaviour was risky. Some of the group were shocked to learn that they had already made themselves vulnerable and began to think about getting tested. One young man, I'll call him "Vusi," was extremely thin and had repeated bouts of diarrhoea. He looked frightened as he listened to Theresa.

I watched the young people as they absorbed her words. HIV had already taken a hold on their day-to-day experience. Some of them had mothers and fathers, sisters and brothers, who were infected or who had died of AIDS, and some, no doubt, were carrying the virus themselves. I didn't know it then, but later we would accompany them to clinics, argue with doctors until the right medication was prescribed, visit their families, and attend their relatives' funerals.

As time went by, it became obvious that Vusi was unwell, and we watched day by day as he lost weight. Each time he arrived at Themba his tiredness seemed to have increased, and sometimes he found it hard to take part in the exercises and rehearsals. Eventually Theresa persuaded him to go for an HIV test, and it turned out he did indeed have the virus even though he'd never had a sexual relationship: he had been raped at the age of fourteen.

Vusi needed to start antiretroviral treatment immediately, but as he had no money, we funded the first four weeks' supply of drugs ourselves. As the end of the month approached, Vusi took the now almost empty pill boxes to the state hospital. After queuing for most of the day, he was eventually seen by a nurse and explained that he couldn't afford to pay again. This forced the hand of the staff at the clinic because they knew that any break in treatment would make matters far, far worse. He was duly given free medicine and his life was saved, but if we'd waited for the state to provide the first drugs, he would almost certainly be dead now.

The CD4 count blood test measures how healthy, or not, a person's immune system is. The Government had recently bowed to pressure and agreed to fund antiretroviral medication (ARVs) for people with a count lower than two hundred, but the drugs were only intermittently available. Hundreds of thousands of people, mostly young and potentially productive, died unnecessarily of AIDS-related illnesses because they couldn't afford to pay for the essential treatment. Part of the problem was that the stigma of being seen attending a hospital or clinic was so great that people often refused to get tested, even when they were displaying signs of the virus. Without a test they were unaware of their HIV status, and if positive, continued to infect their loved ones.

It didn't help that the messages coming out of the Government were mixed: The Health Minister, Manto Tshabalala-Msimang, was notorious for advocating a diet of beetroot, garlic and lemon juice to "cure" AIDS. She was known among her critics as "Dr Beetroot". Her negative stance on the use of conventional medicine to combat AIDS not only resulted in the deaths of thousands of people, it was extremely unhelpful for organisations like Themba which were attempting to give people correct, scientifically-proven information.

It was important for our trainees to know as much as possible about the virus if they were to feel confident when presenting plays about HIV and AIDS. They also needed to learn a naturalistic style of acting. This would be a departure for them, and in order to deepen the work on developing realistic characters, I introduced ideas which were unknown to them.

"Stanislavski was a famous Russian theatre practitioner," I said. "He was born a long time ago – in 1863. He wrote books about how to train actors and how to develop a character. He wanted acting to be naturalistic, and for the characters to seem like real people."

"Real?" asked Bongani.

"Yes, so that you'd recognise them as being like someone you might know. He means that everything you do on stage needs to be what that character would do in real life. He wanted actors to ask themselves the question, *If this was really happening, how would my character respond to the particular circumstances in the play?*"

The actor-educators were listening closely, and seemed interested in what I was telling them. I went on, "Stanislavski called his method of training The System, and something like it is used in America and in the UK to train some of the best known actors – even today."

"Like who?" asked Jordan.

"Have you heard of Marlon Brando? Or Dustin Hoffman?"

"Yebo."

"Well, those are two who were trained in Stanislavski's System."

The young people were fascinated by the fact that they were learning about a process that had been developed so long ago and so far away.

Together, Theresa and I worked with the trainee Themba actors and helped them devise and rehearse a number of short plays. The stories were based on real situations that the young people encountered in their everyday lives. They told us of the lack of privacy in the clinics and how people had to queue up for hours together, of grandmothers bringing up eight or more children because their own sons and daughters had died of AIDS, about young men who were sleeping around, about "sugar daddies" and the girls who had sex with them in order to pay for food or school fees for younger siblings.

Theresa and Bongani rehearsing

After a few weeks, Theresa and I identified those actor-educators who we thought might have the qualities to be trained as facilitators. Forum Theatre requires a "go-between" to create a relationship between the actors and the audience, and we needed to train some of the young people for this role. Although I would facilitate during the pilot phase in order to model how it should be done, we knew that ultimately, we would need two actor-educators with facilitation skills for each performance. I believed that a woman of my age (and white, moreover) would be seen as a "teacher" by our audiences, and that would be inappropriate for Forum Theatre.

We thought that Bongani, Jordan, Thato and Mary had the potential, so we approached them and asked if they would like to take on this further training.

Jordan frowned. "I don't know," he said. "I enjoy acting, and I want to go on doing that."

"Thank you, Mama. *Siyabonga*," said Mary, "but I prefer being a character in the play."

The others nodded in agreement.

This was disappointing; I'd hoped they would be pleased to be singled out.

I made a suggestion. "How would it be if you trained as facilitators, but also continued acting in some of the plays? You could learn how to facilitate the ones you're not performing in."

They hesitated. Then, after Bongani said he would give it a try, they all agreed.

After weeks of rehearsal we eventually focussed on just four of the plays that had been created: *Peer Pressure, Truth-Denial, The Wish of the Dying Son,* and *Ignorance Kills.* We rehearsed them repeatedly, swapping parts over so that each character could be played by a number of different actors. This meant we would have flexibility if someone was absent.

To train Mary, Jordan, Thato and Bongani in their extra role, one group would perform their play while the rest of us pretended to be an audience of school children. Working in pairs, the trainee facilitators practised their new skills. It wasn't easy for them to stand in front of their peers and try to imagine that they were learners in school. Sometimes the Themba actor-educators who were making up the "audience" deliberately made things difficult:

"Hey, man, I think using a condom is like eating a sweet with the wrapper on. I don't want to use a condom when I have sex."

"My Mam told me you can get HIV from cups and knives and forks and I believe her."

"Eish, it's not part of our culture to talk about these dirty things."

"Who says you can't get HIV from kissing?"

"My cousin says you catch HIV from a toilet seat."

"My boyfriend is really hot, man. I don't think he can have HIV."

The new facilitators tried to keep straight faces while responding to these sorts of comments, though at times we all dissolved into giggles. What we were dealing with was serious, and messing around like little kids allowed us all to let off steam.

* * *

One Thursday afternoon, just before going home for the weekend, Bongani came to see me in the office. He was looking dejected and serious.

"Hi Bongani, what can we do for you?" I said.

He sat his long frame down in a chair near my desk. He was visibly upset and leant forward with his elbows on his knees and his shoulders hunched up by his ears. His hair was closely cut, almost shaven, and his head hung down, emphasising his prominently rounded cranium. He twisted his beanie round and round in his slim brown hands. They were beautifully shaped, with fine fingers and strong, pink fingernails – they looked like pianist's hands. There was a silence. Theresa, sensing something was amiss, turned in her chair.

"I'm come to tell you … I … I … have to leave … Themba," said Bongani in a low voice.

"What? What do you mean? Leave Themba? Why?"

"It's my Mum and Dad. They say I must go back to work at the Juicy Lucy at the airport. They need me to bring money into the family."

Theresa and I looked at each other in dismay. We knew we couldn't lose Bongani. He was one of the mainstays of the Project now, like an anchor for the group. He was a very good actor and was doing well learning facilitation skills. Also, he was helping out in the office occasionally, looking in the directory to find schools where we might perform. He had once told us that he'd hated being a waiter at the Juicy Lucy café, and had often been treated badly by customers.

"Tell me, Bongani, how much money did you earn there?" I asked.

"Two hundred and thirty rand a week. But that's in tips. They didn't pay me a proper wage."

"And if I could somehow find that same money for you, would your parents let you stay in Themba?"

"Eish, I don't know. They think I'm wasting my time here."

I said, "Go back to your parents and tell them we want to keep you – very much indeed. Tell them I'm going to try to find the same money you would get at the Juicy Lucy and ask them if they'll let you stay with us."

He looked up with a glimmer of hope in his eyes.

"I can't promise anything, Bongani, but I'll do some sums over the weekend and look at what money we've got coming in. I'll see if there's a way we could pay you. But we'd have to make a proper role for you, something like Project Assistant here in the office. Otherwise it wouldn't be fair on the others."

I glanced over at Theresa and she gave a small nod.

"Have a talk with your Mum and Dad and come back and see us after the weekend. I'll try to find the money."

After Bongani left the office, Theresa and I agreed that we had to do everything we could to keep him. Some of the young people had already left the Project, and we now had a tight-knit group working effectively together. Bongani was a central part of that. He provided a mature, solid benchmark against which the others, unconsciously, measured themselves.

I looked at the figures for a long time and worked out that if we took a big risk, we could find the money from the grant the Elton John AIDS Foundation had just awarded us. It would be within the terms of our agreement with them and it would provide Bongani with the means to stay at Themba. After some extra training, he would be responsible for contacting schools and making bookings. The danger was that the Elton John money would run out more quickly. Unless I worked even harder at fundraising we could find ourselves with not enough to keep the Project going.

Bongani managed to persuade his parents and they agreed he could stay. He became our first employee.

Chapter 15

England/Johannesburg, April 2002

Among all the complexities of setting up the new Project in Johannesburg, trying to help manage the Trevor Huddleston Centre, and establishing myself in a new country, I was suddenly called to the UK because my father was very ill. I flew back on 10 April 2002 and when I reached the hospital in Bath, I found my brother and mother sitting close together on a sofa in a pale green room, drinking tea. If my plane hadn't been delayed I would have arrived while my father was alive, but despite hiring a car from Heathrow and dashing up the M4 at one hundred miles per hour, it was all over by the time I walked through the door.

I went to see my father in a room a little way down the corridor. He looked terrible. His chin had dropped, his face was elongated and he'd turned a pasty grey. He was not lying quietly in classic "hero style" with his hands clasped over his chest, but instead the bedclothes were tossed in all directions, and his knees were bent up and out. His pyjama-clad arms were flung away from his body and he looked as if he had died fighting. He'd always had a need to be in control and found it difficult to let go, so dying must have been hard for him – the final surrender. The atmosphere was oppressively hot and there was a sickly, sweet smell. I stared out of the window at the cheerful daffodils in the hospital grounds and longed to open a window to let in the crisp April air.

I pressed my forehead to the glass and without turning around, said, "So you really have died, have you?"

I stood still leaning against the pane and tried to feel him in the room, but there was nothing. I walked about for a few minutes and wondered whether I should take his hand, or kiss his forehead. But he was dead, and I didn't think it would make any difference to him. Only half an hour earlier he'd been breathing and his heart had beaten, and now there was nothing.

"You always seemed so powerful," I said. "We've had our differences, you and me, haven't we? Strange to think you're not here anymore."

I waited. Nothing.

I didn't know how I felt about him being dead – not sad, or relieved, or unhappy. Maybe I was in shock – and I was very tired. I'd had no sleep on the plane. It was difficult to comprehend that this man, my father, who had been such a forceful presence throughout my life, was gone.

I joined my mother and brother.

"Were you with him when he died?" I asked. They nodded.

"It was a struggle," said my brother.

"Yes, it looks like it," I replied.

Two weeks later, after we'd held my father's funeral, I went to the South African High Commission in London and handed in my application for residence and work permits. I had been living in Johannesburg with just a holiday visa, so it was high time I sorted out my official status. It had been a tiresome and complicated mission to collect all the necessary documents and bring them to England, but within a few days I had my passport returned to me with the authorisation stamped inside. It was with enormous relief that I went back – legally – to South Africa.

* * *

A few days after my return, I was sitting down at home to eat my lunch. The table was near the French windows which opened out onto a balcony. The autumn day was warm enough to have the doors open and the sun streamed in. I listened to the grey louries perched high in the branches of the trees in the garden telling me, with their distinctive hollow cry, to go away ... go away ...

go away. It was that empty time of day, between the busy-ness of morning chores and the idle afternoon. My cat was curled up asleep in her basket and I could hear the sound of distant cars as they meandered along the main road, half a mile to the south. The pungent, sugared-almond smell of the purple and white flowers of the "yesterday-today-and-tomorrow" shrub wafted through the open doors.

I thought about my mother and wondered how she was coping now my father was dead.

Suddenly there was an ear-splitting crack. Something crashed through the ceiling, whistled past my head, hit the floor with a heavy thud and disappeared under a chair.

I jumped up from the table, leaving my sandwich untouched. Clare came running in.

"What was that bang?"

We searched the floor and found a shiny, brass object which had rolled into the corner of the room: a bullet.

Looking up I saw a small hole in the pressed steel ceiling. Split edges of metal curled outwards in neat triangular sections, forced out by the velocity of the missile. They looked like the petals of a jasmine flower. The bullet must have missed me by an inch.

Then I did something really stupid – I went out onto the balcony and looked across the garden. As I did so the grey louries flew off, flapping their wings. The grass sloped down from the back of the house towards the cottage and the pool. If the gunman was behind one of the bushes I would have been straight in his line of fire. But as the bullet seemed to have come vertically down through the ceiling, I guessed that whoever had shot it must have been above us.

The house was in the typical single-storey style for Melville: moulded ceilings painted white, pine floors and doors, with walls decorated in cream and terracotta. Having surveyed the garden, I leant over the balustrade and, bending back as far as

I could, tried to make out if there was anyone above me. All I could see was clear blue sky, the straggling pink bougainvillea and the flaking green paint of the corrugated iron roof.

"I think we'd better call the police," Clare said.

I'd been warned that the police often didn't bother to turn up, or arrived so late there was no chance of finding the culprit. But we phoned, and three burly men arrived within fifteen minutes.

"You reported a shooting, ja?" one of them asked cheerfully.

They had a uniform of sorts: grubby blue jeans, bush shirts and big boots. And each had a pistol in a holster on a wide leather belt. They were all bulky men and spoke with thick Afrikaans accents. The tallest man had a big paunch, very black hair and a chin like Desperate Dan. Another had a purplish scar across his cheek. The third was unkempt, with a tear in his jeans and a shirt that smelt unwashed.

"I'll just go and have a look," said Desperate Dan, after I'd shown him the bullet. He took a chair out to the balcony, and with surprising alacrity hopped onto it, then jumped to the top of the balustrade. From there he leapt up onto the high garden wall, and thence to the roof. He clattered around on the hot corrugated iron while Clare and I stood below trying to make conversation with the other two men. We were rescued by a call from above.

"There's a hole up here," Dan yelled. He scrambled down to our level and we trooped indoors to inspect a small indent where the bullet had landed on the polished floor.

"It looks like someone shot into the air, and it just happened to come down through your roof. It happens. There was some guy recently at Ellis Park watching a football match and a stray bullet came from the sky and went straight through his skull. Killed him instantly. You were lucky."

Guns were a part of life in South Africa that I found difficult: all the police were armed, as were most criminals and many white women in the northern suburbs. It was common to read in the newspapers of high-jackings, hold-ups at gunpoint and murders. A customer at our small local supermarket had recently been shot dead while waiting at the checkout to pay for his goods.

"I expect it's one of those munts in Hillbrow," Desperate Dan went on, displaying his ingrained contempt for the black residents of Johannesburg. Hillbrow was the nearby area of deprivation, with poverty, crime, drugs and prostitution. "Ag, man, there's so many Zimbabweans down there now. And they'll all be out of their skulls. It's Saturday."

Many years before, when I'd lived there, Hillbrow had been a white area and the streets had been safe. I used to walk from my flat up the hill to Yeoville where there was a municipal swimming pool ("whites only"), and I had never encountered any problems. Back then Hillbrow consisted of shining high-rise blocks of apartments, with tidy, flower-filled balconies. It was dirty and dangerous now, and despite the municipality's many attempts to improve people's lives, the residents lived in over-crowded, rat-infested conditions. The police made frequent raids to search out illegal immigrants, criminals and drugs, but it remained a hazardous place.

I thanked the officers when they left. They were decent enough men and had done their job efficiently, but I was left with a sense of unease because they seemed to have assumed that I went along with their racism and xenophobia. I still felt like a visitor in the country despite having lived in Jo'burg for five months, and I was hesitant about expressing my own opinions.

I deposited the bullet in the fruit bowl and went back to my lunch.

A few weeks later, when Theresa was in the kitchen, she called out to me, "There's a bullet stuck in this pawpaw. What's it doing here?"

* * *

As the months went by I began to feel more at home. With Theresa and me both at Themba, we were able to move the Project forward quickly. The plays improved, the acting became more naturalistic and the post-play process, which the facilitators managed with me, was well defined. The confidence of the actor-educators increased, and we had an effective well-structured presentation.

On 6 May 2002, we gave our first performance at a high school in Tembisa, Bongani's township. We showed two plays, *The Wish of the Dying Son* and *Your Status*. There were one hundred school children in the audience, but the teachers stayed away. The performance took place out of doors, on a pot-holed, unfenced concrete area that had once been a tennis court. The children stood around at a short distance on meagre grass which sloped down towards the school. The wind carried our voices away and the sun shone directly into our eyes.

Although the circumstances were far from ideal, Bongani and I, the two facilitators, were subsequently able to coax the audience into choosing the play they wanted to see "forumed". They chose *Your Status*. The story involved a character denying he was HIV positive and refusing to go for a blood test. The children participated in bringing the story to a satisfactory conclusion: one of them took the role of the friend of the HIV-positive character and persuaded him to go to the clinic. We managed to engage our audience and they all stayed till the end, even though it would have been easy for them to wander off across the school grounds.

After the performance we gathered in the church hall back in Sophiatown to reflect, and evaluate our very first presentation. The actor-educators were excited and happy.

"I think we did well," said Bongani. "They were all listening, and seemed to be enjoying it."

"Yebo," said Zodwa, animatedly, "some of those learners didn't know much about how you catch HIV. You could tell that from their questions."

"But, eish, it was hard acting with the sun in our eyes," said Tshepo. "Next time I think we must do our plays indoors."

As a non-Zulu speaker, I had found it difficult to understand some of what the children in the audience were saying as they shifted effortlessly between English and isiZulu. However, Bongani had been co-facilitating with me, so I wasn't completely lost. In fact, I was very pleased. What we had achieved that morning was far from perfect, but the interactive theatre process we'd been developing since February had succeeded. Our audience had become involved in the play in the way we had hoped and, most importantly, they had learnt how to keep themselves safe from the virus. A great deal of work was still needed, but I was sure now that we could accomplish what we had set out to do. It was a good feeling.

By the end of May we had performed at fourteen schools to a total of two thousand and sixty-three children and adults. All six of the plays we had created had been forumed during that time, and three of the schools had said they were "desperate" for us to return to work with students across all year groups. It began to look as if we had created something which was not only unique, but also valuable.

Thabo (left) and Tshepo as Mzobo and Tebza in *Class of 2006* (Photo: Anand Madhvani)

The Trevor Huddleston Centre continued to provide us with a home, and the church hall gave us space to rehearse. It was good to be under the wing of the Centre and to be working in Sophiatown, imbued as it was with its history of anti-apartheid activism.

Unfortunately, things were about to change. Thabo Makgoba was invited by the Anglican Church to become the Suffragan Bishop of Grahamstown, based in the Eastern Cape. This was sad news for me personally because Thabo and his wife, Lungi, had become good friends. It was also upsetting for the congregation at the Church of Christ the King, because Thabo was their much-loved priest. But they were proud of him, too.

"What on earth makes you want to go to Grahamstown?" I asked him. "We need you in Jo'burg. Here at the Centre."

He looked down at me and seemed a little embarrassed. "It's a ... a calling," he said, sheepishly.

There was no way I could argue with that, however much I might have wanted to.

I was very sorry to see him go. It was Thabo who had invited me to leave Swaziland and set up the Themba HIV & AIDS Project at the Centre. Although he was often busy with his work in the church and at the university, his influence was always evident. He was a benign presence, and as well as being priest-in-charge, he was the co-director of the Centre.

None of us had any way of knowing that one day Thabo would become the Archbishop of Cape Town and the head of the Anglican Church in Southern Africa, the post that was sometimes referred to as "the Desmond Tutu job".

After he left, everything at the Trevor Huddleston Centre began to feel ragged and confusing. I was never sure if there would be enough funding to keep Themba going, and Theresa, who I relied on to share the training of the young people, was often unwell. She was, in any case, only supposed to be working part-time – partly because there wasn't enough money to pay both of us full-time, but also because she was still involved with work in the UK which she did online.

I was constantly trying to catch up with myself, and was torn in different directions. I was managing the day-to-day organisation of the Project and trying to get it onto a stable footing, as well as working hard to raise more funds. At the same time, I needed to be with the young people helping them to develop the plays and the post-play process. *And* I had to go to every performance because I was not only the chief facilitator, I was also the driver.

It didn't help that there was no effective management at the Trevor Huddleston Centre. Thabo had left, and Tricia, the other director, only appeared intermittently because she was based in the UK. I found myself being asked to take on responsibilities within the THMC which were inappropriate. I had no authority to make decisions on the Centre's behalf, and should only have been concerned with the Themba HIV & AIDS Project.

In July I took a week off and drove to Grahamstown for the Arts Festival, and to see Thabo and Lungi. On the way, I decided to visit the tiny village of Mvezo, Nelson Mandela's birthplace in the Eastern Cape. I turned off the main highway onto a dirt track, and drove for many miles through the barren, dried-up terrain. I passed clusters of circular rondavels with thatched roofs. Some of the huts were painted turquoise, others were cream with a deep maroon stripe along the bottom. The area had hardly changed since I'd first travelled this way in 1964 with the Cambridge Shakespeare Company. Then it had been called the Transkei, and it was here that my life-long love affair with South Africa had begun. I hadn't known then that this was Madiba's homeland. Madiba is the affectionate name that Nelson Mandela was known by.

As I drove, local people stopped and waved. They pointed along the road, guessing that I was going to Mandela's homestead. It was unusual for a white woman to drive off into the *bundu* on her own.

"Madiba?" the women called out to me, as I passed. They were wrapped up in thick skirts with warm shawls tucked over their jumpers. Their heads were covered in *doeks* and they had daubs of white paint on their faces to ward off the strong winter sun.

"Yebo," I called back, "Madiba, siyabonga." They smiled and nodded, indicating I should continue along the road.

The rondavels disappeared as I went on. Now I was by myself in this vast wilderness, the brilliant blue sky arcing far above me. A wide river bed held a desultory trickle of water. On and on I went, mile after mile, until I began to wonder whether I would ever reach my destination. The hills and valleys rolled by, with only a few scrubby bushes growing in the dry earth. The sand and dust from the dirt road billowed out behind my car and drifted away into the bush.

In the distance I saw what looked like a mirage. Something shimmered in the dip of the hills like imagined water on a hot tarred road. It grew and grew, and as I drew near I could see that the gleam came from a large structure reflecting the sun. I drove closer, stopped the car and clambered out. The building was a series of partitions made of reeds or canes, about twelve feet high, with chunks of grey slate making up the base on which they stood. Between the screens were sheets of glass with portraits of Nelson Mandela etched on them. A plaque on one wall told me that this was indeed the birthplace of Madiba. Half a dozen black and white goats roamed in and out of the screens. The silence was intense, emphasised by the light sound of the goats' hooves delicately treading the earth, and the ticking of the car's engine as it cooled.

Suddenly I spied someone running from the brow of a distant hill. The figure sprinted towards me, and as he came closer I could see he was a ragged, barefoot boy. He looked about ten years old. He skidded in the dust and halted beside me, breathing heavily, and held out a small school exercise book with a grey paper cover. Where had he come from? There were no rondavels to be seen, no huts, no dwellings of any kind. Did the boy stay all day, maybe sitting under a distant thorn bush, waiting for the sound of a vehicle?

"Please?" he asked.

I opened the pages to discover a few names with dates. It was the visitor's book.

The boy showed me the place where the rondavel of Mandela's childhood had been. It was just possible, among the short grass and rocks, to make out that there had once been a small circular hut there. I asked and mimed if I could take a stone from the earth and the boy nodded.

I was glad I had made the journey. It felt like a pilgrimage, and reinforced my determination to keep going at the Project, however challenging things might be.

* * *

Back at Themba, Theresa was unwell with a variety of aches and pains, so Razaan came and helped out with training the young people. She was one of the friends from Cape Town whom we'd met in 1997 at the International Conference on Conflict Resolution in the Magliesburg Mountains. We needed Razaan as I was due to go to England. It was time to join the rest of my family to bury my father's ashes.

Many years before, I had promised my mother that she and I would one day take a trip to Italy. She had reminded me of this shortly after my father died, and I had booked a holiday for us in Florence and Venice. Although I was worried about Themba, I couldn't let her down, so after we'd interred my father's ashes we flew off to spend ten days together. I tried to remember when I had first started calling my mother "Jane" rather than "Mum". It was probably after I'd married. My husband had been considerably older than me, and it would have sounded silly if he'd called her "Mum".

Away from Themba I gained a sense of perspective. Sitting in a café looking across the Grand Canal towards the Rialto Bridge, I told my mother about the Project. As she had worked in the theatre herself, both as an actress and as a drama teacher, she appreciated what I was attempting to do.

She seemed to understand my need to be in South Africa, but looking at me quizzically she said, "I am sorry you'll always be a bit schizophrenic, not knowing whether your home is England or Africa."

I hadn't thought about it like this.

"Maybe it's more of a privilege than a burden," I said. "It's good to feel at home in both countries."

Jane had always loved visiting new places, and I hoped that now my father had died she would travel more. All the time I was living in southern Africa I felt guilty and sad that I was not at home to spend more time with her. After all, she was now eighty-five years old, and despite being sprightly and energetic, she wouldn't live forever.

The time came for me to say goodbye to my mother and return to Johannesburg. I arrived to discover that Themba was in a better place than when I'd left a few weeks earlier. I didn't know whether this was because I'd had a break and had a more positive outlook on things, or because between them Razaan and Theresa, who had returned in my absence, had moved things on. They were both highly skilled trainers, and were providing excellent training for the actor-educators and facilitators. The young people were developing confidence and self-assurance. The "product" that we had spent so long creating was more structured, the plays were well-designed and conveyed the messages we wanted to get across. Themba was developing into a distinct Project with its own unique identity.

The year ended with an *indaba* – a meeting between me, Theresa and our Advisory Board. Some of the Board members were Quakers, like Margaret Roper (a strategist who ran her own development company) and Dudu Mtshazo (who was head of ethics and professional practice at Baragwanath Nursing School in Soweto).

It was especially valuable that I was part of the network of the Religious Society of Friends both in the UK and in South Africa. Themba was indebted to the British Quakers for spiritual nourishment and for money, and now that the Project was up and running, the Johannesburg Friends gave us a huge amount of support. The Blue Idol Meeting in England had recognised my "leading" as a "concern". This is Quaker parlance for a "prompting of the Spirit" which usually begins with an individual and develops into a piece of work that a whole Meeting adopts. Setting up the Themba Project was seen by Quakers, both in the UK and in Johannesburg – and by me – as part of my spiritual journey. This led other people to view what I was doing as sound. It also gave me the strength to carry on when things were difficult.

Together with the Advisory Board, we worked on a strategy for the next twelve months. The first year had sometimes been extremely challenging, but on reflection, I realised we had achieved a great deal. We had begun the Project, run a pilot, honed and developed the work, and performed to thousands of learners and their teachers. We were welcomed in schools and colleges and we knew from the feedback we received that our presentations were valued. Many schools asked us to come back, and our reputation was growing. Despite Theresa's absences, my unexpected trips to Europe and the UK, and never having enough money, we had survived. The young people who had stayed with the Project now "held" it. Their skills, knowledge and confidence had increased over the year and they were more and more able to make decisions and influence direction.

We had almost certainly helped save some lives. I expected the following years to be exciting and challenging as we moved

Themba forward.

Jane, my mother, came out to South Africa for an extended visit and she and I went to Zanzibar for Christmas. It turned out to be the last Christmas she was able to enjoy.

Chapter 16

Johannesburg, January–May 2003

War in Iraq was looming and the world was on edge. My friend Jenny, from Swaziland, was in hospital in Pretoria suffering from leukaemia. While not at Themba, I spent all my spare time outside the American Consulate in Johannesburg protesting against the war, or travelling the hour's journey to and from Jenny's bedside. We talked about life and death and whether people had souls which lived on after they died. Jenny was sure they did. We chatted about our "failed" marriages, our children and our hopes for the future. And we remembered the ideas we'd had of setting up a women's theatre group in Swaziland. We were both sad that we'd never worked together.

As Jenny's health deteriorated, the situation in the world worsened. It seemed we were all holding our breath.

One evening I sat quietly with Jenny. She was seriously ill by this time, and unable to get out of bed or talk much. The chemotherapy had left her with no hair, but even though she was so unwell, when she smiled I could sense her resolute spirit. Together we listened to the CD I'd lent her of Tracy Chapman's *Unsung Psalm*.

"I want this played at my funeral," said Jenny. "I know I've made mistakes in my life, but I've tried to live right."

"And you've succeeded," I replied. "Let's hope your funeral won't be for a while yet."

Jenny regarded me, smiling faintly.

She had chosen not to try for a bone marrow transplant and I had to face the fact that she was dying. I left the hospital in tears and made my way to the American Embassy on the outskirts of Pretoria where I'd been told there was to be a major anti-war demonstration. It was dark by now, and I drove around the huge white building a couple of times, but could see no protest. I parked my car, got out, and went to speak to one of the guards. Behind the white wall surrounding the Embassy were tall acacia trees and lawns of bright green grass. It looked like a film set starkly lit up by floodlights. Security people wandered around the site; there was very little traffic and no one on the street. It was eerily quiet.

"Do you know anything about a protest?" I asked a guard.

"I think they're all at the Union Buildings," he said.

I made my way into the centre of Pretoria and drove through the park, past the enormous statues, and up to the vast semi-circular government building, also brilliantly floodlit. The cupolas on the roof stood out vividly against the night sky. I waited for a while, but all was silent and there were no people about so I drove back to the US Embassy on the outskirts of town. A couple of police vans had arrived, and half a dozen officers stood around in their uniforms, chatting and smoking. They told me the demonstration was at the State Theatre in the middle of town, so I set off once more.

It was teeming with rain by now and the night was gloomy and dark, which matched my mood. I drove down the slope into the underground car park, but instead of protestors, I was met by hundreds of people spilling out of their cars and heading for the theatre, dressed up in smart clothes, laughing and chatting. I wondered whether the police had been ill-informed, or had deliberately sent me on a wild goose chase.

I gave up, left Pretoria and drove back to Johannesburg, weeping all the way. Baghdad was bombed on 19 March with no United Nations mandate, and the world seemed to have gone mad. A few days later Jenny's son, Jiggs, phoned me at the office to say Jenny had died in the night. He was inconsolable.

The anti-war protests continued, but my heart had gone out of it. All I could think of was Jenny and how unfair it was that the world had lost such a good soul. My mother had said to me once, "Those whom the gods love, die young." The gods must have loved Jenny very much.

* * *

Themba was now more than a year old, and I immersed myself in work to try to overcome my grief at Jenny's death. Some of the young people had left the Project because they had been offered a college place or found a job, or because they were unable to cope with the demands we made on them. We expected punctuality, regular attendance, commitment and a willingness to develop the programme. In return they received training they wouldn't find anywhere else, and a small stipend.

One young man, Obey, left to set up his own business – a poodle parlour. Seipati joined the South African Navy. A few just drifted away and we never discovered what happened to them. One had to go because we discovered he was cheating on his travelling expenses. This was a hard decision: the young people had so little money that I could well understand the temptation to bump up a travel claim, but it was important for everyone to know that lying and dishonesty could not be tolerated. The young people who remained formed a tight-knit group, able to respond flexibly to the varied demands made on them in the different schools we visited.

I concentrated on teaching acting (voice, movement and characterisation), and the ideas and theories of Stanislavski. The actor-educators were learning to abandon their somewhat melodramatic style and were now acting more naturalistically. Theresa devised a structured programme of training and taught HIV and AIDS, sexual health, antiretroviral medication, the dangers of drugs, alcohol and smoking, and the importance of a good diet and a healthy lifestyle. Together we developed Forum Theatre techniques and helped the actor-educators devise a range of plays, each with a story around HIV and AIDS. These stories were drawn from their own lives and those of their friends and families in the townships. Some of the original plays were cut from the repertoire, others were improved, and new ones created. The HIV situation in South Africa was constantly changing, and our plays had to reflect this.

Theresa and I spent many hours with the actor-educators and, informally, bit by bit, we introduced them to the stories of their own country. We realised that many of the young people who had joined us at Themba had very little knowledge or understanding of South African history, thanks to the Bantu Education system. It was through us that they learnt how apartheid had been structured, and they began to understand what had been done to their forebears – and to them. The irony was not lost on any of us: Theresa and I were both foreigners, both white, and yet we were the ones teaching them about South Africa's troubled past.

Tshepo was the most politically aware: as a child he had been subjected to the indignities of apartheid. He told me, "I remember the police coming to my uncle's house. I was asleep and they kicked me out of bed with their boots. I was about seven or eight."

"That's appalling, Tshepo," I said.

He shrugged and said, "My family was involved in politics."

As a result of their minimal education, the cognitive ability of the young people had had little opportunity to develop. Until they came to Themba, they had never been encouraged to think for themselves, to hold opinions, or to envisage their futures. We helped them improve their literacy and numeracy skills, and showed them how to budget – vital knowledge when they had so little money.

Through long discussions, we set about encouraging them to have their own opinions. We wanted them all to fulfil their potential. Our thinking was based on Paulo Freire's books, *Pedagogy of the Oppressed* and *Pedagogy of Hope*. Freire believed that people should bring their own knowledge and experience to the process of learning, and that education should be a dynamic practice rather than simply the imparting of facts. He was passionate about helping people reflect critically upon their world, and thus be active in changing it. Augusto Boal, whose Forum Theatre principles we were following, had based his work on Freire too.

* * *

It soon became clear that the young people were having their own thoughts and ideas about the Project. One day a small delegation came to the office to talk to me and Theresa.

"We've been thinking," said Bongani, "and it seems to us that Forum Theatre isn't enough."

I had a feeling I knew what was coming, but I asked, "Enough? What do you mean?"

Mary answered for the group, "You've taught us about how Boal created Forum Theatre, and how he wanted to improve the conditions of people in the factories. I know we've adapted it to HIV, but we're not sure Forum Theatre is working for us."

"What do you suggest?" Theresa asked.

"We're in the business of saving lives," joined in Bongani, "Forum Theatre is fine, but we think we need to do something more. We should be giving our audiences *facts* about HIV and AIDS."

"Yes," said Zodwa, "it's all very well for them to come up with solutions for the plays, but I don't think the people are learning enough about HIV."

"We need to *teach* them," said JR.

The whole thrust of Forum Theatre is that the members of the audience, through the process of interactive theatre, find their own solutions to the problems presented within the plays. Any sort of didactic approach is anathema to the philosophy. But Theresa and I could see that the young people were right. There was so much ignorance that many South Africans regarded HIV as a death sentence. Antiretroviral medication was only erratically provided by the state hospitals, and many people were so afraid of stigma that they refused to go to the clinics. We agreed that the Themba Project needed to address this, and over the following weeks we began to devise our own unique way in which we could be both entertaining and educational.

We experimented with lots of ideas and introduced colour-coded cards with words for sexual behaviour on them: green cards for activities like kissing and hugging; orange for using a condom; red for unprotected sex, including anal and oral. Once we'd rehearsed, we introduced the cards as part of the performance and they succeeded in encouraging our audiences to talk openly about sex and HIV.

"So, what do the colours remind you of?" Bongani asked our audiences.

"The ROBOTS!" came back the gleeful response.

"Yebo," said Bongani. "Green for *safe*, orange for *careful* and red for *STOP!*"

We included a "silent moment" towards the end of the presentation, when our audiences would sit quietly while the facilitator invited them to think of ways in which they could keep themselves safe. Another innovation was the demonstration of a series of very short duologues showing how it was possible to say "No" to unprotected sex, and to insist on using a condom. Members of the audiences would come to the front and practise these mini-scenes with the actor-educators.

We decided to call our presentation, "Interactive Themba Theatre," and the actors introduced it with wide arm gestures and lots of drumming, dancing and razzmatazz, as *This Is ITT!*

We performed in primary and secondary schools: Roman Catholic, Muslim, private, state and secular. Although apartheid was officially over, many schools and colleges were still segregated into black, white or coloured. The very up-front, no-holds-barred nature of our performances was challenging for the teachers, but we were invited to all the different types of school because the HIV situation was so serious.

Bongani composed a song, *It's My Life,* which was sung at the end of every performance:

It's my life
I make a choice
Choose to be safe
Abstain, and think twice …

We encouraged our audiences to join in with the singing, reading the words from leaflets we handed out. Children were heard repeating the song as they left the classroom after they'd watched Themba. All we could do was hope the message would get through and they would stay safe.

* * *

One day Theresa and I sat down together in a little tea shop in Melville, a somewhat old-fashioned place with flowery curtains and bone-china cups and saucers. Through the window we could see the Zimbabwean street hawkers sitting on the pavement with their delicate beaded animals, waiting for tourists to pass and buy their wares. The men chatted with each other in a comradely way. Theresa and I discussed the future of Themba. We knew our respective roles needed to be clarified, rather than muddling on as we were.

As I sipped my Earl Grey and ate my Victoria sponge, Theresa abstemiously drank her green tea. We agreed that I would become the "executive director" and Theresa the "training manager". She was a superb trainer and facilitator, and more than able to develop the plays and the I.T.T. process without my input. But I was sad to give up working closely with the actor-educators and the trainees. I missed them as I drifted inexorably into a management role.

In May, Theresa was unwell again. She went back to the UK for an appointment with a doctor specialising in neural problems: all the typing she'd been doing was causing her arms and neck to seize up and she needed treatment. Razaan was standing in once more as a facilitator and trainer, so the actor-educators went out each week to perform at different schools. But they were getting restless.

A group of them came to see me to say they were unhappy, and demanded that they receive four hundred rand a week each or else they would leave. I spent hours working out exactly how much money we had, down to the last cent, and called a meeting to show everyone what our financial situation was. I presented them with all the information I had about our income and expenditure, and explained how funders ring-fenced their grants. I showed them that if we upped their stipends, we wouldn't have enough money to continue the Project, which would mean Themba would close down. Only one chose to leave.

Theresa was due to return, and I looked forward to her coming back: I felt I was holding everything together on my own. But instead of her welcome reappearance, I received a telephone call to say she'd collapsed on the way to Heathrow with pneumonia and had been refused a "fit to fly" medical certificate. I felt weighed down – I needed to share with her the demands the actor-educators had been making.

I was horribly aware that the Themba HIV & AIDS Project and the Trevor Huddleston Memorial Centre mirrored the way most companies, businesses and NGOs were set up in South Africa – and I didn't like it. At the top, the bosses were almost invariably white, as were most of the senior management. Lower down were the poorly paid black workers. It seemed that no amount of hand-wringing would change the situation. I knew that the training our young people were receiving at Themba would stand them in good stead in the future, but it was unfair that I was paid considerably more than them. It was only an accident of birth that put us in these different positions.

I knew my limitations, too: I was "old enough and ugly enough" (as my father would jokingly have said) to have learnt that I needed a certain level of comfort to be able to function effectively. I tried to justify to myself my salary, my house, my car and my full belly with the knowledge that I would be no use to the young people if I was deprived of any of that. But I still felt deeply uncomfortable.

I awaited Theresa's return so I could discuss all this with her, but it was not to be. Themba was to be left leaderless for a while. On 26 May my brother phoned from the UK to say my mother had had a stroke. I was on the plane that evening, desperate in case there was a repetition of what had happened with my father and I would arrive after she'd died.

* * *

Jane's stroke had been severe and she was unable to speak except indistinctly in the tiniest whisper, but she could understand what was being said to her. She had lost the ability to swallow and by the time I arrived at the special unit of the local hospital, she'd had a "peg" inserted into her stomach so she could be given nourishment via a tube.

It was deeply distressing to see her in this condition, and once more my feelings of guilt reared up. What was I doing living in South Africa when my Mum was elderly? Why hadn't I arranged to come back and live in the UK? I stayed by her bedside as much as I could in the following days, held her hand, smoothed her forehead, and talked quietly to her.

One afternoon my brother and I had a meeting with a doctor. He was a tall, broad man, dressed in a tweed jacket with leather patches at the elbows and baggy mole-skin trousers. His voice was loud and authoritative, and he reminded me of some of the large "White Rhodesian" men I'd met.

"The best thing to do," the doctor boomed, "is simply to let you mother pass away. If we remove the peg, she'll just slowly starve to death. It shouldn't take too long."

Mike and I stared at the doctor, then turned to each other in shock. Our lovely, lively, kind mother had disappeared, and had been replaced by an old lady lying unmoving in a bed. And now this brutal man, this so-called doctor, was telling us to just pull the plug and let her die? We were speechless.

I talked to my mother about the "peg". She was sitting propped up now in a special chair. Her hair, which until recently had remained fair, had thinned and turned grey, and her smile – which had always been slightly crooked – was lopsided and droopy. She was wearing a hospital gown, and she seemed to have shrunk. She could do nothing for herself, was semi-paralysed, had very little speech and would probably never walk again. I kissed her forehead and sat down on a small stool in front of her. Despite the delicacy of the subject, I had to speak loudly because her hearing was not good.

"Jane," I said, "you know you've had a stroke don't you?"

She nodded slightly.

"And you're being fed by this tube in your tummy."

She nodded again.

"Because you can't swallow."

She inclined her head.

"Well, the thing is this. Are you happy to keep on being fed through this tube? The doctors say that if they take it out, you would slowly fade away. Is that what you'd prefer? Or would you like them to leave the peg in?"

She sat still, and I could see she was contemplating what I had said. She looked at me with a shadow of that quizzical look she'd always had.

"If they keep the tube in, it will keep you alive, but we don't

194

know how much better you will get. It's possible you'll stay much like you are now."

Again she sat, thinking. I waited. I knew she was now in exactly the situation she had always said she wanted, at all costs, to avoid.

"Would you like them to keep the peg in, or should they remove it?" I asked.

After another long pause she said quietly, but quite distinctly, "I want the peg."

I stayed for two weeks, visiting the hospital every day, and my children came to see their grandma. There was little sign of improvement, and very reluctantly I returned to South Africa leaving my brother and sister to liaise with the hospital and to see Jane whenever they could. I was distraught. We'd always been very close and had had a wonderful mother-daughter-friend relationship. We had our love of the theatre in common, as well as our teaching experiences. She was a Quaker, too, and we had often gone on peace marches together and stayed at the Greenham Common Peace Camp. I wanted to remain in England, but knew it would be irresponsible to give up on Themba now. I would be letting everybody down.

Razaan and Jabu had kept things going while Theresa and I had been away in the UK. Although Theresa was now back at Themba, she was only working two days a week, mainly because that was all the funding we had for her post. I picked up the threads of my life in Johannesburg and worried about my mother – and about the knife-edge financial situation at the Project.

On 18 June my brother phoned to say that Jane had been moved out of the stroke unit and into the main hospital because she was haemorrhaging and unlikely to live. Once again, I took the plane, this time convinced that my mother would die. My son Andy met me at Heathrow and we raced up the M4 to the hospital.

Jane looked as though she would leave us at any moment. She was stretched out flat on her back on a hard bed and had lost a lot of blood. There were tubes pumping more blood into her, but her face was pale grey. Her skinny white arms lay on the hospital sheet which was tucked up near her chin. She looked unconscious, and there was no reaction when I spoke to her. I held her hand, and Andy and I sat each side of her bed quietly weeping.

I stayed in England for three weeks, and slowly and miraculously my mother's health improved.

"She must be as strong as an ox," said one of the nurses.

Jane was moved back into the stroke unit, and when I knew she was out of danger, I reluctantly returned once again to South Africa.

I was met by good news: The Joseph Rowntree Charitable Trust had awarded us a three-year grant. And not only that – I discovered that as a result of an article I'd written for the Quaker magazine, *The Friend,* four thousand pounds had been donated by Meetings, Trusts and individual Friends. We were going to be all right for a while.

* * *

Late one afternoon when everyone had left the Centre except Theresa and me, we heard a scream from outside and dashed out to investigate. There was a small garden at the front of the building with a couple of dense bushes and a few cactus plants. Lindiwe (not her real name), one of our actor-educators, was half-hidden behind a shrub. Tumelo (also a pseudonym) was standing in the middle of the dried-up grass, breathing heavily and looking distraught.

I opened the sliding glass doors and called out, "What's happening?"

Lindiwe began to cry, and Tumelo turned away. They both

seemed very upset and I guessed they'd had a row. Theresa and I went into the garden; I put my arm around Lindiwe and led her indoors. Theresa followed with Tumelo, holding him by the elbow. I led Lindiwe to the sofa in the reception area, and we sat down. Tumelo looked aggressive and desperate. Theresa stood calmly by his side. I could see a dark red bulge emerging on Lindiwe's forehead, just above her left eye.

"What's this all about?" I asked gently.

Neither of them spoke. Lindiwe brought her hands up in front of her face.

"Has Tumelo hit you, Lindi?"

She nodded, gasping for breath, but didn't speak.

Tumelo squatted down on his haunches, leaning his back against the wall. He said, "You see, I love this woman. I love her. She's the only girl I ever … I love her. Come on Lindi. We'll go now. I'll take you."

Lindiwe sat with her head in her hands, rocking backwards and forwards, crying.

All of a sudden, Tumelo seemed to collapse. He slid sideways and slumped down on the hard floor.

He thumped his chest. "It hurts. It hurts my heart. In here. I love her." He looked up and went on aggressively, "You know what she's been doing? She's been having men. She wants to go to Cape Town. And it hurts *me*."

He was quiet for a moment, then said, "Come *on*, Lindi. Come *on*. You're coming with me."

Theresa said quietly, "Tumi, when you hit someone, everything changes. You know that, don't you? Go now, and come in tomorrow so we can talk. We'll get Lindiwe home. Come outside with me."

"I won't do it again, Lindi. You know that don't you? I love you. You know I won't do it again."

Lindiwe lifted her head and looked at him. Her eyes were puffy and swollen. A dark purple bruise was developing on her face.

"Go home, Tumi," she said. "I don't trust you. I'm not going with you. Go home."

Tumi looked at Lindiwe pleadingly, leant across and put his hand on her knee. She flinched. He took his hand away and said, "I love this woman. But she's cheating on me. She has these men phoning. They give her money."

In a flash, Lindiwe was on her feet, glaring down at him. "Who?" she shouted, "Who gives me money?" She turned to Theresa. "My mother gave me money and he thinks it's these men. What men? My next-door neighbour came round. He thinks I'm having an affair with him." She looked down at Tumi and yelled, "Who gives me money? Who's phoning me?" She slumped down on the couch, breathing heavily. "Go home, Tumi."

Tumelo sank back and leant against the wall. He said quietly, "I gave up everything for you, Lindi. I love you." He was nearly in tears.

Theresa took him by the hand, helped him up and led him to the door. "Come now, Tumi," she said, "You must go home. We'll look after Lindi. Come back tomorrow morning. We'll talk."

He went outside then turned back to gaze at Lindiwe. He looked broken as he slunk away.

We made a cup of tea for Lindi with lots of sugar. When we were sure the coast was clear, we all piled into my car and set off. We decided not to go to Lindiwe's house in case Tumi came to find her there. Instead we went to her sister's home in Katlehong, a township I was not familiar with. The light was fading as I drove down endless narrow streets, past small *spaza* shops, shacks and single-storey breeze-block houses. There were no street lights and it was now night-time.

"Stop over here," said Lindiwe, "I'll walk the rest of the way. It's only just round the corner."

But we couldn't leave her there. A crowd of people, mostly

men, were milling around in the smoky dark, silhouetted against a dim light from a ramshackle wooden building which I guessed was a *shebeen*. Some of the men were carrying tin cans which were no doubt filled with beer. The scene looked sinister, like something out of a TV crime drama, and the atmosphere was tense. There had recently been a series of rapes in the area and it would be dangerous for Lindiwe to walk past. She was already feeling vulnerable and nervous.

"We'll take you all the way," I said, and drove gingerly through the crowd. With my white face clearly visible through the windscreen I felt dangerously exposed. We found her sister's house and left Lindi there, telling her not to come in the following day. Lindiwe gave us directions to get out of the township by a different route and thankfully we reached the highway without incident.

The next morning, we listened to Tumelo. Theresa and I had explained to the young people at the beginning that we had no objection to them forming relationships, but if they did, they were not to impinge on the work of the Project. We reminded Tumi of this, and he agreed that his behaviour had been unacceptable. We had to ask him to leave. This was a serious blow – not just for him, but for Themba, because he was one of our best actors and was beginning to learn facilitation skills. He was a valuable member of the group. Tumelo was always someone who wanted – and believed he deserved – more from life, but that couldn't excuse his behaviour towards Lindiwe.

A couple of days later, Lindi told me Tumi was threatening to kill her, then himself. She said he was also saying he would "expose" the Themba Project in the media. He wanted to show the world how Themba had "exploited" him and the other actor-educators. Lindiwe said that some of his threats were personal to me. I was sure he knew where I lived so I phoned the police for advice. I also emailed the members of our Advisory Board to tell them what had happened, and I asked the security guards who roamed up and down my street to look out for Tumelo.

When I spoke to him on the phone he was very angry and said, "You've messed with a black man once too often, Kim." Real gangster-speak. I was sad that he seemed to have reverted to his old gang culture, and worried that Lindiwe was at risk. He could harm her, as well as the Project.

Nevertheless, the work continued, and for the time being, I was able to stop worrying so much about money. We ran a series of auditions, and recruited forty new young people to start as actor-educators. These recruits were whittled down to eleven during the initial period and they began their intermediate training. Theresa was back more or less full-time now, and concentrated on developing the new trainees. I began to feel Themba had a future, and wrote a discussion paper for our Advisory Board with ideas for ways forward. When I presented it to them in August, they were extremely positive and complimentary. I hadn't expected them to praise me for my "dedication, tenacity and vision". It was good to have this feedback after so many struggles. Things were beginning to go well.

The only worry in the back of my mind was Tumelo, but I never heard from him again. Lindi stayed on at Themba and she told me, looking relieved, that she and Tumi had stopped seeing each other.

Theresa was unsure how long she would be able to continue with the Project. She was suffering from crumbling vertebrae and repetitive strain injury in her wrists. Her arms, neck and back were painful. It was hard for her to sit at the computer and type, so she was experimenting with voice recognition software. It wasn't successful, as her New Zealand accent meant that the computer had to be trained to recognise her pronunciation – a process that was laborious, frustrating and time-consuming. After the brief month when she'd been around a lot more, she was once again down to just one day a week. She went to St Benedict's for a weekend's retreat to give herself time to think.

I worried that she might come back to tell me she'd decided to return home to England or New Zealand. Now Bongani and Mary were doing well training the new recruits, maybe Theresa would feel she had done enough to set the Project on its feet, and could leave.

I hoped she would decide to stay.

Chapter 17

England/ Johannesburg, August 2003–July 2005

My brother kept me up to date with my mother's condition so I knew of her ups and downs. Her health swung from worse to better to worse again. I couldn't help comparing her situation with that of people in South Africa. If they were unwell and weren't able to afford private health care, their situation was grim. State hospitals were underfunded, and thousands of people died of AIDS and other conditions because they couldn't pay for medication. Young, potentially productive people were denied the care they deserved, while an old lady in England was being given the best the NHS could provide. Although I loved my mother dearly, it all felt topsy-turvy.

At the beginning of August, I went back to the UK to see Jane. Amazingly, she was sitting up and wearing a pretty summer dress rather than the hospital gown I'd last seen her in. We were able to have an almost normal conversation, even though her voice was very weak. We talked about death and dying.

She said, "I've already died once, you know."

"Died?"

"Yes. I died but decided to come back because I wanted to see you."

"I'm very glad you did," I said.

"I used to think people lost consciousness, but now ..." her voice trailed away.

"Now?" I prompted. "What do you think now?"

But she didn't reply. She looked at me with a long hard stare.

I said, "It's a mystery."

She nodded.

The next day, when I asked the nurses and my brother

about Jane, they said that the conversation I'd had with her was unusually lucid, and normally she was drowsy and uncommunicative. During my two weeks in the UK, I never again saw her so alert.

* * *

Back at the Trevor Huddleston Memorial Centre things were far from easy. I was dragged into all the muddle and resentments when I should have been concentrating on Themba – especially as we were now in the middle of an external evaluation funded by Oxfam. Ma B, who was employed not by Themba but by the Centre, had been rude to some of the actor-educators; she'd also been gossiping about them, though she denied it. Busi was doing extra hours, without pay, because the Centre administrator had left. The email address no longer worked. The volunteer who was due to arrive from Canada needed letters from the Centre in order to get her visa. I finished up writing them and faxing them to her, even though I had nothing to do with her placement.

Other frustrations arose. I had at last raised enough money to kit out the actor-educators in green Themba T-shirts, black jeans and smart *takkies* (trainers), to give them a professional appearance. The uniforms were awaited with excitement, but then the supplier phoned to say he didn't have the necessary equipment to create our logo and couldn't source the right size jeans for the girls. I had to start all over again with another company. I was signing cheques almost daily (or so it seemed), and each one depleted our resources. I had hoped that Razaan would come back to the Project for a few months to help out, but she emailed to say she'd decided to stay in Cape Town.

What with one thing and another, it all got too much for me. One day when the phone was jangling, the computer had broken down, some actor-educators were waiting to see me, and I was been harried by the finance director of the Centre for financial information which I didn't have and wasn't even supposed to have access to, I just burst into tears. At least now everyone knew I wasn't invincible.

I asked myself again why I was doing this, and the answer came back *because you wanted to be in South Africa*. I knew that what we had created was valuable, but without a major injection of cash we couldn't continue. My diary says:

> *This is the crunch moment when so many NGOs go under. But we* ***won't***. *I know I can do it – with help. We have a fantastic Advisory Board and we can **and will** ride this difficult time.*

In September I had a formal meeting with Colin, the evaluator from Oxfam, for him to give me feedback about the Project. I was nervous about what he would say, but I needn't have worried: he was very positive.

It was gratifying to hear his comments. Although I was stressed and worried, it was clear that the work was good. The actor-educators were benefitting, too: they had gained confidence and self-awareness as well as knowledge about HIV, and they had acquired new skills in acting and communication. Themba had now worked with over twelve thousand people – learners and teachers – giving performances in schools. Colin's evaluation said that this was "exemplary" given the small number of staff.

Themba was developing fast, so we recruited a senior trainer – Mpone. The Trevor Huddleston Centre was expanding too, and there wasn't enough room for the different projects: we were all crammed into the little bungalow in Ray Street. Although we had the use of the church hall three days a week for our training, everybody needed space to grow. I knew I would be sad to leave the historic area of Sophiatown, but the time had come for us to branch out on our own. I had always managed Themba as a separate entity within the THMC, and we had our own Patrons and Advisory Board. We had a distinct accounting system, too, and had a different financial year-end, which made things extremely complicated while our accounts and those of the Centre were interlinked.

It was time for me to look for new premises.

Over the next few months, I searched across Johannesburg for somewhere for Themba to move to. We now had two theatre companies, and they were "boxing-and-coxing" in the church hall. When one group was rehearsing or creating new plays, the other was out in schools performing. Theresa had introduced a system of feedback and the actor-educators were asked to evaluate each activity they were engaged in. Their critical-thinking powers were developing.

December came, and I heard from my brother that my mother had been moved to a nursing home. I went back to England to see her at Christmas. The home was gentle and quiet, and the staff were sympathetic and dedicated. My brother told me he had been very upset when he'd helped move Jane to her room in the home because he knew this would be the place where she would eventually die. I felt bad that I hadn't been in the UK to help with the move. Once again, I was torn between wanting to stay with my mother and needing to be responsible for Themba. I stayed for two weeks, but then had to return to Jo'burg.

* * *

In March 2004 I was still on the hunt for new premises. I had an appointment at the Windybrow Theatre in Hillbrow to discuss the possibility of us moving there. I'd promised to drive to Soweto after the meeting to pick up Theresa and some overseas visitors who had come to see Themba's work. I stopped my car in Wolmarans Street in the centre of Jo'burg to look at the map – I wasn't sure of the best route to the township. It was not a safe area of the city and I should have known better.

A man approached me on the near-side and mimed asking

for a cigarette. He was tall and gangly and wearing a dirty jacket which looked baggy on his meagre frame. I shook my head, and lifted my hands in an apologetic gesture.

"I'm sorry, I don't smoke," I mouthed.

There was a massive bang and a crash, and the window smashed. Shards of glass flew everywhere, and an arm reached into my car. It seemed to telescope out as it grew and lengthened. A hand grabbed the strap of my handbag, which I had not hidden carefully enough under the passenger seat.

I yelled, "Leave that alone!" but the thief dashed off along the pavement, my bag swinging behind him

"Fuck you!" I screamed, and put my foot on the accelerator. The car lurched forward onto the kerb and almost smashed into a tree. I changed to reverse and slewed backwards down the road like a mad woman. It was a one-way street, and other cars veered in both directions to avoid me, hooting their horns.

"Bastard! Bastard!" I screeched.

I shifted into forward gear and turned left, making a U-turn into a garage. The man was nowhere to be seen.

"Did you see that guy running down here?" I yelled. "He's got my bag."

The people in the forecourt stared at me and shrugged.

I sat in my car trembling, breathing heavily. My money, and more importantly, my cards and my cheque-book were in that bag. Luckily, I always kept my cell phone in a pouch on my belt, and my house keys on a ribbon around my neck.

I phoned Theresa.

"Hi," I said. "Sorry, but I won't be able to fetch you. I've been mugged."

"What?"

"Well, I don't know if you'd call it mugging, but my passenger window is smashed and my bag gone. I've got no money, and almost no petrol. I was just on my way to buy some."

"Shit," she said. "Are you OK? Don't worry about us. We'll

get a combi-taxi back."

"Right. I'll try to get to the Centre and borrow some petty cash."

"Are you all right, though?"

"Yes, I'm fine. A bit shaken up, that's all. It's such a bugger."

I was angry with myself. I had been driving a Swazi-registered car and looking at a map in a part of Jo'burg near Hillbrow that was known to be dangerous. It was my own fault because it would have looked as if I was an ignorant visitor. I had become too blasé and would need to be more watchful in the future.

One of the paradoxes of living in South Africa was that while I needed to be constantly watching my back, I felt more of a sense of freedom than I did in England. There was a laid-back attitude towards rules and regulations, a far cry from the "Health and Safety" obsession in the UK. Although it was against the law, I frequently didn't bother to do up my seat belt in the car. I knew this was reckless and dangerous, but it gave me a foolish feeling that I was somehow in charge of my own destiny. And being in charge of my own destiny meant I sometimes did really stupid things.

* * *

At last! After a long search, in April I found a large office on the second floor of a 1960s building in Juta Street, Braamfontein, in the centre of Johannesburg. It was a bit small for our purposes, but it was ours. There was room for a couple of desks in one corner and enough space for the actors to rehearse. The rent was just manageable, thanks to the Joseph Rowntree Charitable Trust which had agreed to cover core costs. We bought second-hand office furniture, packed up all our files and training materials, said goodbye to Ma B and Busi, and went down town.

A few weeks after we'd moved in, we noticed that as we were locking up our office at the end of the day, a number of young women were arriving in the lift. They were dressed in very short skirts, with low-cut tops showing a lot of cleavage. They wore a great deal of make-up, and their hair was extravagantly styled. Some of them carried mattresses, blankets, cushions and exotic wraps under their arms. They sidled into the room across the corridor from us.

We always greeted each other as they exited the lift while we waited to enter. "*Sanibonani*, how are you?"

"We're very well, thank you, and how are you?"

One evening Theresa and I discovered a man unloading a video camera and other equipment, carrying it in behind the girls. We guessed that this was some sort of sex chat-line, and the young women were being filmed as they talked with clients on the telephone.

"At least it's safe," Theresa said. "They're not going to catch HIV by having sex on the phone."

* * *

When I'd set up Themba I hadn't reckoned on spending my time searching for premises, meeting with accountants and auditors, asking for help from recruitment agencies, writing job descriptions and employment contracts, managing staff, arranging AGMs, creating work-place policies and networking with other organisations. I had simply seen me and Theresa training a few young people in Forum Theatre, helping them develop plays about HIV and then taking them into schools. But now Themba had grown and was an established NGO, and I had to take responsibility for both its success and its survival.

Comic Relief and the Elton John AIDS Foundation were funding us, and we were given a three-year grant from the Anglo American Chairman's Fund. Individual Quakers and Meetings of the Religious Society of Friends in the UK continued their support, as did the Joseph Rowntree Charitable Trust and the Bishop Simeon Trust. Thanks to Elton John and the BST, we purchased a minibus and hired a part-time driver. I no longer had to attend every performance and was freed up to spend more time in the office, writing funding proposals and reports.

Kim, Tshepo, Sir Elton John and Lunga with the Themba minibus in Soweto

Themba stayed in Juta Street for six months, rehearsing, training, giving performances in schools and developing the skills of the young people. Theresa was once again in relatively good health and we auditioned and recruited two new training groups, TG3 and TG4. Once they were "out on the road" as actor-educators, we developed long-term relationships with certain schools. We also began negotiations with the Boksburg Youth Correctional Centre a few miles to the east of Jo'burg. This was a special interest of Theresa's because in England she had worked extensively in prisons. She was glad to use her expertise, and with Bongani and Mary she developed new performances and workshops for the young inmates.

Themba was moving from the initial setting-up stage to a place where we were consolidating and being noticed. Other NGOs contacted me to learn about our particular methodology, and schools and colleges approached us directly to ask us to work with them. This was a welcome reversal from how we had begun. Then Bongani and I had had to search out schools ourselves and ask for permission to perform.

The Project was becoming established and I was more confident about its future, so in May I flew to England for a couple of weeks to visit my mother. My brother and sister were clearing her house, and had begun the process of selling it. The money was needed to pay the fees at the nursing home.

"What'll happen when all the funds are gone?" I asked my brother.

"We'll cross that bridge when we come to it," he replied. "Somehow we'll have to find a way to cover the costs ourselves."

It was painful and upsetting emptying Jane's house, full as it was of mementos from our childhoods. It felt wrong to be getting rid of her things while she was alive. As I was clearing out some old copies of the *Encyclopaedia Britannica*, a painting slid out of one of the volumes and dropped to the floor. It was a watercolour illustration done by my grandfather for a children's book: *There was an Aged, Aged Man* from *The Book of Nursery Rhymes*. The paper was thick, approximately A4 size, with curling edges, and the colours were bright and cheerful. In my mother's handwriting, written in pencil on the back, was my name: *Kim*. I looked through each edition and found two more paintings, one with *Mike* scribbled on it, and another for *Hazel*. I handed them over to my brother and sister. They were as surprised – and pleased – as I was. Jane's father, Charles Folkard, had been a well-known children's book illustrator, with a style similar to Arthur Rackham's. Originals by him were worth – to us – a great deal more than money.

After spending as much time as I could with my mother, I went back to Johannesburg. I was reluctant to leave Jane, but I was needed at Themba. I had to continue to raise funds.

* * *

Bongani and Mary were now involved in every aspect of the organisation, but Bongani's skills as a trainer, facilitator and actor were needed full time, so we relieved him of much of the admin work and recruited "Mam" Bongi Chabeli as our office manager and book-keeper. Mam, Ma, or Auntie were terms of respect used by young people towards an older African lady. They would often call me Ma Kim, or even Gogo, a deferential term used for a more mature woman.

Mam Bongi was heavily built, about fifty-five years old, and had worked for many years in the NGO sector. She soon settled into her role and helped me with the time-consuming and frustrating legal business of registering Themba as an official Not-For-Profit Organisation (NPO). Eventually, after filling in mountains of forms, we managed to open our own bank account, independent of the Trevor Huddleston Centre.

I could see that our new office manager was going to be a real asset, both to me and to Themba. As a South African, Mam Bongi was used to dealing with the complex bureaucracy of many institutions, and she was also a Zulu speaker. Unlike her, I found it almost impossible to stay unruffled in the face of the bureaucratic indifference we encountered, and I often got impatient and cross. When I talked to friends about my reaction, they came up with the well-worn, sardonic comment, "It's a training opportunity." No doubt this was true, but as there was little training given in the workplace, staff continued to be rude and inept.

I hoped that at Themba, with all the coaching our young people were receiving, we were helping in a small way to reverse the incompetence and lack of organisation in the country. But it was like trying to turn an enormous, heavy elephant around with our bare hands.

Thanks to our funders, we finally had enough money to pay salaries, so rather than keeping Bongani and Mary on stipends, they became proper employees: Assistant Trainers. The day Mary received her first pay slip, with the tax showing, she danced around the office singing, "I'm a tax payer! I'm a tax payer! I'm a true citizen of the New South Africa." I doubted whether a first-time tax-payer in the UK would have responded like this, but South Africa was being governed by the anti-apartheid heroes, and many young people were proud and grateful to be contributing to society.

Now we had staff with employment contracts, job descriptions and remuneration, Theresa and I developed an appraisal system with Key Performance Indicators. It was relatively easy to introduce these to the younger employees, because they had no experience of the workplace, and we explained that the KPIs were designed to help them grow in confidence and improve their skills. Mam Bongi, however, thought that these appraisals were a way to catch her out if her work wasn't good enough, but she came round eventually and could see their value.

Both Theresa and I knew it was important to introduce the KPIs. Themba was a serious enterprise now, and we wanted it to be a role-model not only for the young people within the organisation, but also to set an example to other NGOs, some of which were still managed in a somewhat amateurish way. We worried constantly that we were imposing a "western" style of doing things, but nevertheless decided we needed appropriate systems of management in place. We knew from our own experience this would ensure Themba was well-run and would therefore be more likely to have a future.

Having rapidly outgrown our office in Juta Street, I once again found myself searching Jo'burg, looking for a suitable space to move to. Eventually I discovered a solid, square concrete building just around the corner: 58 Jorissen Street, Braamfontein. There were two storeys available for our use, and the room we would use for rehearsals was enormous. Importantly it had no pillars holding up the floor above. I had seen dozens of rooms which would have been ideal if only they hadn't been encumbered with these supporting columns: we needed a large, open space for rehearsals and training. When I took Theresa to see what I'd found, she skipped back and forth across the bare concrete singing "There's no pillars, there's no pillars, eeyi, eeyi-o" to the tune of *Old MacDonald Had a Farm.*

"So this will do, then?" I asked, smiling as I watched her dancing over to the windows.

She stopped and looked out over the Jo'burg skyline towards the Nelson Mandela Bridge. "Yebo! Yes. Definitely."

Then she turned to me. "But can we afford it?"

"Just about. I'll have to go on raising money, but we'll manage somehow." I crossed my fingers behind my back.

We rented part of the first and all of the second floors. Our rehearsal room was next door to a charismatic Nigerian church. Luckily it was usually only open on Sundays when we weren't around, so the worshippers were free to glorify the Lord for hours – very loudly, and with no inhibitions. Sometimes, as I drove through the streets of downtown Jo'burg, even on a weekday, I would hear singing, stamping and drumming as the evangelical congregations in one or other of these places of worship praised their God.

I had no idea that the move to Jorissen Street would have such a profound effect on Themba and the young people. By chance, the Drama Department of Witswatersrand University was just across the road. Warren Nebe was head of its "Drama for Life" programme, and three of the Themba actor-educators were able to enrol as students, even though they didn't have the usual entry requirements. Their experience at Themba was accepted in lieu of academic qualifications, and I was thrilled that Themba had provided the opportunity for these young people to move into higher education and work towards a degree. As children, they had all come through the Bantu "education" system so they had never dreamed of being allowed through the hallowed portals of this previously white-only University. They would have expected their paths in life to follow the same pattern as their parents, and they'd been destined for work in menial jobs, very likely as cleaners, cooks, or gardeners for white masters. Or worse: working in the mines. Before coming to Themba, they had never been helped to learn, and certainly had not been expected to *think*. Again, it felt as though my own journey was being echoed through these young South Africans.

Bongani was the first to graduate and I felt enormously proud and grateful that Themba had been a catalyst for his achievement. This was a world away from the expectations of the young man who had come to tell Theresa and me he would have to go back to work at the Juicy Lucy.

* * *

Relocating to our new home felt as if we were growing up. We had the rooms carpeted, bought more second-hand office furniture and installed heaters. Next on the agenda was a proper business plan for the coming years. Themba had been muddling along step by hesitant step since we'd begun nearly three years earlier, but now we were established, we needed to get ourselves more organised. I asked a friend, Brendan Finnegan, who was a "brander" to create a professional logo for us based on the design my brother had drawn in 1995. A few weeks after we'd moved, Theresa and I again met with Margaret Roper and Dudu Mtshazo, two of our Board members. They provided us with gentle and nurturing love as well as hard-headed practical support.

The four of us looked in detail at how Themba was structured. I was the director, and Theresa the lead trainer. Bongi was the office manager, Mpone the senior trainer, and Bongani and Mary were assistant trainers. Then there were the actor-educators, the driver, occasional volunteers and the office cleaner. In addition, we had our Patrons and the Board of Directors. I would have preferred a less hierarchical organisation, but at least it was efficient. We had systems in place where everyone had an equal opportunity to be heard and could contribute to how Themba was developing. I thought we were doing as well as we could.

I told Margaret and Dudu how torn I felt about being in South Africa while my mother was in her nursing home in England. We agreed that I would continue as director for a further year, and in the meantime, we would appoint an assistant director whom I could mentor and who would be ready to take over from me when I began to withdraw in 2005. Part of the reason I wanted to begin to take a back seat was in order to avoid "Founders Syndrome". There were too many NGOs where the person who had set things up stayed on, and on, and on, preventing innovation and creating a culture of "we've-never-done-it-like-that-before". I was keen to avoid this for Themba, and felt that if the Project had a future it would need to be in South African hands. I hoped that my mother would live long enough for me to spend a part of each year with her.

I wrote a job description and person specification for the new post of assistant director, and a schedule of advertising, interviewing, recruiting and induction was agreed with the Board. It was cheering to think that within a short space of time we would begin the process of passing on the Themba HIV & AIDS Organisation (as it was now called) to a new generation.

But I was wrong to feel optimistic about the future.

On Boxing Day 2004, a massive earthquake created a terrible tsunami. It caused devastation around the Indian Ocean, and the deaths of more than 300,000 people. One of these was Jane

Holland, the daughter of Richard and Sheila Attenborough, our founding Patrons. Their granddaughter, Lucy, also died.

I was on a short visit to Cape Town that Christmas, and I remember seeing through the window of a newsagent's shop a photograph of Richard's face filling the front page of the *Cape Argus*. He looked utterly devastated. I stood stock still, staring at the picture, the tears pouring down my cheeks.

This appalling tragedy turned out to be the precursor of the most difficult year in the life of Themba – a year that was deeply unhappy, and extremely challenging for us all.

* * *

Everyone at Themba felt that the best way to thank Richard and Sheila for their support was for us to continue working to help reduce the spread of HIV. We began to implement the business plan put together with the help of Margaret and Dudu, and in March interviewed applicants for the post of assistant director. The actor-educators, as well as members of the Board and a human resources agency, were all involved in the recruitment process. We held interviews with a number of candidates, showed them around our premises and introduced them to some of the young people. The applicants who were short-listed watched training taking place, and also saw a performance. Then we held formal interviews. On 11 May the man we'd appointed, "B", began work. His CV and references looked good, and he appeared to be experienced in NGOs. We were confident he would be an asset to Themba.

At first all seemed well. B appeared to be friendly and attentive. He sat behind the desk we had acquired for him, looking very much at home, stroking down his thick black moustache as he read through the Themba documents I'd given him. He was a stocky, coloured South African, with neatly cut hair, greying at the temples. We all had high hopes for him. He was introduced to everyone, and he greeted them all affably. Theresa and I had meetings with him to explain the collaborative way in which we worked. Travelling to schools in our minibus with the actor-educators, B watched a number of performances to understand our unique interactive theatre process. He attended rehearsals and sat in on some of the sessions where new plays were developed. During his induction (which he said was "impressive") he had meetings with members of the Board, with Bongani and Mary, and with the young people. He smiled a lot and shook hands with everyone he came in contact with. He seemed keen to get to know all aspects of the organisation.

When he felt ready, I gave him a few straightforward tasks while I began to make tentative plans to work part-time. But by July, cracks were beginning to show. Some of the young people came to me to say they were unhappy with B's behaviour at performances, and we noticed he was making a large number of private calls from the office phone and his personal mobile in work time.

I could do nothing about B, however, because I had to fly to England. My mother was dying.

Chapter 18

England/Johannesburg, July–December 2005

Sally, my daughter, met me at Heathrow and we drove to the nursing home in Wiltshire. My brother Mike and sister Hazel had already been there for some days and they were exhausted. Hazel left soon after I arrived: she needed to get back to Yorkshire. She had things to do at home, and it was a long drive. Mike, though, stayed for a while longer and explained what had been happening.

"I think when I told her Uncle Ted had died, she decided to stop eating altogether. I believe she's had enough and just wants to let go."

Ted was Jane's older brother and had died in April. Since then Jane had kept her mouth firmly closed whenever food had been offered, and gradually she had become weaker. I knew this, of course, because I had been in constant touch with Mike. Jane's ability to swallow had returned about a year earlier, and I'd been able to feed her when I'd visited. She had once again been able to enjoy the sensation of taste, and – importantly for her – a cup of tea.

When Jane had begun to refuse food, the staff at the nursing home had suggested re-introducing nourishment via the tube in her stomach, but Mike, Hazel and I believed that would be wrong. All decisions about Jane's life were taken by other people, from when she was woken up in the morning to whether or not she had her hearing aids in place. The only choice she had left was to not eat. She had made her wishes known some years earlier when she'd made a Living Will and this explained quite clearly that she was not to be kept alive if she was unable to make her own decisions about her care.

Mike tenderly said goodbye to Jane and left to go home to his family.

Sally and I entered the room and sat on either side of Jane's bed. She lay motionless under the cotton blanket. I looked at my mother's face: her closed eyes were sunken and her cheek-bones prominent under pale, slightly blueish skin. She seemed peaceful, and she wasn't breathing. We watched her, but there appeared to be no breath whatsoever.

My eyes met Sally's. She whispered, "Do you think she's died?"

"I don't know," I said. My stomach felt like lead.

We sat and waited. I stroked Jane's forehead, the way she used to stroke mine when I was a child and felt unwell.

Suddenly she heaved a great in-breath, and shuddered as the air left her. Then she was still once again. A nurse came in.

"Quick," I said, "my mother just took in a great big breath, and now she's not breathing at all."

"It's OK," said the nurse gently. She led me to one side of the room. "It's called Cheyne-Stokes breathing. She's been like this for a couple of days. It happens when someone is near the end. It doesn't usually go on as long as this, though. I think she's been waiting for you."

I went back to the bedside and held Jane's hand, but didn't trust myself to speak.

After a while I looked up and said to Sally, "You need to get back to London, don't you? You'd better go. I'll be all right here."

"Are you sure?"

I nodded.

Sally kissed her grandmother goodbye and left. I stayed with my mother. I sat by her bedside, trying to take in the fact that she was dying. I thought back to the occasion when, some years ago, we'd gone on a beautiful walk in the country near my Sussex home. As we'd neared my house, she'd stopped suddenly and said, "I've finally grown up. But I think you knew that, didn't you?" She'd been seventy years old at the time.

"I knew there was something different about you." I said. "You seem to have been chirpier lately, and I've seen you sometimes smiling to yourself."

"I saw you grow up when you were about forty," she said. "I knew I had to do the same. It's just taken me a bit longer, that's all." She'd given me that quizzical smile.

"So what difference has it made to you – to have 'grown up'?" I asked.

"Simple, really," she said. "Now, when Pip wants me to do something, I think about it and decide for myself whether I will or not. In the past I just automatically did what he said." Pip was my father.

I remembered another walk we'd taken one summer when we'd been caught in a sudden storm with thunder, lightning and a howling wind. Instead of trying to find shelter, we'd each found a large, flat rock to stand on, and in the pouring rain had lifted our arms and faces to the heavens and quoted from *King Lear*, yelling into the swirling air: *Blow winds and crack your cheeks! Rage! Blow! You cataracts and hurricanoes spout. Till you have drench'd our steeples, drown'd the cocks!*

We'd run home, soaking wet and giggling.

My mother was comatose for two more days, drawing in great gulps of air, breathing out as if it was her last, then lying still. I was at her bedside most of the time. She died on 16 July at five o'clock in the morning.

The nurse said I should remove my mother's jewellery. "It's best," she said, "you never know what will happen to valuables." I gently lifted Jane's head to remove the chain she always wore around her neck with the two little silver charms I'd given her: one, a small fish I'd bought her on a holiday we'd shared in Tunisia, the other, the drama masks symbolising the comedy and tragedy of life. It was the very last thing I would do for her.

I drove into Bradford-on-Avon and waited in the park for

the funeral directors to open. I have no recollection of how I arrived there. As I sat on the bench I saw Jane gliding across the grass in her pale blue denim dress, her handbag slung over her shoulder. She was strolling away from me towards the river. She had always walked fast, determined to arrive at her destination. But on this beautiful day, with the early morning sun on her back, she seemed to be in no hurry to get to wherever she was going. I watched her as she moved away across the grass. I very much wanted to call her back.

* * *

After Jane's funeral, I returned to Johannesburg and the problems with B. In early August he was more than halfway through his probationary period and we had a supervision meeting.

Referring to the notes I'd taken of what other members of staff had said to me, I began by asking him to explain what he'd been overheard saying on the phone.

"From what I have been told, it seems you think your job is *a nightmare.* I understand you have been heard to say, *I'm the deputy director, the director's in England* and, *these people are paying themselves in pounds in the UK.* These calls were made on 1 August. Can you tell me about them?"

I waited for an answer, but B just sat at the table in the meeting room looking glum.

I continued, "I gather you have also said, *It's not right, I want to put a stop to it ...* Can you explain all of this, please?"

B denied it, and said, "This is just tattle-taling." I imagined he meant "tittle-tattle" or "telling tales" but it came out wrong. He went on, "This is absolutely and totally untrue. I've never worked in an open plan office before."

"I don't understand what you mean," I said.

He answered, "I think the atmosphere in the office should be more relaxed."

I moved on to another area of concern.

"I gather you were reading a newspaper when you were supposed to be watching a rehearsal," I said. "The young people thought it was disrespectful to pay so little attention when they were hard at work. Can you tell me about this?"

He said, "I don't remember reading a newspaper. When was this supposed to have happened?"

I referred to my notes but he hurried on, "In any case, surely you can see this is nit-picking?"

B was in a position of seniority, and it was important for him to be a role model for the young people. "A culture of mutual respect is what Theresa and I encourage and expect at Themba," I said. "We need you to understand this."

He didn't respond, but sat looking down at the Key Performance Indicator appraisal documents on the table in front of him. He clicked the top of his biro in and out with his thumb.

We moved on to some letters B had written and sent out to potential funders asking for financial support. They'd had a number of grammatical and spelling errors. I showed him copies. "This really isn't acceptable," I said, "and it harms Themba's credibility when communications go out of the office with mistakes in them."

He agreed. "Yes, I'm sorry. It won't happen again."

"And another thing," I continued, "I've been told you have been calling some of the young women *girlies*. Is this true?"

He nodded and said, "I have difficulty remembering people's names."

"Do you think this is the right way to address young women?"

He didn't reply, but shifted his body and looked uncomfortable.

"I would like you to stop using the expression *girlies*, please, because it's belittling and disrespectful. You are in a position of authority and I need you to find a way to remember people's names."

Next, I took him to task for arbitrarily changing some of the figures in a budget without consultation. "We all need to work together on fundraising applications so there are no misunderstandings," I said.

The discussion continued for more than two hours and although it never became heated, at the end B said, "I will fight. I want to know who it is who has said these things. I will take them to court if necessary." He stood abruptly, gathered up the documents in front of him, and marched back to his desk.

A few days went by and the atmosphere deteriorated. I attempted to get on with work, but it wasn't easy as the mood in the office felt strained and awkward. Although I tried to separate my worries about B from my grief at my mother's death, I couldn't help thinking about Jane as I tried to concentrate.

Things went downhill fast, and soon I had a phone call from one of the directors to say that B had started a grievance procedure against me. I was sure in the logical part of my mind that there was no case to answer, but on the other hand I felt sick.

The problems with B worsened: documents went missing, he didn't attend meetings, work wasn't completed and he refused to be managed. I'd had experience in the past of managing a "failing" employee and I knew that the best way was to give as much help and support as possible. I tried to do this with B, but began to despair of finding a way to improve matters. Things finally came to a head when he was asked by members of the Board to provide them with certain papers, which he failed to do. I explained to B that because the Board had needed the information urgently, and because he hadn't been at his desk, I'd tried to access the documents on his computer. When he heard this he was so angry he stormed out of the office and left the building. He didn't return.

In early September, the Themba Board held the grievance meeting that B had requested. Although I was sure the directors had faith in me, I still worried and fretted about the outcome.

It was as if I'd been thrown back to my schooldays when I'd sat outside the headmistress's office waiting to be told off about some real or imagined wrongdoing. The Board found there was no grievance to answer and B was issued with a notice of a disciplinary hearing to take place in a week's time.

This investigation was held over four full days in our small, stuffy meeting room, with B, an external chairperson, David Dennis, a well-known actor and member of the Board, and me all crammed in uncomfortably together, seated around a large oval table. These were some of the most difficult and painful days of my life. I hated having to "accuse" B of all his misdemeanours and failings. He had been offered the opportunity to have a friend to support him, but he'd declined. He fidgeted with the various papers he'd brought to the meeting, losing his place and dropping documents on the floor. He tried to answer the "charges" against him, but became ruffled and confused as he attempted to defend himself. I could see a fine line of sweat above his moustache.

After the meetings were over, we waited two weeks for the report from the arbitrator to arrive. It was a tense fortnight. When the bulky document finally came, I was relieved to read that the conclusions were all in Themba's favour. B was judged as having performed poorly and being incompatible with the organisation. The recommendation was that B be dismissed as of 31 October 2005.

I breathed a heavy sigh. I had felt very alone during this whole process, despite the support of members of the Board and friends checking regularly that I was alright. Theresa, too, had done what she could, and she, together with Mpone, Bongani and Mary, had held Themba together while I was preoccupied.

The matter should have ended there, but B decided to take Themba to the Commission for Conciliation, Mediation and Arbitration (CCMA). I was horribly aware that I was a white English woman and Themba had dismissed a South African man of colour. I worried that in the atmosphere of post-apartheid South Africa this could be regarded as racism rather than a genuine workplace dispute.

In early December the investigation took place at the offices of the CCMA. The glass-fronted building in the centre of town was an intimidating block of about twenty storeys. Inside, the walls were dull cream with a wide dark red stripe along the bottom, reminiscent of the colour of the paint on the rondavels in the Eastern Cape. I tried to keep an image of my journey to Mandela's birthplace in my mind as office workers bustled up and down the tiled floor clutching files, their shoes clacking on the hard surface. I felt extremely uncomfortable waiting in the corridor outside an office, sitting next to B. There were only two chairs and they were much too close together. I wanted to move mine away from his, but I didn't want to give him an excuse to make a snide remark. I could sense from his fidgeting that he was feeling awkward, too.

B attempted to make conversation.

"So how've you been, Kim, since I saw you last?"

"Fine, thanks."

"Everything OK at Themba?"

"Yes."

I didn't know what he expected. He seemed not to realise we were facing a final showdown and that one of us would emerge the loser. Polite chat was hardly appropriate in the circumstances.

Eventually we were called in to the Commissioner's office and sat facing each other across a wide document-strewn table.

I explained that we'd already had a four-day disciplinary hearing, and there was a sixty-page report from the external arbitrator with the recommendation that B be dismissed. During this meeting B made it clear what he wanted: a year's salary in lieu of notice. He knew, though, that Themba didn't have that kind of money and if the decision went in his favour it would close us down.

The Commissioner dismissed the appeal and told B that if he wanted to take things further, he had thirty days to decide whether to go to arbitration. This would be a formal, public, tape-recorded hearing. If the court agreed at the end of it that B's case was what they called "frivolous and vexatious" then he would have to pay costs.

It was a stressful thirty days' waiting to find out what would happen. I didn't know whether B would risk it and take us to court. Once the deadline had passed, however, and B had made no further contact, the great weight I'd been carrying on my back lifted. I had spent nearly a year dealing with the stress B's appointment had created, but now, thankfully, the whole saga was over.

I began to notice my surroundings again, and could breathe. It was summer.

* * *

All through this worrying time, the Themba HIV & AIDS Organisation itself had been doing well. By now we had given performances to over thirty-eight thousand people, most of them schoolchildren. We had performed in a huge variety of spaces from vast soulless community halls, to tiny stuffy classrooms. We had a well-defined selection and training programme for actor-educators, and we'd begun a series of post-performance workshops in schools, community-based organisations and in the youth prison at Boksburg, east of Johannesburg. Participants learnt how to protect themselves from the virus, deal with stigma, lead a healthy lifestyle and support their families and friends. We encouraged everyone to overcome their fear and go for a blood test. Antiretroviral medication was becoming more freely available at the clinics, and a positive result from an HIV test was no longer regarded as an immediate sentence of death.

Bongani and Mary had grown up: they were no longer the

hesitant, nervous youngsters who had come to our first auditions in 2002. In their place were two mature, intelligent, thoughtful, and skilled adults.

Lack of money, though, was still a major headache.

One evening in mid-December, Theresa and I attended a talk by Clem Sunter at Wits University. Clem was a highly-regarded business strategist and author of the best-selling book on strategy, *The Mind of a Fox*. Earlier in the year he had given us his time and expertise *pro bono* to help us with our planning. By coincidence – another of the many coincidences that made us feel Themba was being "held" by the universe – Clem drew up in the car park alongside me.

"Oh, hi, Kim," he said as he disentangled his long legs from his shiny red Mini Cooper. Clem was grey-haired with an open, smiling face. He stooped and reached into the boot of the car. There were a number of boxes full of *The Mind of a Fox* and his newest book, *Games Foxes Play*.

"Here, let us help you with those," I said.

Clem, Theresa and I walked across the car park together carrying the heavy packages. I looked up at him.

"How are things going at Themba?" Clem asked in his gentle English-sounding voice.

"To be honest, Clem, I don't know how we're going to survive," I said. "We haven't enough money to pay even the basic bills. I'm going to have to send people home early for Christmas."

Clem had been the Chair of the Anglo American Corporation, and was now leading their charitable foundation. He stopped, looked down at me and said, "We can't let that happen, Kim. I'll speak to Margie and see if they can bring the next portion of your grant forward. Will that help?"

"It certainly would," I smiled. "Thank you very much."

Clem kept his promise. The Anglo American donation arrived before the end of the year and was more generous than I had expected. It would tide us over until the next tranche of Comic Relief funding came in January.

It was heartening to end what had been a terrible year on such a positive note. Once more it began to look as if Themba had a future. I looked forward to 2006.

Chapter 19

Soweto, April 2006 This is I.T.T!

The smart white Themba mini-bus is emblazoned with the names of two of our sponsors: the Elton John AIDS Foundation and the Bishop Simeon Trust. I drive through the maze of streets in Soweto and we travel past shacks, modest houses with corrugated iron roofs, churches and small *spaza* shops until we arrive at the Orlando West district. Huge pink and purple billboards line the streets shouting their message: "STAY SAFE! USE A CONDOM! KNOW YOUR STATUS!"

People roam up and down the rutted pavements carrying plastic bags of shopping. Many of the women have babies strapped to their backs, and street-traders have laid their wares out on the dusty ground. We pass the newly opened Hector Pieterson Museum and Memorial, just two blocks away from where the schoolboy was shot and killed. The late-summer sun is bright and shines warmly on the red-brown brick of the museum, contrasting with the stark grey slate of the memorial. Hawkers have sprung up, selling mementoes to the few tourists who wander about. Some of them stop and buy beaded jewellery or carved animals.

Theresa is in the back of the combi with the actor-educators. Tshepo, who lives near this area, is with me in the front and gives me directions as I drive. When we arrive at the school I park in the rubbish-strewn playground. We unload our metal screens, banners, costumes and props and walk across to the main building. The children who are milling around the compound greet us with cries of excitement, and welcoming hands help us carry our gear inside.

I go to find the Principal, only to be told by the school secretary that he has gone to a meeting. This is becoming such a common occurrence I wonder if the head teachers of the schools we visit are deliberately absenting themselves. I suppose that if there is any comeback from disgruntled parents or governors after our performance, the Heads can truthfully say they weren't there so can't be blamed. Themba's reputation has spread, and some adults are nervous about our openness and the way we talk about HIV, sex and condoms. The school is expecting us, however, and a teacher shows us to a classroom. We begin to sort out our stuff, erect the screens and hang up the shirts which will be used in the play.

The actor-educators, neat in their uniform of emerald green Themba T-shirts, black jeans and *takkies*, run through the voice and movement warm-ups. They practise the Tai Chi Theresa has taught them, and become focussed and grounded. They no longer need instruction from Theresa or me. It is heartening to see that they have become so self-reliant.

The drumming begins. Children spill into the grimy room, most of them heading straight for the front. Although this is a primary school, some of the learners look as if they could be fifteen years old, while others are probably only ten or eleven. We have arranged a hundred or so chairs in rows; they are plastic, orange, and dirty, with pieces of hardened greyish-white chewing gum stuck under the moulded rims.

The Themba actors pick out some of the smaller children and lead them forward so they can get a good view of what is about to happen. Three teachers gather in one corner looking uncertain, their authority usurped by the actor-educators. They seem nervous, not knowing whether they should assert themselves or leave everything to the theatre company. Two are women, but the other – a short, plump man – has a stick tucked under his arm. He looks as if he would like to thwack some of the more boisterous pupils. He controls himself, however: corporal punishment is now officially outlawed in South Africa, but canes are still carried by some teachers as a threat.

Big boys saunter in, talking and smirking. They arrange themselves on the heavy wooden desks which have been piled up at the back of the room to make space for a theatre-style arrangement for the performance. The older girls swagger in, skirts turned over at the waist to reveal their thighs, and white school blouses stretched tight across burgeoning busts. Their grey knee-high socks and black lace-up shoes look incongruous on these near-women. The young men call the girls over to perch with them on the desks, while the younger children sit giggling at the front, turning around in their seats to chatter to each other.

The anticipation grows as the volume and speed of Bheki's drumming increases, and dust motes dance in the beams of sunlight flooding through the cracked windows. There are posters peeling off the grubby walls, and a few books are piled haphazardly on a set of broken shelves by the teacher's desk. The classroom is hot.

Bongani erupts from the back of the room. He runs through the crowd of excited students and into the acting space. He turns around, flings his arms out wide, and calls the name of the next performer: "Thabo!"

Thabo dashes to the front, turns, holds out one arm and shouts: "Zodwa!"

Zodwa races in: "Tshepo!"

Tshepo sprints forward and introduces: "Mary!"

Mary dances in: "Mpone!"

And so it goes on – "Lunga," "Bongiwe," "JR," "Mkhonzeni" – until there are ten actor-educators dancing energetically in front of the students. The drumming stops, the actors stand in a line, and Bheki joins them as his name is announced. There is a burst of applause. When it dies away, the actor-educators stand in silence while Mary comes forward to light the HIV/AIDS candle, a fat cream-coloured candle with a red AIDS ribbon pinned to the front. She pauses for a moment, holding the lighted match. As she puts it to the wick, she says, "I light this candle to remember all those who have died of AIDS, and those who are living with HIV."

The children are quiet. Even the older adolescents at the back have stopped their gossiping to watch and listen.

Now the actor-educators sing a topical, popular song and the whole audience joins in, clapping their hands, tapping their feet, singing and swaying with the music.

When the song is over, Bongani and Mary take a step in front of the other actors who sit down on the chairs placed in a row along the back of the performance area. Tshepo, Thabo, JR and Zodwa take down white school shirts and blue and grey striped ties from the screens and put them on over their Themba T-shirts. Bongani tells the audience his name and says that they are about to see a short play entitled *Class of 2006*. He briefly explains a little about what's going to happen, and then with a burst of energy, he flings his arms wide and announces, "THIS IS ITT!"

Tshepo and Thabo take their places in the acting space and the performance begins. It is only ten minutes long, and tells the story of Mzobo (played by Thabo) who is a "player" with the girls. He and his friend Tebza (played by Tshepo) are in school, waiting for lessons to begin. Lebo (JR) enters and takes Mzobo to one side and hesitatingly tells him her news:

Lebo: *Yeah, that's the thing I wanted to talk to you about.*
(with difficulty) I'm ...
(Mzobo moves towards her to comfort her)
Mzobo: *Come on baby, you can talk to me; I'm your man.*
Lebo: *I ... I'm HIV positive.*
(Mzobo moves away from her, in silent shock)
Lebo: *(Desperately) Mzobo. Say something!*
Mzobo: *(Accusingly) So – you have been sleeping around, ne?*
Lebo: *No! You are the only guy I have ever slept with.*
Mzobo: *You know what? From today I'm no longer your boyfriend.*
Don't call me, don't come near me. Just stay out of my life!

The play moves on with Lebo's friend, Nthabiseng (Zodwa),

comforting her, and Tebza trying to persuade Mzobo to go with him for an HIV blood test. When the play ends, the story is unresolved and the characters are left in a state of indecision.

Now Mary and Bongani, the facilitators for today, come forward and ask the members of the audience what they would do if they found themselves in the same situation as Lebo and Mzobo. The children look around to their classmates and wonder how to respond.

Then a small hand shoots up from a little boy in the middle of the room. "I'd try to persuade Mzobo to go for a test."

Then another hand from a girl near the front. "I think Lebo should go and talk to Mzobo again."

A third child joins in. "No. Tebza should *make* Mzobo go to the clinic with him."

"So how would he do that?" asks Bongani.

"I'd tell him I needed him to come with me for *my* test," says the boy.

"OK," says Bongani, "so will you come up here and show us what you would say?"

The boy is embarrassed and squirms in his seat. But his friends encourage him, and soon he is in front of all his schoolmates and standing next to Mary. He is small, with big eyes and sticky-out ears, and he has the cheeky grin of a meerkat. The audience is tittering and chattering, but Mary holds up her hand for quiet.

"What is your name?" she asks the child.

"Dumisani."

Mary takes the school tie off Tebza and, turning to the audience, says, "When I put this tie round Dumisani's neck, he is no longer Dumisani – he is Tebza."

Mary checks with the boy that he's OK, and then asks him to talk to Mzobo and try to convince him to go for an HIV test. The little chap is bold and determined, but Mzobo resists at first, sulking and refusing. The audience watches fascinated as their school friend takes part in the play. Eventually Mzobo is persuaded. He puts his hand on Dumisani's shoulder and says, "OK, man, I'll go with you. I'll see you after school."

Mary removes the tie from Dumisani and reminds the audience that he is no longer Tebza. As the boy returns to his seat he is greeted with cheers. "Hey, Dumisani, my man, you told him, OK? Sharp, sharp."

Bongani and Mary bring Lebo back on stage and question her about her behaviour, asking her what she would do differently if she could go back in time. She says, "We were at a party, and went into another room and Mzobo persuaded me to have sex with him. I should have said no, or I should have had a condom with me."

Mary asks the learners how they would behave in the same situation. Lots of boys and girls call out their ideas. Soon Mary picks out one of the bigger girls from the back and asks her to come forward. There are cat-calls and whistles as she threads her way regally through the other children, smiling and waving her hand.

Two chairs are placed in the centre of the acting space and the girl, whose name is Lerato, sits with Mzobo. Mary gives them both party tops to wear. They start the scene with Mzobo trying to persuade Lerato – who has now become Lebo – to have sex with him. She resists:

"No, Mzobo. I won't have sex with you without a condom."

"So, you don't love me?"

"It's nothing to do with whether I love you. I want to keep myself safe."

"Oh, come on, baby."

"If we have sex we must use a condom, and I don't have one."

"Oh, man, a condom is like eating a sweet with the wrapper on."

"No condom, no sex."

"Come on ..."

"No! Mzobo – take me home. It's late."

And she gets up and walks away from him.

There is cheering and clapping while Mary removes Lerato's party blouse and, reminding the children that she is no long Lebo, indicates she should go back to her seat. Lerato swings her hips as she ambles back through her peers looking pleased with herself. All eyes watch her progress.

Bongani comes forward and summarises the story of the play, reflecting back what has been learnt so far. Then he beckons Mzobo to him.

Bongani asks, "Mzobo, do you think it is possible you might be HIV positive?"

Mzobo replies, "Eish, no, man! How can I be HIV positive? It's not my fault about Lebo."

But Bongani persists, "How do you know? Have you been for an HIV blood test?"

"A test? No, man! I'm not going for an HIV test."

Bongani pauses for a moment, and then reaches behind him. An actor passes him a knobkerrie with a band of leopard-print material wrapped around the middle and green ribbons hanging down from the top. Bongani solemnly hands it to Mzobo.

"Mzobo: this is the Truth Stick. Whoever is holding this stick must tell the absolute truth. Do you understand? Now, I'm going to ask you again: do you think you might be HIV positive?" He pauses. "Think hard, and remember: you are holding the Truth Stick."

Mzobo's air of confidence crumbles, and his body slumps. His shoulders droop and he hangs his head. Bongani waits. Everyone in the audience leans forward, expectant, willing Mzobo to speak. There is a hush.

Slowly Mzobo lifts his head and takes a deep breath. "I do wonder if I might be HIV positive," he says in a low voice, "but I don't want to go for a test."

Bongani asks him gently, "Can you tell me why not?"

Mzobo is nearly inaudible, but his whisper carries to the back of the classroom.

"I ... I'm scared."

"You are scared of going for an HIV blood test?" asks Bongani softly.

Mzobo nods his head.

An audience of township school children. (Photo: Anand Madhvani)

Bongani turns to the audience and says, "Most people are scared of going for an HIV test, but it is important that we all know whether we are HIV positive or negative. If we find we are HIV positive we can lead a healthy lifestyle, get medication if we need it, and be very careful not to pass the virus on to another person."

Thabo, the actor, now takes off Mzobo's shirt revealing his Themba T-shirt. He speaks to the audience: "As I take off this shirt, I am no longer Mzobo. I am now Thabo, the actor. I'm going to put the shirt on this chair, and as I do so, I want you to imagine that Mzobo is sitting here. I am going to speak to him."

The audience watches fascinated as Thabo speaks to "Mzobo":

"Mzobo, you must grow up and take responsibility for your

actions. You must go for an HIV test and find out whether you are positive or not. And you must speak to Lebo and make it up with her. Will you do that?"

The question is left hanging in the air.

Bongani asks everyone in the room to stand up and face him. The actor-educators, now all wearing their Themba T-shirts and no longer in character, stand in a row in front of the audience.

Bongani says, "The actors are going to say a line, and we are going to ask you to respond. The line is, *I am HIV positive* and we would like you all together to say, *I still care for you.* Do you understand? We will demonstrate first."

After the demonstration there is tension in the air as the actors face the children, breathe in, and say loudly and with conviction:

I am HIV positive.

The audience responds as requested, but raggedly, *I still care for you.*

Bongani explains that now they will swap over and the audience will say *I am HIV positive* and the actors will reply. There is fidgeting and surreptitious sideways glances, but they join in:

I am HIV positive.
I still care for you.

Everyone sits down again, some of the children looking sheepish. Bongani reiterates, "It is very important that we know whether we are HIV positive or HIV negative. We must encourage people to come out and be open about whether they are positive or negative, and we must support those who have HIV."

Now Mkhonzeni and Bongiwe, Thabo and Lunga, Zodwa and Bheki line up in pairs – one being a same-sex couple – and perform pieces of dialogue, two-lines long. One of them is:

All my girlfriends sleep with me – it's my right.
It's my right to do what I want with my body.

Another:

You don't trust me.
It's not about trust, it's about being safe.

And a third:

I want to have sex with you.
I want to have sex with you, too, and we must use this. She holds up a condom.

Some of the children bring their hands up in front of their mouths hiding their giggles as Thabo and Lunga, two male actors, speak the second of these duologues. The teachers look down at their feet, embarrassed. This is a traditional school where such things are not discussed. It seems that the liberalism of the new South African Constitution has not yet trickled down to this primary school in Soweto, and attitudes are still set against gay relationships.

Mary now invites six learners to come forward to the performance space and each one links up with one of the actor-educators. They repeat the words from the duologues, using small cards as prompts. The children read haltingly; the scripts are in English and unfamiliar, and for all of them English is not their first language. Again, there is nervous laughter as the pupils go back to their seats.

Suddenly I hear an echo to the laughter: learners from other lessons are pouring out into the playground and surrounding the classroom where the Themba presentation is taking place. Children are peering in through the windows, climbing onto each other's backs to get a better view and calling to their friends inside. Some of them are pulling faces and making silly gestures. The three teachers leave and two new ones slide in through the door at the back, letting in dust and heat-laden air. The children in the audience are distracted and wave to their friends outside, but after a few minutes Bongani and Mary restore order by asking everyone to calm down and attend to what is going to happen next. A bell sounds and the noise from the courtyard subsides as pupils wander off to their next class.

The actors line up across the performance space and fire a range of questions directly to the children in the audience:

Is sex before marriage okay for me?
Is sex before I have a life partner okay for me?
Is it against my beliefs?
Is it against the law?
How will my parents feel if they know?
How will I feel the next day?
How well do I know him?
How well do I know her?
Do contraceptive pills prevent HIV?
What if I get an STI?
Is it going to mess up my life?

Next, Zodwa and JR bring out large cards and the actors, standing in line, hold them up for the audience to see. The cards are coloured green, orange and red.

The green cards have these words on them: MASTURBATION, MUTUAL MASTURBATION, NOT HAVING SEX, SAYING I LOVE YOU, HUGGING, KISSING. The three orange cards say, ORAL SEX, THIGH SEX and USE A CONDOM, and the red card is printed with the words PENETRATIVE SEX and ANAL SEX.

One by one each actor steps forward and speaks what is on their card, and Bongani and Mary ask the members of the audience to translate into isiZulu, isiXhosa, Ndebele, Venda,

Sesotho, siSwati, Afrikaans or any other languages they know. There is pandemonium as the children are encouraged to shout out words which they would normally only whisper secretly to each other. The teachers look askance at what they doubtless believe is highly inappropriate behaviour. Soon Mary and Bongani quieten the audience down again and explain the reason for this part of the presentation: it is to help people talk openly about sex rather than inadvertently finding themselves doing it.

"Did you notice the colours on the cards? What do they remind you of?" asks Bongani.

"The robots!"

"Yes. So, what's written on the green cards is safe, the orange cards are a warning, and the red card means STOP or DANGER." He continues, "USING A CONDOM is on the orange card because condoms are not one hundred per cent safe. The only way to stay safe is not to have sex at all."

Bongani now comes forward and stands very still in the centre of the acting space. The actors have put down the cards and are behind him in a straight line, also unmoving. They wait for the restlessness in the audience to subside, and then Bongani says, solemnly and quietly, "Some of us in this room here today are HIV positive, some of us are HIV negative, and some of us don't know yet whether we are positive or negative. I'm going to say a few words and I want you to think about them for yourselves. Please bow your heads or close your eyes and be silent while I say these words."

A hundred heads are bowed. Some of the children bring their hands together as if in prayer, their eyes shut tight and their faces screwed up. Even the teachers have their heads down, their hands clasped in front of them. Bongani speaks slowly, pronouncing every word with care.

"What is one thing I can do, when I leave here today, to keep myself safe and healthy?"

There is complete quiet. Everyone is motionless. The heat in the classroom is intense, and the silence thick.

He repeats the words:

"What is one thing I can do, when I leave here today, to keep myself safe and healthy?"

There is a profound stillness. After a pause Bongani continues. "It is important to remember that what we have done in the past, is what makes us what we are today, and what we do today will determine our future ..."

The young people remain still, with bowed heads, as if making silent vows about how they intend to lead their lives from this moment.

"Thank you," says Bongani after a short while, "you may open your eyes now."

The sombre atmosphere changes as the actors sing their final song, *It's My Life,* and the audience joins in. The words are written on a banner which Tshepo and Lunga unroll. Mkhonzeni, Mpone and Zodwa move among the learners handing out leaflets with the words of the song. As the children disperse, they babble among themselves, and some, as they leave the classroom and make their way across the schoolyard, continue singing:

It's my life – my life
My life.
It's my life.
I make a choice
I choose to be safe
It's my life, my life.
I'll do what is right for me
Stop the spread of HIV
This is my life, my life!
I am wise
I wait now
Abstain
And think twice.

During the journey back to the Themba building in Braamfontein, the actor-educators chat among themselves. Tshepo sits behind me giving directions. Theresa is in the front making notes. There is a sense of satisfaction amongst us. Whenever we hear a child leaving our performance singing the Themba song we feel that we have achieved something. There is a chance that child will remember what we have imparted today, and may stay safe.

On our return, after we've had something to eat, we gather in the rehearsal room for the feedback session. The evaluation method was devised by Theresa together with the actor-educators and she leads. We sit in a circle and one by one we speak in response to the first question:

What did I do well today?

Then we respond to the second:

What might I have done differently?

Sometimes the comments are about the performance and sometimes they are to do with general behaviour. Theresa makes a note of anything that needs to be worked on in future training sessions. When everyone has had the chance to speak to these two questions, we move on to giving feedback for each other:

One thing I noticed that you did well today ...

and

One thing I noticed that you could have done differently ...

We are all aware that at this point someone could say something hurtful or inappropriate, but Theresa has trained them well, and all the comments are made respectfully with a view to learning, both for the individual and for the development of the process.

Everyone in the group has the opportunity to give feedback for everyone else, including me and Theresa. This is the way we all learn – from what we did well and what we might do differently. We have never used the expression, "you (or I) did this or that *wrong*" and we have created a way of learning which is exceptional in South Africa. This method was completely new to the young people when they first arrived at Themba. They had been brought up in an old-fashioned dualistic manner, with a "right" and a "wrong" way of doing things.

I wonder whether this way of giving and receiving feedback will survive when Theresa and I finally leave Themba. Eric Richardson is due to start work with us in May as the new operations manager, and the plan is that he will eventually take over the job of executive director from me. Theresa will be gone by July and I have promised the Board that I'll stay on while Eric is mentored into his post. He had glowing references when he applied, and I am confident he will run Themba well when I finally go back to England.

After we reach the end of the feedback session, all the actor-educators except Bongani go home for the Easter break.

"*Salani kahle,*" they call as they leave. "Stay well."

"*Hambani kahle*", we reply. "Go well. See you after Easter."

Theresa, Bongani and I go upstairs to the Themba office, make mugs of tea, and sit down to go through the list of bookings we've already secured for the next few months.

I watch Bongani's and Theresa's heads bent together as they look over the paperwork, and I feel humbled.

I marvel at what we have achieved.

Testimonial from Mpone Moeketsi, trainer and facilitator at Themba

Kim Hope and Theresa Lynne empowered me to be the woman I am today. I started working at *Themba Interactive Theatre* in 2003 as a Trainer/Facilitator and stayed at Themba for four years. Working at Themba gave me great experience as a young person who had little sense of direction. I am so grateful that I met both of you. I thank you so much for having been part of my journey. There is no class I facilitate when I do not mention you and Themba. God has used you in my life and for that I am humbled always. You should see me in action! I still apply all – I mean all – that I was taught at Themba. You gave me hope that I too can make a difference and live for a greater purpose in the world.

Postscript

I live now in one of the most beautiful parts of England, right in the middle of the South Downs National Park. I am a freelance theatre practitioner and run drama workshops with adults, some of whom have learning disabilities. When I walk on the Downs early in the morning and see the undulating, sensuous hills, the wildflowers, the buzzards and red kites, the butterflies and the occasional hare or deer, I feel my heart breaking open for the beauty of it all. It feels akin to the way the hills and valleys of the Transkei grabbed my soul all those years ago. But this is home, where my family is, and although I miss South Africa terribly sometimes, I am content.

A Showcase of Themba's work was held in July 2006 in the Joe Slovo Courtyard at Constitution Hill, a prestigious venue which houses the Constitutional Court. It had originally been a prison, The Old Fort, and it was where Nelson Mandela and the other Rivonia defendants were held while on trial for treason. Justice Edwin Cameron, one of Themba's Patrons and the most high-profile person in South Africa to have come out publically as being HIV positive, gave a powerful address.

Eric Richardson, the operations manager who joined Themba in May 2006, became the managing director when I officially resigned at the July 2007 AGM. I spent much of that last year dividing my time between the UK and South Africa.

Themba's interactive theatre methodology was the winner of the South African "Investors in the Future – Most Innovative Award" in 2007.

When I returned full-time to England, the Board of Directors of Themba asked me to set up a new charity to raise money for them in South Africa. The Themba Trust UK was launched on World AIDS Day, 1 December 2007, with Lord Richard Attenborough as our host and generous benefactor. We marked the occasion with

245

a reception at the South African High Commission in Trafalgar Square, London: this was the dinner Richard had promised me when I'd first asked him and Sheila to be Patrons back in 2001. Six actor-educators – Bongani, Mary, Bheki, Tshepo, JR and Mkhonzeni – came from South Africa and performed for the London audience, and later that week for the staff at Comic Relief. Dame Janet Suzman gave a moving speech, and Hugh Masekela played his flugel horn. Archbishop Desmond Tutu made a DVD which was shown at the event, appealing for funds for Themba. Richard's speech concentrated largely on the opportunities afforded by education, and he praised the way in which the actor-educators had been trained and educated at Themba.

On World AIDS Day 2008 the Themba Trust UK held a fundraising tea party at the House of Commons with Lord Chris Smith, one of the Patrons, as our host. In 2009, Sweetness Buthelezi, the assistant managing director at Themba, came to speak at a major fundraising dinner which was held at the South African High Commission with Terry Waite CBE, as our guest speaker.

The Themba Trust UK has now been laid down, but during its life it was able to transfer welcome funds to Themba in South Africa.

On 15 February 2008 I revisited South Africa at the invitation of the Gordon Institute of Business Science which described me as a social entrepreneur. I gave a breakfast seminar for NGO personnel on the subject of "How to Avoid Founders Syndrome". I was invited back by Themba in 2012 for the tenth anniversary celebrations. I have returned twice since.

* * *

Bongani is married to Lele and they have two children, a boy and a girl. He dreams of setting up his own NGO one day, using the arts for social transformation.

Mary had three daughters. She worked in Human Resources. She died in March 2017.

Thabo joined Themba in 2002 as part of Training Group 2. He became the main "culture carrier" for the organisation, working with all subsequent managing directors.

"Vusi," who contracted HIV after being raped when he was fourteen, has become a father thanks to the innovative use of antiretroviral medication which was given to his (HIV negative) wife. Both wife and baby are HIV negative.

Lunga's dream was to be a film-maker and he achieved a place at film school. He was later killed in a car crash.

Seipati is a Lieutenant Commander in the South African Navy.

Tshepo is the heritage coordinator at the Dr A.B. Zuma Museum in Sophiatown, which is linked to the Trevor Huddleston Memorial Centre.

Theresa now lives in New Zealand.

Eric Richardson retired from Themba in 2010. Warren Nebe became the new Director, dividing his time between Themba and the Drama for Life programme at the Wits University Drama Department. He was later succeeded by Justin Holcroft.

David Dennis has become an even more famous actor in South Africa as a result of his 2018 award-winning performance in *Priscilla Queen of the Desert*.

Lebo Mashile is a highly successful performance poet, actress and TV presenter and has won numerous prestigious awards.

Jabu Mashinini of TALK travels the world providing help and guidance to major international companies.

Stephen Gray, one of the young directors of the Cambridge Shakespeare Tour, is an esteemed poet, critic, playwright and novelist in South Africa. Sandy Dane, the other director, returned to the UK and acted in a number of "Carry On …" films.

Babington House School is thriving and is no longer just "An

Establishment for Young Ladies". Boys are now admitted to the sixth form and the latest (2016) Independent Schools Inspectorate report said the "the quality of the pupils' academic, and other achievements, and the quality of their personal development is excellent."

The Trevor Huddleston Memorial Centre is active in Sophiatown and Soweto. It has new premises, and continues with a number of Projects for young people and adults in the community (www.trevorhuddleston.org).

The Shewula eco-tourism camp has succeeded, and welcomes guests from all over the world (www.shewulacamp.org).

BoMake-Gone Rural is the organisation founded by Jenny Thorne in Swaziland. It employs over seven hundred Swazi women dying and weaving grass and making artefacts for the home. It has been the recipient of many prestigious awards and has numerous community development initiatives (www. goneruralswazi.com/bomake).

The Bishop Simeon Trust is a UK charity which, together with local partners, helps vulnerable children in South Africa. Their youth programmes use a range of creative arts to explore different issues in the lives of young people, one of which is HIV/AIDS. They use forum theatre, community film making, grassroots comics, dance and song, to create a safe space to explore sensitive issues in a constructive manner, focussed on critical thinking (www.bstrust.org).

Glossary

These words and phrases are Afrikaans, isiZulu, SiSwati, Sesotho or isiXhosa. Some are slang, some *tsotsi-taal* (tsotsi = gangster/taal = talk/language).

asseblief – please
bakkie – open-back small truck
bayethe! – Hail to the King!
bobelas – hangover
boerewors – spicy sausage
braai – barbecue
bundu – rural area
bunny-chow – half a white loaf with middle scooped out, filled
    with curry
dankie – thank you
doek – headscarf
eish! – exclamation to express frustration, surprise or disapproval
hamba kahle – go well (singular) meaning "goodbye"
hambani kahle – go well (plural)
indaba – meeting or gathering
isifebe – slag
Jozi – affectionate nickname for Johannesburg/Jo'burg
kakhulu – very much (as in thank you very much)
kokies – felt pens / markers
mealies – corn on the cob
mealie meal – porridge made from mealies
naartjies – small tangerine-like oranges
pap – also called mealie meal, porridge made from corn flour
robots – traffic lights
salani kahle – stay well (plural) meaning "goodbye"
sala khale – stay well (singular)
sanibonani – hello (plural) literally means "I see you"

shebeen – informal drinking place

siyabonga – thank you

sawubona – hello (singular)

spaza – small makeshift shop sometimes attached to private home

swaart gevaar – "black threat"

takkies – trainers/plimsolls

tsotsi – gangster

umfundisi – teacher

wena – eh wena, literally meaning "you"

yebo – yes

Appendix

Forum Theatre and Interactive Themba Theatre (I.T.T.)
Drama games and exercises
Forum theatre

Augusto Boal, the Brazilian Theatre Practitioner (1931–2009), devised the interactive theatre process known as Forum Theatre. Actors present a short play or scene in which the protagonist does not achieve his or her goal and there is no clear solution to the "problem" presented in the play. Audience members can say "STOP!" if they wish to change the action and make a suggestion for how the play could move towards a satisfactory conclusion. The actors attempt to do what is suggested, but will ensure that a resolution to the dilemma is not achieved. Then people from the audience are invited to join the actors on stage to assume a role within the drama. The play continues with audience members taking one or other of the parts and attempting to change the outcome by making new choices.

By its nature, Forum Theatre is not didactic, but instead offers audiences the power to create their own satisfactory resolution for the situation in the play. However, when the actor-educators at Themba brought their concerns to us about Forum Theatre being "not enough" we introduced more "teaching" in an attempt to demonstrate to our audiences what was safe and unsafe behaviour. We wanted to encourage people to go for an HIV test so they would know whether they were HIV positive or negative.

* * *

Interactive Themba Theatre (I.T.T.)

I.T.T. is a development of Forum Theatre and uses a number of different activities both before and after the performance of the play.

Before

- Drumming – to create a lively and entertaining atmosphere.
- Introducing the actors in a loud and exciting fashion with each actor running through the audience as their name is announced.
- Lighting the HIV/AIDS candle with the words, *I light this candle to remember all those who have died of AIDS and all those living with HIV.*
- Singing a topical song which the audience knows. This has a three-fold purpose: to enliven the atmosphere after the solemnity of lighting the AIDS candle; to have the audience members "hear" their own voices in the space (and thus be more ready later to join in with the presentation); to create a shared moment between audience and actors to break down the barrier between them.

After

Following the play, when it has been explored through facilitated interaction with the audience:

- Questioning the actors while still in character. For example: *Mzobo – do you think you might be HIV positive?*
- Truth stick – where the character must speak the absolute truth while holding the stick.
- Actor speaks to his own character. For example: Thabo *As I put this shirt on the chair I want you to imagine Mzobo is sitting here* – and then he speaks to "Mzobo" - *You must grow up, and go for an HIV blood test.*
- Audience and actors face each other and take it in turns to speak these lines *I am HIV positive* and *I still care for you.*

- Actors line up in pairs and speak short duologues together. For example: *All my girlfriends sleep with me – it's my right/ It's my right to do what I want with my body*. Then children from the audience come to the acting space and join the actors in speaking these lines.

- Actors line up across the space facing the audience and fire a range of questions directly at them. For example: *Is sex before marriage okay for me?* or *How will my parents feel if they know?*

- Coloured cards are shown to the audience with different sexual activities on them. Some are red – danger: PENETRATIVE SEX and ANAL SEX; some are orange – careful: ORAL SEX, THIGH SEX, and USE A CONDOM; some are green – safe: MASTURBATION, MUTUAL MASTURBATION, NOT HAVING SEX, SAYING I LOVE YOU, HUGGING, KISSING. Members of the audience are encouraged to call out these words in their own mother tongue. The purpose of this is to hear the words "out there" so that people have the tools to talk about sex before engaging in it.

- Silent moment: the facilitator comes forward and speaks to the audience: *Some of us in this room here today are HIV positive, and some are HIV negative, and some of us don't know – yet – whether we are positive or negative. I'm going to say a few words and I want you to think about them for yourselves. Please bow your heads or close your eyes while I say these words.* [Pause.] *What is one thing I can do, when I leave here today, to keep myself safe and healthy?* [Pause.] *What is one thing I can do, when I leave here today, to keep myself safe and healthy?*

- Singing the final song *It's My Life* with the words distributed among the members of the audience who join in.

* * *

Selected Drama Games and Exercises used in our Workshops and Training

- The Sun Shines On Anybody Who ... This game (aka The Big Wind Blows On Anybody Who ...) was used in almost all the workshops that we held for conflict resolution and non-violence, and later at the beginning of the training of new groups of trainee actor-educators in the Themba HIV & AIDS Organisation:

All participants sitting on chairs in a circle with one spare chair close at hand. The leader steps into the centre of the circle and explains:

We're going to play a game called The Sun Shines On. The person standing in the middle – I will start – says, "The Sun Shines On anybody who ..." and then you say something which is true for you. For example, I might say, "The Sun Shines On anybody who – has a brother" (because I have a brother) or "The Sun Shines On anybody who – went to see a movie in the last week" (because I went to the movies). Then anyone in the circle who this is true for too must jump up and go to another chair. The person in the middle moves quickly to an empty chair and then someone else is left in the centre. He or she then begins again with "The Sun Shines On anybody who ..." and says something that is true about themselves.

The game begins. You run it for a while. Some people will find it difficult to think of anything to say when they are in the middle, so you introduce a new "rule". *Anyone who wants to, if you can't think of something, say "SUNBURST!" and then we all get up and dash to another chair.*

Run it a bit more. Then introduce a new rule when appropriate: *Here's another rule: you can't just slide from one chair to its neighbour. You must move at least to the next but one.* At this point (or earlier if it's getting rowdy), you say, *Please look after yourself and other people. We don't want anyone getting injured.*

When you think the group has had enough, rather than stopping the game in an arbitrary fashion, you just quickly grab the extra chair, slide it into the circle, and sit down on it. Then everyone will discover that they all have a chair and the game ends in surprise and laughter.

This game is useful at the beginning of a workshop, and especially with a new group because:

- The person in the middle is looked at by an "audience"
- The person in the middle has to speak loudly – particularly so those behind can hear
- The person in the middle has to think quickly
- There is physical movement
- Energy is created
- There is a lot of laughter
- You find out things about people
- You finish up with everyone sitting next to someone they weren't sitting next to at the beginning of the game – you mix people up.

A note of caution: you don't know what people might reveal about themselves. For example: "The Sun Shines On anybody who ... is HIV positive" or "who has lost both parents" or "whose sister died last week." It is a good idea when introducing the game to explain to people that they should only say things about themselves that they are happy for the group to hear. Mostly, though, people tend to keep it light.

- Line-ups:

This exercise is usually used near the beginning of a workshop. It encourages people to move around the space, they learn things about each other and start to collaborate. It begins with simple fun and progresses to something more serious, introducing issues pertinent to the workshop.

Participants are asked to line up across the room one behind the other in order of their height from shortest to tallest. Then in order of their hair colour: *This end of the room we'll have the lightest and over there will be the darkest* then eye colour: *This end pale blue, then through turquoise, green, hazel, brown, and dark brown.* This line-up gets people looking deeply into each other's eyes to work out where they should be in the line. A good beginning for collaboration.

Next in order of the date of their birth. This has to be done in silence, so you say, *This is where you'll stand if you were born in January, and right over there is December. You have to guess where you'll be standing without any talking, indicating, or holding up fingers or mouthing the date of your birth.* People shuffle up and down the line trying to work out where their birthday is, then they slot themselves in. With some groups it is worth remembering that there may be participants who do not know the actual date of their birth, so you might need to say something like, *If you don't know when your birthday is, or you decide you'd like a different birthday, just choose a date and stand where you think that date is.*

When everyone has placed themselves – in silence – on the line, you stand near 1 January and ask people to call out the date of their birthday. As they do so, you move down the line. They can rearrange themselves if they want to (they usually do). Surprisingly often we found we had "twins". This game creates laughter, a sense of belonging, and again provides a little more information about the others in the workshop.

Now you say, *We're going to move on now, and instead of lining up with hair colour or date of birth, I'm going to ask you to stand in a line in response to a statement I will say. So if you strongly agree with the statement, you'll stand right over here, if you definitely disagree, you stand over there, and if you are not sure or don't have an opinion either way, or any knowledge of what the statement is about, you'll stand somewhere in the middle. So, if you are not quite sure, but you think maybe you agree or disagree then you'll be somewhere along the line towards one end.* Now check that they all understand.

Start off with innocuous or safe statements, like: *The summer is my favourite season* or *I really enjoy watching football.* Then the participants move to where they think they should be on the line depending on their opinion. These are for practice only. Check that everyone understands which end of the line is which. People are still working in silence.

Now you move onto statements which are relevant to the workshop. For example:

> *I think everyone should have an HIV test so they know whether they are positive or negative.*
>
> *I believe the Health Minister when she says garlic and lemon juice can cure AIDS.*
>
> *It's safe to have sex as long as you use a condom.*

Once everyone is somewhere on the line for each of these (and subsequent relevant statements) ask them to talk in pairs or small groups and tell each other why they are standing where they are standing.

Continue with different statements until just before the energy in the group begins to wane.

This exercise is effective because it moves people around and gives them the opportunity to express their opinions without having to speak out loud in front of the whole group (which can be intimidating).

A note of caution: very occasionally you might find that just one person is down one end (maybe strongly disagreeing) and everyone else is bunched up on the other end. This can make the solo person feel very vulnerable, so as soon as you suspect this is about to happen, go and stand by the individual and draw them towards the main group. Then you can all have a discussion about what made people stand where they stood and they can all listen to each other's point of view.

• Mapping:

Again, this gets the group moving around and also learning more about each other.

Place a chair in the middle of the room. Say: *This chair represents where we are now – in the Peace Centre in Cape Town* (for example). *That way is north, that is south, over there is west and that way is east.* You indicate the different points of the compass and check that everyone understands. You may need to explain that a particular area or suburb is in that direction, or remind people where certain landmarks (or even other countries) are in relation to the chair. Then you ask the participants to go and stand where they were born. Some people will move right away from the centre and go as far north-west as they can (for example). Some may stay right in the middle if they were born in Cape Town. Others will place themselves approximately where they were born in relation to Cape Town. (Theresa and I would place ourselves as far apart as possible and right up against the walls of the space, because I was born in Northern Ireland and Theresa in New Zealand.)

Now you ask the people nearest to each other to have a short discussion about where they were born. Sometimes you find that two people in your workshop were born in the same hospital.

Next you ask them to stand where they were living when they were, say, five, or ten or eighteen years old. You can choose these arbitrary times. Give people the opportunity to think about this before they move. Some will hardly move at all, others will travel a great deal. Each time they are at a particular stage in their lives, they stop and talk to those nearest to them. Some will have moved because of family tragedy, others because someone got a new job or because they went to college (for example).

A note of caution: this needs to be handled sensitively because you are asking people to recall moments in their lives which could possibly be painful. Keep it moving and watch for upsets. This is not a therapy session and you have a responsibility to ensure that everyone in the workshop feels safe.

• Milling:

There are many different reasons for "milling" around the space. You may want the participants to learn *STOP!* or *FREEZE!* when they are expected to stand stock still at a given signal (an important drama discipline). Or you may want them to learn to spread out and use the whole space, walking around without bumping into each other and always ensuring the space is filled with people and no gaps are occurring. Or possibly you will be asking them, at a signal, to get into groups of three, four, five etc. Sometimes you will use milling when you want people to walk at different speeds, or as different characters, or with exaggerated movements. Another exercise involving milling is:

• If You Were a Colour What Colour Would You Be?

The group walks around the space, not bumping into each other, and always attempting to ensure that no big spaces appear amongst them and they are at all times fairly equidistant from each other. You strike your "signal" and everyone stands still. You tap one participant lightly on the shoulder and ask, *If you were a colour, what colour would you be?* The participant has to answer immediately, without thought. *Red!* is a very common answer. Ask the group to continue milling. Then the signal to STOP again and you tap someone else on the shoulder and ask, *If you were a tree, what kind of tree would you be?* In England the response is very often, *an oak tree!* but in South Africa it might be a Marula or Thorn tree. Then the group continues milling and you stop them and ask each in turn: *If you were ... a book, a newspaper, a piece of furniture, an article of clothing, a vegetable, a plant, a poem, a flower, a building, a play, a famous person ...* whatever you can think of.

The purpose of this exercise is to free the imagination. Because the response must be immediate, it is not thought through intellectually but arrives spontaneously. Sometimes the answer is a complete surprise to the person who is responding. Also, the group begins to understand about use of space: they must be aware of each other and the environment they are working in.

Another "milling" exercise is:

• Find the Moment:

The group mills around the space, and at your signal they all stop at the same time. Then at your signal they begin walking again. You do this three or four times making sure that the lapse of time between your signals is varied. Then you explain to the group that you are no longer going to signal to them when they should start walking and when they should stop. The group as a whole will "Find the Moment" when it feels it wants to begin to move and when it wants to pause, and when it wants to move again. Usually there is some scepticism about whether this will work or not. But it does, and can feel uncanny. It is important to tell the group that no one is to "lead" but that all, when the moment feels right, will start to move at the same time.

• Pattern Ball:

The group stands in a circle. Go around with each person saying their name. Then you gently toss the ball to one of the group and say their name as you throw. They then throw the ball to someone else and say the name of that person. And so on. The names are called randomly and you need to make sure that everyone is included. Have a bit of practice so you can see if anyone is finding catching difficult. (If they are, you may need to stop the game at this point and move onto something else.) Now explain that the pattern the ball makes as it is thrown to each person (and the names called) is to be repeated, so everyone has to remember who they threw the ball to (also who they caught it from). Once the order (the pattern) is thoroughly established through repetition, you can reverse the order if you feel like it, so everyone is throwing the ball in the opposite direction. Now go back to the original order until it is very well learnt by everyone in the group. With a group which is experienced in drama games, you can now introduce a second ball (with a different colour) and start a new pattern. Once both patterns have been learnt, both can be done at the same time, thus there are two balls moving across the circle all the time. With people you've worked with for some considerable time it might be possible to introduce a third ball with a third pattern, but this is very challenging. To make it even more challenging, you can go into reverse.

The purpose of this game is to help people learn each other's names and also to develop concentration and coordination. Be gentle with those people who find catching and throwing difficult. Small leather juggling balls are ideal for this game as they are a good weight, size and colour.

- Name Games:

We used a number of name games (in addition to the above). These are played at the beginning of a workshop or when new people have joined.
    a. Go around the circle and say your name and tell us something about your name. You discover fascinating information about people with this. For example, "I was

named by my grandmother" or "I chose my name for myself" or "I was born in June so my parents called me June" or "My name is Trouble because I was such a trouble to my mother when I was being born" or "My name is Wednesday" (or Precious, or Gracious, or Sweetness or Blessing – all names we met in our workshops).

b. Adjective names (with thanks to the Alternatives to Violence Project): go around the circle and everyone says their name preceded by a *positive* adjective with the same initial *sound*. For example: Colourful Kim, Terrific Theresa, Gorgeous Gloria, Jolly James, Kind Claire, Magnificent Marie. Sometimes people find this challenging if they have low self-esteem. When someone can't think of a positive adjective to go with their name, then the rest of the group helps and makes suggestions until an acceptable word is found. If someone uses a *negative* adjective (for example, Horrible Henry) they are challenged by the group and helped to find a positive word (maybe Happy Henry).

- Concentric Circles (again with thanks to AVP):

You'll need enough chairs for everyone in the group. Arrange the chairs so there is an inner circle facing out and an outer circle facing in, so that each chair has another one in front of it. Ask half the group to sit on the inner circle of chairs (facing out), and half to sit in the outer circle (facing in). Thus everyone is sitting opposite someone else. (It is useful to have a co-facilitator if there is an odd number of participants. If you are the only trainer then you will need to put yourself in the outer circle and sit opposite someone in the group, but this is never satisfactory.)

Now explain that all the inner circle people are "A" and all the outer circle are "B". Once everyone has absorbed this, explain that all the As are going to speak to the Bs opposite them about a subject that you will give them. Bs are to *only* listen, not speak.

Bs should make it clear by their body language that they are listening (nodding, leaning forward, looking at their partner's face, etc.) but they are NOT to speak and join in and say things like "Oh, yes, that happened to me, too" (or whatever). Later they will swap over. When everyone is clear about this, explain that you will be timing each section so both the As and the Bs have equal opportunity to speak.

Now you say again that the As will speak first on the subject you will give them, and when you've timed them they will swap over and Bs will speak on the same subject. Depending on the experience of the group and the purpose of the workshop, begin with fairly straightforward subjects. For example:

Something I really enjoy doing

or

A place where I feel happy

Once both As and Bs have spoken on the subject, you ask *either* the As or the Bs to stand up and move around the circle one place. Thus, they find themselves in front of a different partner. Now that people are in front of someone new you give them the second subject, this time more to do with the purpose of the workshop. For example:

Something that makes me angry

or

A time when I felt I was let down

And so on, with both the As and the Bs doing the moving round. (Make sure both As and Bs move so they have the opportunity to stretch their legs – unless you have someone in one half of the group for whom movement is difficult. You will have to remember who moved and in which direction, otherwise this doesn't work.)

You can, if you wish, at the end of each "session" of speaking/listening ask the participants to find a way of thanking their partner and saying goodbye before moving on to the next person. Similarly, you can ask them to find a way of greeting their new partner.

Timing: it is surprising how long a minute is when you are speaking without being interrupted. Start with just a minute or two and lengthen the time of each "session," but don't let any of the different "sessions" become too long. It is challenging for the trainer/facilitator to keep tabs on the timing and on how this exercise is going if you are one of the participants.

Speaking/not speaking: you need to tell everyone that if they don't wish to speak out loud to their partner then they can "take this time" to just think to themselves about whatever the subject is. Then the "listening partner" simply sits opposite silently conveying support.

The purpose of this exercise is:

a. to have an opportunity to be heard and to speak uninterrupted on the subject. It is rare that we speak and the person we are speaking to simply listens. It can be very affirming to be listened to intently. Conversely it can feel intimidating. As the facilitator, you need to be aware of the possibility of people becoming upset.

b. it is rare that we just listen without "rehearsing" our response in our heads. This is a creative listening exercise where we give our wholehearted attention to the person speaking.

The facilitator needs to be very sensitive to the group and the individuals in it and gently bring the activity to a close if it feels as though this is causing upset.

- Rainstorm:

This is played towards the end of a workshop as a gathering exercise after much activity.

Begin in silence. The group stands in a circle. The facilitator stands in the centre of the circle. The facilitator starts, and slowly turns, looking at each participant in turn. Only when she is looking at the person in the circle does that person join in with the action the facilitator is doing. Thus, the sound gradually develops, increases and builds, as the different sounds/actions overlap with each other. We start by rubbing our palms together to make a soft swishing sound. Then the "rain" begins, pitter-patter, with the clicking of fingers. It increases as we slap our hands against the front of our thighs. Finally, the thunder comes with loud stamping on the floor (while still slapping thighs). Hold this noise for as long as you can – the stamping and slapping together can be tiring. Then the sounds are made backwards as the "storm" subsides until there is calm. Everyone stands still in the circle, holding a moment of silence. If this is done on a sprung floor the noise is impressive and sounds just like a thunder storm.

Another way of leading this is for the facilitator to stand with the participants in the circle and begin the exercise with the rubbing of the hands. The person standing next to the facilitator copies what she is doing. Then the next participant copies the person next to them, and so on. Each time the facilitator changes the action (from rubbing palms to clicking fingers, from clicking fingers to slapping thighs etc.) the next person changes, and the next, and on around the circle. Again, this means that the sound is built up to a thunderous storm and then subsides to silence. Doing it this way quite often goes "wrong", though, because participants tend to copy the "leader" rather than their neighbour.

The purpose of the Rainstorm is to bring the whole group together for a communal, creative exercise. It is important to tell the group that no talking, laughing or exclamation is allowed as the storm builds and subsides. This is simply because it spoils the effect. At the end of the storm, hold a moment or two of silence before breaking the spell.

- Working in Metaphor:

A metaphor is a thing which is a representation or a symbol for something else. We used the "swimming pool" metaphor at the Quaker Peace Centre in Cape Town to help participants understand their place in the organisation in which they were working. For example, the woman who "swam" away from the deep end when she no longer felt "out of her depth".

Working in metaphor can be a powerful indicator of how people are feeling about their situation. If we had worked in "reality" using discussion and role-play, it would have been more challenging for the participants to say what they wanted or how they were feeling. Metaphor provides some distance and thus makes it possible for people to express their true hopes and desires (and fears) without directly confronting a situation.

- Working in Silence:

There are a number of reasons for asking people to work in silence:

The removal of the ability to speak compels participants in a workshop into a more equal relationship with each other.

Participants in a workshop may have a number of different first languages or mother tongues.

When people work without words, they become more aware

of themselves in relation to others in the group.

People are more aware of their body language, and the body language of the other participants.

- Evaluation:

There are many ways of evaluating a workshop. Here are two:

a) Brainstorm:

You use a flipchart and draw three sections on it (in the shape of an upside-down Y). Then you draw one of these pictures in each of the three sections: ☺ and ☹ and 💡. You invite the participants to call out what they think should go into each section, and write it up. The light bulb indicates a "lightbulb moment" when someone has learnt or discovered something new. The other two sections are for participants to say what they enjoyed or what they found difficult or challenging, or that they didn't enjoy. When facilitating a "brainstorm" you need to tell the participants that there is no discussion of people's contributions. After the calling out is over, however, you can have a full discussion when group members can elaborate on what they have said earlier.

b) Thumb-thing:

This is a short, fun, participatory way of evaluating a workshop (as long as all the participants have working right hands and arms).

The group stands in a circle. You explain that each person (either in turn going around the circle or randomly) will say a word or a short phrase to illustrate their feelings about the workshop they have just experienced. You need to say that every word or phrase that someone says is simply heard and not challenged or agreed with. Everything is acceptable. As each person speaks they stretch out their right arm, holding up their right hand in a fist with the thumb pointing upwards.

If someone wants to say a phrase, it needs to be kept *very* short. Some people start off on a long explanation of what they did or didn't like about the workshop and people who already have their arms out in the circle will find it difficult to keep holding them up!

When everyone has spoken, there is a circle of thumbs pointing up towards the ceiling/sky. You ask everyone to turn their thumb to the left and slot it into the fist of the person on their left. To achieve this, you may need to ask people to turn slightly, and come in a bit to make the circle smaller. You now have a circle of hands, all tightly linked together. You all bend your knees a little, squatting or bending down with the hands getting closer and closer to the floor. Now you start a low hum which, as the circle of hands lifts higher and higher, the noise increases and turns into a great yell of exhilaration. As the hands reach the limit of their height, they all release with a great yell. We used to shout "Bayethe!" which is a Zulu Royal salute.

Also remind people to look after themselves and each other and not stand on each other's feet as they fling up their arms up and move backwards.

* * *

I acknowledge that these exercises are not new or unique to Themba. Theresa and I brought our own experiences as teachers, trainers, therapists and participants to the workshops we ran together. Other drama practitioners use these same or similar games and exercises in different contexts and for their own purposes.

Acknowledgements

I am grateful to many people: to all the actor-educators who had the courage to join the Themba HIV & AIDS Organization, and especially to Bongani Sihlangu, Tshepo Letsoala, JR Semelela, Zodwa Mathembula, Mary Mpho Masita, Thabo Nhlapo, Mkhonzeni Fumba, Bheki Simelane and Moleko Lesiba Komelane. To Eric Richardson and then Warren Nebe, Sweetness Buthelezi and Mam Bongi Chabeli who, with the help of the Board, managed Themba after I left. To other staff and volunteers: Manya Gittel, Lebo Mashile, Manuela Piotti, Clare Roberts-Lamont, Fiona De Villiers, Dineo Seleki, Augustine Mugisha, Mpone Moeketsi, Wendy Landau, Shahana Chattergee, and to Simon Morare, Themba's driver. To the people who served on the Board of Directors: Justine Limpitlaw, Margaret Roper, Adolphus Madonsela, and Maya Koboka.

To the original Advisory Board: Mark Hiller, David Dennis, Lucky Mazibuko, Dawn Joseph, Dr Anthony Kinghorn, Professor Alan Whiteside, Dudu Mtshazo.

The Patrons: Lord Richard and Lady Sheila Attenborough, Lord Chris Smith, Dame Jocelyn Barrow, Dame Judi Dench, Dudu Mtshazo, Sibusiso Mamba, the Honourable Mr Justice Edwin Cameron, Archbishop Emeritus Desmond Tutu, Anna Carteret, Dame Janet Suzman, Professor Alan Whiteside, Laurence Nodder, Dudu Mtshazo, Archbishop Thabo Makgoba and Pieter Dirk Uys (aka Evita Bezhuidenhout) who were wonderfully supportive and lent their names to Themba. In particular Richard and Sheila Attenborough who agreed to become Patrons before Themba existed, and who were also generous with financial help. My grateful thanks to you all – you are never forgotten.

The funders who made the work possible, and who supported Themba (and me) as I struggled to keep the organization going: Comic Relief, The Elton John AIDS Foundation, The Joseph

Rowntree Charitable Trust, The Anglo American Foundation, The Bishop Simeon Trust, The British Council, The South African National Lottery, many Quaker Meetings and Quaker Trusts in the UK and individual Friends.

Most Reverend Dr Thabo Makgoba, Anglican Archbishop of Cape Town, was the part-time Director of the Trevor Huddleston Centre and Priest-in-Charge of the Church of Christ the King in Sophiatown when he invited me to come from Swaziland to Johannesburg to set up the Themba HIV & AIDS Project. I am deeply grateful to you Thabo, and to Lungi.

To Tricia Sibbons, who achieved that first crucial grant from Comic Relief and nurtured Themba from the beginning, and to Stuart Craig and Martin Keat of the Bishop Simeon Trust.

To Sisters Jane, Maureen, Patricia, Pam and Erica OHP, of St Benedict's, Rosettenville - grateful thanks and love to you for your spiritual nourishment, your laughter, and your generous hospitality.

To Theresa Lynne, who, with courage bordering on foolhardiness, accompanied me on this journey – to you, much more than thanks.

I would like to acknowledge the new members of the Board: Glenda White, Sudeshan Reddy, Pat Masithela, Timothy Maurice Webster and Dale Smith. And Yusaf Justin Holcroft, past CEO of Themba Interactive, Initiatives for Life.

Friends: among them Jabu Mashinini, Judy Connors, Razaan Bailey, Tessa Edlemann, Genni Blunden, Kathryn Leafe, Jennifer Kinghorn, Margaret Roper, Justine Limpitlaw, Manya Gittel, Luke Pato, Chris Knott, Beverley Meeson, Val Rowling, Lesley and Bren Finnegan. More than thanks to the 'Woodbrooke Seven': Mary Lou Leavitt, Mary Synott, Maria Brown, David Atwood and Gordon Matthews – I owe you more than I can say. And special thanks to Ken and Hazel FitzSimons for lending me their apartment in Spain so I could write undisturbed, and for their unwavering friendship.

Stephanie Norgate (my supervisor at the University of

Chichester MA in Creative Writing course), Dave Swann (my academic advisor) and Alison MacLeod gave me invaluable support while writing this book - for which very many thanks.

My writing group: Janet Denny, Yvonne Phillips and Jane Venn, for your patience, inspiration, ideas and feedback.

My editors: Helen Holleman in South Africa and Stephanie Cross in the UK.

I also acknowledge the Friends Higher Education Adult Grants Group who helped me financially during the MA course at the University of Chichester.

I am obliged to Paul Hughes of the Roseland Observatory, Cornwall, who researched for me the position of the Southern Cross in the sky the night I returned to Swaziland from Johannesburg in 2001.

My 'beta' readers: Mary Synott, Vita FitzSimons, Lesley Finnegan, David Reid, Kersti Wagstaff: grateful thanks.

And finally, thank you to all the schools, colleges, youth correctional centres, workplaces, churches, community groups, theatres, prisons and hospitals who opened their doors to Themba and allowed us to break the silence around the taboo of HIV and AIDS. You showed courage when you invited us and you cared enough to join us in our determination to save lives.

Permissions

Thanks are also due for the use of the following extracts and illustrations:

Extract from *Cry, The Beloved Country* by Alan Paton.

Permission kindly given by the Ewing Trust Company (Alan Paton Will Trust) South Africa.

From Cry, The Beloved Country by Alan Paton Published by Jonathan Cape Reprinted by permission of The Random House Group Limited. © 1948

From CRY, THE BELOVED COUNTRY by Alan Paton. Copyright © 1948 by Alan Paton. Copyright renewed © 1976

Framespotting
Changing How You Look at Things Changes How
You See Them
Laurence & Alison Matthews
A punchy, upbeat guide to framespotting. Spot deceptions and
hidden assumptions; swap growth for growing up. See and be free.
Paperback: 978-1-78279-689-3 ebook: 978-1-78279-822-4

Is There an Afterlife?
David Fontana
Is there an Afterlife? If so what is it like? How do Western ideas
of the afterlife compare with Eastern? David Fontana presents
the historical and contemporary evidence for survival of physical
death.
Paperback: 978-1-90381-690-5

Nothing Matters
A Book About Nothing
Ronald Green
Thinking about Nothing opens the world to everything by
illuminating new angles to old problems and stimulating new
ways of thinking.
Paperback: 978-1-84694-707-0 ebook: 978-1-78099-016-3

Panpsychism
The Philosophy of the Sensuous Cosmos
Peter Ells
Are free will and mind chimeras? This book, anti-materialistic
but respecting science, answers: No! Mind is foundational to all
existence.
Paperback: 978-1-84694-505-2 ebook: 978-1-78099-018-7

Punk Science
Inside the Mind of God
Manjir Samanta-Laughton
Many have experienced unexplainable phenomena; God, psychic
abilities, extraordinary healing and angelic encounters. Can
cutting-edge science actually explain phenomena
previously thought of as 'paranormal'?
Paperback: 978-1-90504-793-2

Vagabond Spirit of Poetry
Edward Clarke
Spend time with the wisest poets of the modern age and of the
past, and let Edward Clarke remind you of the importance of
poetry in our industrialized world.
Paperback: 978-1-78279-370-0 ebook: 978-1-78279-369-4

Readers of ebooks can buy or view any of these bestsellers by
clicking on the live link in the title. Most titles are published in
paperback and as an ebook. Paperbacks are available in traditional
bookshops. Both print and ebook formats are available online.

Find more titles and sign up to our readers' newsletter at
http://www.johnhuntpublishing.com/non-fiction

Follow us on Facebook at
https://www.facebook.com/JHPNonFiction
and Twitter at
https://twitter.com/JHPNonFiction